PUBLIC RELATIONS RESEARCH ANNUAL
Volume 1

PUBLIC RELATIONS RESEARCH ANNUAL
Volume 1

A publication of the Public Relations Division, Association for Education in Journalism and Mass Communication.

EDITORS

James E. Grunig
Larissa A. Grunig
University of Maryland

John V. Pavlik, Pennsylvania State University
Catherine Pratt, Ohio State University
Ron Pearson, Mount Saint Vincent University
J. David Pincus, California State University at Fullerton
Shirley Ramsey, University of Oklahoma
Carol Reuss, University of North Carolina
Michael Ryan, University of Houston
Charles T. Salmon, University of Wisconsin
Peter Sandman, Rutgers University
Linda H. Scanlan, Norfolk State University
Benno H. Signitzer, University of Salzberg
Holly Stocking, Indiana University
Gerald C. Stone, Memphis State University
H. Leslie Steeves, University of Oregon
Elizabeth Lance Toth, Southern Methodist University
Judy Van Slyke Turk, Kent State University
Lowdnes F. Stephens, University of South Carolina
James K. VanLeuven, Colorado State University
Steven L. Vibbert, Purdue University
Jon White, Cranfield Institute of Technology
Betty Houchin Winfield, Washington State University
Donald K. Wright, University of South Alabama
Eugenia Zerbinos, University of Maryland

PUBLIC RELATIONS RESEARCH ANNUAL
Volume 1

Edited by
James E. Grunig
Larissa A. Grunig

LEA LAWRENCE ERLBAUM ASSOCIATES, PUBLISHERS
1989 Hillsdale, New Jersey   Hove and London

Lawrence Erlbaum Associates, Inc., Publishers
365 Broadway
Hillsdale, New Jersey 07642

ISBN 0-8058-0312-2
ISSN 1042-1408

Printed in the United States of America
10 9 8 7 6 5 4 3 2 1

Contents

Preface

This volume of the *Public Relations Research Annual* is the first issue of what we believe will be the foremost scholarly publication in public relations. The Public Relations Division of the Association for Education in Journalism and Mass Communication (AEJMC) published three issues of an experimental journal, *Public Relations Research and Education (PRR&E)*, from 1984 to 1985. Publication of *PRR&E* demonstrated that public relations scholars are producing high quality academic research and that there is a need for a publication dedicated exclusively to that research. As a result, the division voted to contract with Lawrence Erlbaum Associates to publish the *Annual* as a stronger and permanent replacement for *PRR&E*.

Scholarly research on public relations has made great progress in both quantity and quality in the last 10 years, and we believe that this first volume of *Public Relations Research Annual* demonstrates that public relations has emerged as a strong domain within the discipline of communication. The *Annual* is published by the Public Relations Division of AEJMC, but it also has received the support of the Educator's Section of the Public Relations Society of America (PRSA), the Educator Academy of the International Association of Business Communicators (IABC), and the Public Relations Interest Group of the International Communication Association (ICA), and the Commission on Public Relations of the Speech Communication Association (SCA). Chapters in this first volume have been presented at annual meetings of three of these organizations.

The principal purpose of the *Annual* is to publish academic research on public relations. There are many trade publications and semi-scholarly journals already in the field. We have no intention of competing with them, nor do we think we should compete with them. The intended audience of the *Annual* is people who do academic research on public relations or who use it in their teaching and practice.

We hope, therefore, that innovative teachers and practitioners, as well as re-searchers, will read the *Annual*. Teachers should be able to use the chapters in this and future volumes to move their classes beyond anecdote to theory and research. Practitioners should find the conceptualizations and criticisms of public relations found here to be useful in providing a systematic framework for their work.

We promise no miracle formulas for the practice of public relations, however. A body of knowledge, in public relations as in other fields, develops slowly and in fits and starts. In the *Annual*, scholars will advance new ideas and support and refine them with original research. Other scholars will criticize those ideas and propose others—again supporting their proposals with research. Sometimes we will see progress. At other times, we may see regression. In the long term, however, the body of knowledge in public relations will progress; and we believe this and subsequent volumes of the *Annual* will reflect that progress.

We want to stress that the *Public Relations Research Annual* will be a *research* publication. All chapters should report original research or develop theories from original research reported previously. We believe that reviews of programs of research and theory-building reviews of research by several scholars are especially important to a discipline. Thus, we will have at least two major reviews in each volume.

There are two reviews in this volume. In the first, Culbertson integrates re-search by several scholars on the concept of breadth of perspective—an important effect of public relations. Grunig and Grunig, in the second review, summarize, and integrate the results of 14 studies of why organizations practice public relations as they do.

The remaining chapters in Volume 1 describe original research. The chapters by Pearson and Childers are based on critical methodology. The chapter by Olasky is both historical and critical. The remaining chapters are based on the methods of social and behavioral science. This distribution shows that all methodologies are appropriate, including social scientific, historical, critical, and legal. Likewise, all methods of scholarly observation are appropriate, including surveys, experiments, case studies, and historical and legal cases and trends.

We are proud to present Volume 1 of *Public Relations Research Annual*. We believe it is a tribute to the field of public relations, a reflection of the progress in one of the newest and most important communication professions.

James E. Grunig
Larissa A. Grunig

PART I

RESEARCH REVIEWS

Chapter 1

Breadth of Perspective: An Important Concept for Public Relations

Hugh M. Culbertson
Ohio University

This chapter argues that "breadth of perspective" is an important concept for public relations practice and research. The author first encountered the notion some 22 years ago in a sociological essay (Warshay, 1962). Recently it has served as a focus of his own research.

The first two sections of the chapter define *breadth of perspective* and discuss its role in several disciplines. A third section looks at its use in two sociological studies with public relations overtones. Then the author summarizes findings related to breadth of perspective in three of his own recent projects.

DEFINITION

Warshay defined *breadth of perspective* as the variety of responses that one calls to mind before tackling a problem. He saw a perspective as a symbolic structure that an actor brings to situations. The structure was said to consist of meanings or concepts, ideas, and values in differing states of clarity and coherence. A perspective serves as a frame of reference in defining situations (Warshay, 1962).

In light of this and other literature that is noted later, it is suggested that a person's breadth of perspective can be high in approaching an issue or topic only if there is:

1. Awareness that more than one definition, stand, or conclusion is possible and is probably accepted as valid by significant persons or groups. In his classic

definition of *public*, Herbert Blumer (1953) specified that members must confront an issue, disagree about how to define and deal with it, and discuss it (apparently leading to a recognition that differing views exist). Grunig and Hunt (1984) see this definition as consistent with their "behavior molecule" (pp. 143–145) concept for public relations planning.

2. Awareness that there are, in all probability, differences between one's own position or definition and that of other people. This would be defined as a moder-ate or low (at least, less than perfect or the highest possible) congruency in the coorientation model of Chaffee–McLeod (1968).

3. An inclination to take others' views into account, as well as one's own, in making communication decisions and carrying them out (Culbertson, 1983a).

4. Knowledge of arguments and ramifications that support viewpoints opposed to (or at least, different from) those to which one subscribes.

REVIEW OF LITERATURE

In addition to its "home discipline" of sociology, the notion of breadth of perspec-tive has shown up, as reported later, in the work of psychologists concerned with flexibile, adaptive cognitive behavior. Also, it has played a role in an innovative mass-communication study by Chaffee and Wilson (1977) on diversity of people's news agendas as well as in research on knowledge level (Edelstein, 1973), and on uncertainty as a motive to seek information (Blood, Becker, & Carey, 1984).

In the public relations area, Grunig and Hunt (1984) discussed four models of public relations practice in their recent text. They focused heavily on a "two-way symmetric" model (p. 41–43) that they regarded as at least the fourth step in the evolution of public relations. Practitioners have long spoken eloquently of public relations in this light, they suggested, but few have practiced in the two-way symmetric mode until quite recently.

Analytically, two-way symmetric public relations appears to involve operating in what Lee Thayer (1968) has called the diachronic mode. At base this involves:

1. Entering a transaction with some thought of knowledge, opinions, or behav-ior that one hopes to bring about in one or more transaction "partners."

2. Having a willingness and inclination to change objectives vis-à-vis these partners as one learns more about them and their contexts.

3. Having a willingness to change one's own beliefs and behavior as a result of what the partners do and say. In public relations terms, this often involves chang-ing client policy or practice—striving to live right, as well as to let people know you live right, as spelled out in one definition of the public relations function (see Simon, 1980, p. 6).

This analysis clearly places a premium on recognition by a communications source that he or she probably has a definition that differs from that of receivers. Thus, *breadth of perspective* lurks beneath the surface of Thayer's definition.

Such lurking also exists in Grunig's (1976) information-systems theory. In particular, the concept of problem recognition has a high value when one recognizes uncertainty with regard to a conclusion or decision. This, in turn, seems to imply a recognition that two or more conclusions are at least possible and merit consideration.

Symbolic-interactionist sociology offers perhaps the most compelling rationale for paying attention to breadth of perspective, although not a very clear statement of what the concept means or how it can best be measured.

As described by George Herbert Mead (1955), an infant (here labelled P) becomes a functioning human largely by:

1. Behaving.

2. Observing how others react to that behavior.

3. Imitating that behavior by others, incorporating it (and accompanying evaluations and assessments of P) into P's own cognitive and behavioral repertoire.

4. Thus gaining the tools to define himself or herself. Furthermore, because two or more others are normally taken into account, the maturing P learns that he or she can be defined and assessed in two or more ways. This realization, in turn, suggests that any one definition of P is arbitrary—not absolute and beyond question. Such definition permits P to see himself or herself *as object*—as something to be evaluated and altered or reinforced adaptively in light of probable outcomes.

As an aside, historian Daniel Boorstin (1971) said that there is danger of exaggeration and insincerity—and of widespread cynicism—when people construct pseudo-events designed to gain publicity and impress others. Maybe so. However, Erving Goffman (1959) argued persuasively that we all play to audiences almost constantly so people will attend to, approve of, and/or respect us. A pseudo-event, such as a new-car unveiling, differs in degree (being designed for many people and a chain of publics rather than for one or a few people), but not in kind, from what all people do on a date, in a meeting, and so on.

Two other interactionists, Ralph Turner (1956) and Thomas Scheff (1964), have honed in on breadth of perspective, without calling it that, in seminal articles. Turner (1956) spelled out three standpoints in increasing order of complexity and maturity:

1. The *first-person* standpoint. Here, the role-taker, P, imitates the behavior of some other person whose role he or she takes. The result is more or less automatic acceptance by P of the other's assessment as his or her (P's) own. Infants tend to

engage in such role-taking, as do adults when mental illness leads them to lose sight of the difference between reality and fantasy.

2. The *third-person* standpoint. Here, P attends to another's assessment but sees it as separate and distinct from P's own. The separateness of the two or more viewpoints becomes salient, permitting P to compare P's view with others' and to alter his or her definition or question others' as seems appropriate and functional.

3. The standpoint of *interactive-effect*. Here, P considers the joint implications of his or her own definitions and those of others. Subtle intricate relational behavior—the stuff of good literature and drama—can result. For example, a salesperson P can behave so as to make a potential customer feel that P is "plain folk." The result of such a strategy may be a sale—if the potential customer likes ordinary people—even though P may continue with some distress (dissonance) to see himself or herself as a sophisticate and not plain folk.

Turner (1956) used the term *reflexive* to denote role-taking in which P defines O's perception of P. And Scheff (1964) has noted an important dimension of reflexivity based on the fact that P can, in a special case of reflexive role-taking, define O's perception of P's perception of O. The situation is analogous to that of a TV set tuned into a program on which the camera is pointed at the set, which in turn contains a smaller picture of the same set, which in turn contains a smaller picture of that picture, and so on in an infinite regress limited only by one's ability to detect small images.

Such depth of reflexive role-taking can be illustrated by a horrible ethnic joke involving two Russian laborers who are feuding with each other. P, the role-taker as defined here, assumes the following about his enemy, O: (a) O is afraid of P and would not like to spend a weekend in a city where P is located; (b) O recognizes that P does, in fact, consider O to be a liar; and (c) O recognizes correctly that P dislikes O strongly and intends to gain revenge against O for a past misdeed.

Against this background, P comes home from work on a Friday and announces to his wife that the two of them are going to a resort in Minsk for the weekend.

"O has been telling people at the shop that he's going to Minsk this weekend," P tells his wife. "Now, O knows I think he is a liar. Thus, if he tells people he is going to Minsk, he probably assumes I'll think he is, in fact, going to Pinsk. He knows I'll probably go where I think he is in order to exact revenge, but he surely doesn't want to be where I am so this can happen. Thus, he apparently wants me to believe he's going to Pinsk so he can spend a safe weekend in Minsk. He can't fool me: he's going to Minsk."

Much the same notion is expressed in the lyrics of a country song heard on American radio in the late 1970s. The song deals with a fellow and a girl who meet in a cafe. The girl leaves the cafe in her motor vehicle, and the fellow follows her in his. The girl sings the following lyrics about her behavior during the ensuing ride:

I was looking back to see
If you were looking back to see
If I was looking back to see
If you were looking back at me

Clearly, such fascinating subtleties in perspective-taking merit careful study by practitioners seeking to understand and improve their all-important "sensitivity" to others—an important aspect of interpersonal communication skill.

Also in the interactionist tradition, Pelz and Andrews (1967), in a large-scale study of research-and-development laboratories, found that productive scientists tended to have *frequent* contact with a *wide variety* of colleagues. This held whether productivity was measured in article output, citations to one's work by other scholars, or rated esteem. The productive scientist also tended not to do research full-time. Teaching and administrative work appeared to help give (or perhaps reflect) a needed variety of perspectives.

Pelz (1975) suggested that exposure to diverse viewpoints *challenges* the scientist. This, in turn, is said to build creative tension only when coupled with a sense of autonomy from organizational demands and recognition for past achievements. Autonomy and recognition help give a sense of *security* needed to pit one's own ideas against other views in a constructive way.

Strauss and Rainwater (1962) expressed related alarm about the growth of new specialties in chemistry. As subfields proliferate, inter-specialty communication is apt to decline. As a result, the discipline may lose a unifying theoretical focus and a creative clash as well as integration of viewpoints. This concern, expressed by many chemists in a nationwide survey, surely has a familiar ring to communication scholars (Rubin, 1977).

In his organization theory, Hage (1980) suggested that a concentration of varied specialists within a complex organization aids creative innovation. Many organizational theorists, including Likert (1961) and Argyris (1973), have also stressed free, open, purposive communication among diverse organization members as pertinent to a wide variety of organizational tasks and outputs.

In a branch of social psychology far removed from interactionism, work on the authoritarian personality dating back at least to Adorno, Frenkel-Brunswik, Levinson, and Sanford (1950) and to Rokeach (1960) has stressed a notion very similar to breadth of perspective.

In this tradition, slavish adherence to one set of world-shaping beliefs (called "central beliefs" by Rokeach, 1960, p. 75) was seen as leading to inflexible behavior as well as to a lack of effective, flexible attention to one's environment. These factors, in turn, help bring about stereotyping and unchanging, prejudiced behavior toward large, varied groups of people.

In a more recent extension of the authoritarian-personality tradition, Hampden-Turner (1971) argued that willingness to risk one's own view via active, questioning exposure to diverse others is a key element in the innovative, courageous, existential sort of person whom he admiringly called "radical man" (p. 389).

Proposing a quite different sociological interpretation, Stewart and Hoult (1956) attributed the inflexible, limited behavior and beliefs of high-authoritarians partly to restricted social environments of such people (who, after all, tend to come from isolated rural areas and homogeneous urban ghettos that do not encourage inter-religious or inter-ethnic exchange).

Given this background, according to Stewart and Hoult (1956), the high-authoritarian often does not share meanings or experiences with diverse others. Thus, he or she tends not to take novel or diverse perspectives into account. Further, when the parochial isolate does make such an effort, performance tends to be ineffective because the individual can do little but view different cultures in formulaic, stereotypic ways.

In political sociology, Lipset has focused on two notions relating to breadth of perspective. Cross-pressures from different social groups and perspectives often lead people to withdraw from politics, he argued (see Lipset, 1960, pp. 203–216). At the same time, the perceived opportunity for upward mobility (moving to a class level preferable to and different from one's own) can encourage people who perceive that they disagree with authority figures to "work within the system" in a democratic way (see Lipset, 1960, pp. 253–258). Also, Shils (1956) argued that political extremism often develops in the absence of "mutual adaptation of spheres rather than the dominance or submission of any one to the others" (p. 154).

In the international realm, Schramm (1967) is one of many who have viewed communication as an important part of social-political-economic development because it prepares people to play new roles and assume new responsibilities.

With this quick (by no means exhaustive) overview of varied disciplines and traditions, we now turn to public relations applications.

TWO PR-RELATED STUDIES

A great deal of symbolic-interactionist work, based largely on the participant-observer technique and in-depth interviewing, looks and reads like insightful PR case-study material. Such research seems especially pertinent to the practitioner who, in following the two-way symmetric model, must take into account and deal with executives' and employees' socialization and training as well as superficial publicity for and awareness by broad, general publics.

Bucher and Stelling (1977) investigated graduate programs, largely in psychiatry and psychological counseling. Their findings challenged the common belief that graduate education is generally a highly regimented process in which an all-powerful faculty molds neophytes in its own image and with its own particular governing perspective.

In some cases, students developed their own perspectives and derived self-assessments from these. Then, students chose internship supervisors and/or major professors who seemed apt to validate already-existing self-assessments and criteria. Student and faculty perspectives, then, were seen as separate and rather independent. Student evaluation consisted of hunting for a match between the two, not of the faculty sanding off edges of square student pegs in order to fit these pegs into pre-determined, round, faculty-created holes.

Matthews (1979) has done a book-length study of what might be called the public relations posture of day-care facilities for the elderly. In the wake of 1974 federal legislation, the United States committed funds to constructing and running such centers. This required a new breed of professionals (or at least, expansion of an existing breed) to run the centers.

The conventional wisdom held that the professionals were supporters and servants of the elderly, with the two groups sharing a common definition of where each was going, how, and why. However, Matthews' participant-observer data convinced her that the professionals and the elderly had conflicting perspectives that lay at the heart of potential problems.

In one center, for example, elderly "customers" sought to be active in politics in the tradition of the Gray Panthers. (After all, 70-year-olds aren't all senile and decrepit just because a law so defines them.) Far from being supportive, the professionals covertly opposed the political bid by withholding information from the elderly (see Matthews, 1979, p. 156).

Why? Matthews contended that the professionals' jobs and the legitimacy and importance of their work hinged largely on the dependent, inferior status of the elderly. This is not a pretty picture if reporters happen to latch onto it, Matthews implied, and it's not a healthy setting for the birth of a profession based, by definition, on a concept of broad, genuine public service (Rivers & Schramm, 1969).

We now turn to a brief summary of elements that reflected the notion of perspective diversity in three recent studies involving the author.

SUMMARY OF THREE
RECENT STUDIES

Newspaper Study

In late 1979 and early 1980, the author interviewed 258 reporters and editors on 17 varied American newspapers (Culbertson, 1983a). A major purpose was to test and further explicate the widely quoted finding of Johnstone, Slawski, and Bowman (1976) that American journalists adhere in varying degrees to two viewpoints about their work: (a) a *neutral* or traditional view stressing speed, objectivity, and traditional journalistic writing style (the inverted pyramid, the summary lead, short sentences and paragraphs, etc.); and (b) a *participant* view calling for somewhat subjective interpretation as to causes, meanings, and implications of events.

In the author's study, there appeared to be a clear-cut traditional viewpoint along with two other, clearly distinct belief clusters: (a) an *interpretative* view emphasizing careful research and basically using the scholar as a role model; and (b) an *activist* position allowing for promotion within news columns of a cause or ideology.

In trying to figure out what these viewpoints meant as to news-judgment behavior, we proposed the news-orientation model—a kind of bastard offshoot of the Chaffee–McLeod (1968) coorientation model. As shown in Fig. 1.1, this model calls attention to three elements: the journalist's own assessment of what constitutes news, the journalist's perception of audience assessments, and the journalist's news-judgment decisions as reflected in projected or actual news play. One can obviously construct three measures of similarity, each focusing on one pair of variables in the model:

1. *Congruency.* The degree of similarity between the journalist's own assessment and that which he or she attributes to the audience. Stamm and Pearce (1971) and Brown, Becker, and McLeod (1976) have emhpasized congruency because it is a "link to reality" that is useful in assessing one's relations to others so as to structure communication behavior.

2. *Followership.* The extent to which one's news-judgment choices coincide with the audience's preferences as defined by the journalist.

3. *Autonomy.* The level of similarity between the journalist's own preferences and his or her news-judgment priorities.

We expected, based on a review of applied-journalism literature, that tradi-tionals would have little time or specialized expertise to develop clear-cut, firm

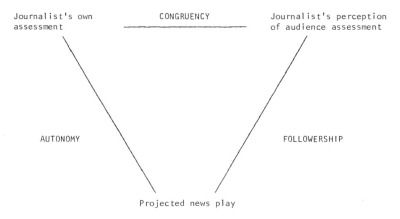

FIG. 1.1.   The news-orientation model.

positions of their own (see Epstein, 1975, pp. 16–17). Further, we believed that they would have been socialized to set aside or ignore what perspectives they had in order to remain "objective" (Charnley, 1966; Ryan & Tankard, 1977).

Given the lack of well established, useable personal viewpoints, it seemed, *traditionals* should tend to show *high congruency* between self and audience (based partly, perhaps, on an inclination to take the audience into account in the near-absence of other bases for developing whatever personal views they might construct). *Interpreters* and *activists*, on the other hand, would likely have research- or cause-based perspectives that could stand as alternatives to audience beliefs, *reducing congruency*.

In light of the foregoing, and a strong tendency on their part to view media outlets largely as profit-oriented businesses, *traditionals* should feel compelled to *follow* perceived audience preferences rather closely in making news-judgment decisions. *Interpreters* and *activists*, on the other hand, should have alternative bases to consider in news judgment, leading to relatively *low followership*.

In a nutshell, these hypotheses were generally supported (see Culbertson, 1983a, p. 20). However, predictions relating to the third variable in news-orientation, *autonomy*, were not borne out—a puzzling result.

It's probable that some developments in modern journalism (the advent of precision journalism [Meyer, 1973] and new journalism [Johnson, 1971], as well as interpretative reporting) may lead gradually toward higher autonomy among journalists. At the same time, the ratings-oriented consulting business and publisher concern about declines in per-capita circulation (Robinson, 1978) may tend to increase followership. In any case, the possible tug of war between autonomy and followership lies at the heart of many issues in applied communication.

Interpretative and activist trends appear to be reducing congruency and followership vis-à-vis audiences of at least some journalists. At the same time, PR types following the two-way symmetric model are presumably convincing clients more than ever to take audience viewpoints into account and follow them. Such trends could change the character of press-source relations in the years ahead.

Public relations people, like journalists, undoubtedly experience some tug of war between following their own and following audience viewpoints. In PR, such concerns may be especially challenging and complex because of a need to attend to clients and numerous publics when making many communication decisions.

Osteopathic Study

In a second project, the author and Guido H. Stempel III examined the PR posture of osteopathic medicine in Ohio.

Taking the two-way symmetric model to heart, we conducted two surveys— one of 252 doctors of osteopathic medicine (DO), a regular-interval sample drawn from the Ohio Osteopathic Association membership list; and another of 415 Ohioans selected through random digit dialing.

Drawing on psychological association theory (Woelfel, Cody, Gillham, & Holmes, 1980), we argued that a belief might warrant particular attention in PR practice if: (a) people who held it also defined doctors of osteopathy as credible when compared with "establishment" MDs—the competition; and (b) DOs and the general-population sample disagreed, on the whole, with respect to the belief and related topics.

For illustrative purposes, we focus here on one topic that met both criteria— osteopathic manipulative therapy, the massaging of bones, joints, and muscles. Long a cornerstone of osteopathy, manipulation is now seen by most DOs as an important but ancillary type of treatment suitable only with a limited class of ailments. DOs now get virtually as much training as MDs in the use of drugs, surgery, radiation, and related topics. Furthermore, DOs are licensed, *total-care physicians*—a fact not understood by everyone.

We asked each DO to estimate the percentage of his or her patients who had manipulation in the DO's own office during the past 12 months. There was considerable variation, indicating that the profession's own viewpoint on when to manipulate needed clarification (a fact readily admitted by many DOs in focus-group sessions and in-depth interviews). On the average, physicians estimated that they had manipulated 32% of their patients.

In the general-population study, Ohioans guesstimated whether Ohio DOs today manipulate all, most, some, very few, or none of their patients. In all, 38% said all or most—clearly denoting far more than the 32% figure provided by DOs themselves. Thus, about two-fifths of the general sample substantially over-estimated the apparent use of manipulation.

This constituted a genuine PR problem in light of another finding. Good–bad evaluation of manipulative therapy correlated positively with perceived DO credibility where people felt that physicians manipulate some, few or none of their patients (gamma = .52, p < .01), but not with respondents who felt that DOs manipulate all or most of the time. Apparently, then, people wanted manipulation only on appropriate occasions and saw a potential problem with its over-use (see Culbertson & Stempel, 1982, pp. 51–53).

Other data also indicated clearly that DOs knew of differences in perspective between themselves and the public. Such awareness, in turn, seemed persuasive in seeking physician support of a PR program. In follow-up consultation with leading physicians, we found them especially open to suggestions for action when we gave them evidence that physicians and public perspectives differed plus evidence that their colleagues had "breadth of perspective" in that they knew of and expressed concern about these problems (Culbertson & Stempel, 1982).

State-Issues Survey

In a third study, Culbertson and Stempel (1986) interviewed 451 Ohioans in the fall of 1983 about three controversial state issues on the November ballot. Respondents were chosen via random digit dialing and interviewed by phone over a 3-week period ending 2 days before the November 8th election. One state issue would have increased the minimum drinking age in the state from 18 to 21. Another would have repealed a 90% boost in state income tax passed by the state legislature several months earlier. The final issue covered would have required a 60% majority in each house of the legislature to pass future revenue bills.

Several weeks before interviewing, we obtained campaign literature from the four interest groups spearheading campaigns for and against the three issues. (The tax issues were packaged together, with all leaders but by no means all voters apparently assuming that a vote for or against one would go along with a similar vote on the other.)

Prior to data collection, each interviewer became familiar with the arguments, pro and con, listed in the literature. Then, arguments were sought from respondents, via unaided recall, by asking questions such as:

> Various politicians and citizens have been discussing pros and cons for state issues 1, 2, and 3 in recent weeks. Now we'd like to know what arguments come to your mind on both sides as you think about these issues.
>
> First, consider issue 1, which, if passed, would raise Ohio's minimum drinking age to 21 years. What specific arguments come to your mind as supporting issue 1? (Please give any arguments you can—whether you accept them as valid or not.)
>
> (Respondent answered. Then interviewer probed by saying, "Any other arguments in favor of issue 1?".)
>
> Now, please give arguments which come to mind as opposing issue 1.

Interviewers checked arguments given that were on the prepared list and jotted down others (rarely offered, as it turned out) in a miscellaneous category. We had asked each respondent whether he or she favored, opposed, or neither favored nor opposed each issue. Thus, we were able to count the number of arguments advanced in support of, and the number opposed to, his or her own position. The "opposed to" figure gave at least a rough indication of awareness of and concern with a perspective opposed to one's own.

This strategy resembled the one used by Edelstein (1973) in a study of beliefs about the Vietnam War. He defined a person's knowledge structure as complex where that person could give both positive and negative values of a proposal to end the conflict.

Arguments given for one's own position outnumbered those for the opposing view by 2 or 3 to 1 for each issue. This held for both pro- and anti-respondents. Thus, Ohioans, on the whole, did not show very well-rounded, balanced mastery of pro and con positions.

In a further analysis, we asked people how often they viewed local and state political news on TV (frequently, sometimes, seldom, or never). And we included a similar item about newspaper use.

Multiple-regression analyses with education and other situational variables (see Fig. 1.2 and 1.3) controlled yielded the following basic results:

1. Media use did not predict argument generation (in total, for own position, or for opposing position) with the sparsely covered drinking-age issue.

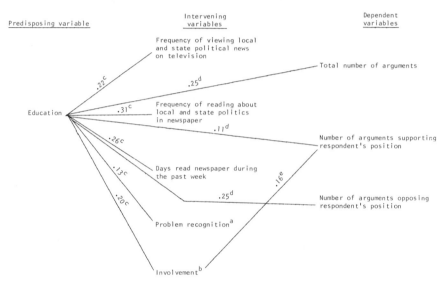

FIG. 1.2. Path model of factors correlating with argument generation on 1983 Ohio state issue about raising drinking age.

Addendum to FIG. 1.2

[a]This variable stemmed from one item asking how much effort the respondent felt was needed to make up his or her mind on whether the issue was good or bad. Response options were a great deal, some, a little, and no effort at all.

[b]This variable stemmed from a single item asking to what extent the respondent saw a connection between him or herself, personally, and the state issue. Options were strong, moderate, weak, and none at all.

[c]This is a zero-order correlation between education, the sole predisposing variable, and one of the five intervening variables.

[d]This is a standardized regression coefficient linking education to a dependent variable with all intervening factors controlled.

[e]This is a standardized regression coefficient linking one intervening variable to one dependent measure with the other intervening factors controlled.

All coefficients reported are significant at $p < .05$. All significant paths are shown.

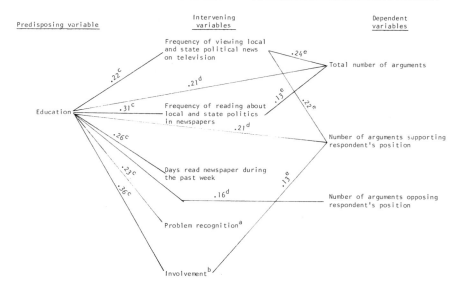

FIG. 1.3.   Path model of factors correlating with argument generation on 1983 Ohio state issues on tax revenue.

Addendum to FIG. 1.3.

[a]This variable stemmed from one item asking how much effort the respondent felt was needed to make up his or her mind on whether the issues were good or bad. Response options were a great deal, some, a little, and no effort at all.

[b]This variable stemmed from a single item asking to what extent the respondent saw a connection between him or herself, personally, and the state issues. Options were strong, moderate, weak, and none at all.

[c]This is a zero-order correlation between education, the sole predisposing factor, and one of the five intervening variables.

[d]This is a standardized regression coefficient linking education to a dependent variable with all intervening factors controlled.

[e]This is a standardized regression coefficient linking one intervening variable to one dependent measure with the other intervening factors controlled.

All coefficients reported are significant at $p < .05$. All significant paths are shown.

---

2. Looking at the two tax issues lumped together, frequency of TV use for news on local and state politics predicted total-argument generation ($b = .24$) and production of arguments supporting one's own view ($b = .22$). Newspaper use for local and state politics predicted only total-argument production (with a marginal b of .13). *Neither newspaper nor TV use correlated significantly with generation of arguments opposed to one's own view.*

3. Education, on the other hand, correlated with all three argument-generation variables, even with media use and situational factors controlled, on the tax issues.

Another analysis yielded intriguing results that relate to opposing arguments. We asked respondents the following on the combined tax issues:

> Now, let's move on to issues 2 and 3, both dealing with state tax legislation. Issue 2 would require a three-fifths majority in the Ohio legislature to pass revenue or tax laws. Issue 3 would repeal the income-tax increase passed in January 1983 by the Ohio legislature. Would you say you have gotten the most information about issues 2 and 3 from newspapers? Radio? Television? Magazines? Other people you've talked with? Public meetings? Or where?

This item permitted us to identify 120 TV-dependent respondents and 121 newspaper-dependents vis-à-vis these issues. TV use did correlate with number of opposing arguments produced ($r = .14$, $p = .09$) for newspaper-dependent persons. This association held with education partialed out. However, neither media-use variable correlated with generation of opposed arguments among TV-dependent persons. Apparently, when newspaper-dependent folks used the media (including TV), they did so in a thorough, critical way that at least sometimes helped make them aware of perspectives opposed to their own. This squares with the often-noted (but also often-ignored) notion that practitioners should not judge the probable impact of a medium solely on the basis of total audience size.

SUMMARY AND CONCLUSIONS

As shown in Fig. 1.4, research and theorizing to date suggest at least five possible mechanisms or processes through which various antecedents may affect the third and fourth components of "breadth of perspective" listed earlier. These components are willingness to take others' views into account and knowledge of arguments and viewpoints distinct from one's own. (Theory about and evidence relating to components one and two, awareness that differing views are possible and exist, seem limited at present.)

Where the number before a given paragraph (following) appears on a line within Fig. 1.4, the process described in that paragraph appears to link a given "breadth component" with an antecedent connected to it by the line. Processes are as follows:

1. Three levels of analysis varying widely on a micro–macro continuum suggest that a feeling of low self-confidence and/or of being threatened in a given situation can reduce willingness to expose oneself actively, honestly, and fully to diverse viewpoints. At a very macro level, Henry (1965) blamed much of what he called "wooly mindedness" and deceit in America on the society's emphasis on

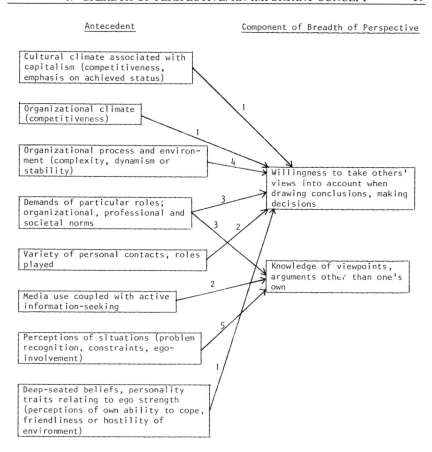

FIG. 1.4.   Antecedents suggested in behavioral-science literature as contributing to two components of breadth of perspective. (The number appearing above a given line denotes the paragraph on pp. 28–31, which describes a mechanism linking the antecedent and consequent connected in the figure by that line.)

achieved rather than ascribed status. This is said to contribute to and stem partly from competitiveness inherent in capitalism. Such a climate, he argued, leads to heavy emphasis on functionality (whether something works) rather than truth-seeking. At the micro level, psychologists in the authoritarian-personality tradition have frequently mentioned a lack of self-confidence and ego strength (and an associated feeling that the world is a hostile environment) as bases for parochialism and lack of openness to diverse views (Adorno et al., 1950; Hampden-Turner, 1971; Rokeach, 1960). And in organizational theory, Argyris (1974) has cited competitiveness and attendant feelings of being threatened within a given organization—the "win–lose dynamic"—as a key to much organizational inefficiency associated with a failure of managers to communicate fully with each other and pertinent publics.

2. Two areas of research center on a combination of past exposure to diverse messages and felt need to seek information actively as antecendents. Sociological and organizational studies reviewed earlier suggest that playing varied roles and making varied contacts sometimes enhance inclinations to take varied viewpoints into account. And data reported earlier (Culbertson & Stempel, 1986) on public response to a state-issues referendum campaign suggested that media exposure correlated with generation of arguments opposed to one's own view where and only where the respondent was newspaper-oriented (hence probably relatively active as an information seeker, based on past research) (Blumler & McQuail, 1969; Patterson, 1980; Weaver & Fielder, 1983).

3. At times, the demands of particular roles played, along with related organizational, vocational, and societal norms, have appeared to bear on taking others' views into account. In the author's research on news personnel summarized earlier (Culbertson, 1983a), adherence to traditional ideas about the role of modern journalism went along with reported inclinations to follow one's audience. In Matthews' study of old folks' homes, "custodial" professionals appeared to ignore or downgrade the viewpoints of the elderly partly because their (the professionals') legitimacy hinged in part on a belief that the elderly were incapable of having important aspirations and goals (see Matthews, 1979, pp. 155–158). Also, the civic attitude scale presented by McCombs and Poindexter (1983) appears to tap a set of beliefs, apparently quite widely held in Western societies, stressing the need to be informed about arguments from varied locations and viewpoints—transcending one's personal, localized interests.

4. Organizational theories advanced by Hage (1980), Grunig (1984), and others suggest that complexity and dynamism or stability of an organization's environment—as well as of its inner workings—bear in complex ways on tendencies to be diachronic or synchronic, to ignore or heed the divergent views of key publics.

5. Grunig's (1976) earlier work on information-systems theory, centering on problem recognition, constraints, and level of personal involvement as factors to be considered when individuals and organizations define particular situations, at least hinted that active information-seeking can, under some circumstances, aid learning about diverse options (i.e., perspectives). One facet of such learning may be "hedging," holding of diverse views with differing attitudinal implications (Grunig, 1982; Grunig & Stamm, 1979). Hedging appears to entail holding of differing (perhaps inconsistent) views as one's own—a possible by-product of Turner's (1956) role-taking from a first-person standpoint. Breadth of perspective, however, entails accepting one view as one's own and recognizing a difference between that and other positions. Such recognition, it appears, requires what Turner (1956) would call role-taking from the third-person standpoint.

In the author's state-issues study (see Culbertson & Stempel, 1986), personal involvement correlated positively and significantly with generation of arguments in support of respondents' own views on all issues. There was no correlation between involvement and number of opposed arguments produced. Problem and constraint recognition did not predict any argument-generation variables, but this cannot be considered a meaningful test of Grunig's theory. In general, a high proportion of respondents rated problem recognition as low, and constraint recognition as high. Few people fell in the category of problem-facing (high problem and low constraint recognition), which the theory suggests should entail intense, active information seeking.

Certainly, the theoretical clarity of empirical support for such mechanisms varies. However, the model in Fig. 1.4 would seem promising as a basis for organizing and stimulating future research.

An important goal for future research, it would seem, is to determine whether, in fact, the four suggested components of breadth of perspective correlate so that concept can be viewed as a single dimension. Included here are awareness that different views are possible, that they do exist, that viewpoints other than one's own often need to be considered when making plans and drawing conclusions, and of arguments opposed to one's own view.

The author's three projects noted earlier have dealt separately with the last three of these components; the newspaper-attitude study (Culbertson, 1983a), which focused on taking views other than the journalist's own into account (tapped by followership); the osteopathic study (Culbertson & Stempel, 1982), with awareness that views opposed to one's (in this case, physicians') own do exist; and the state-issues study, with knowledge of opposing arguments. Unfortunately, two facets of breadth of perspectives were seldom analyzed in the same project so as to permit examining inter-correlations among them.

One element not stressed here but clearly needing attention in future studies is *accuracy* of perception of viewpoints other than one's own.

Bowes and Stamm (1975) have suggested that, in public relations, accuracy in the absence of agreement between client and public can prove to be important. Furthermore, as Klapper's (1964) often-quoted and never fully debunked statement of the minimum-effects model of mass communication implied, changing opinions so public and client agree may be difficult at best. However, improved accuracy of public perception regarding a client's stands and policies may often be an attainable goal because it does not require change in the public's own attitudes and opinions.

It is also clear that level of congruency between own and other's view can create PR problems. Perfect (the highest possible) congruency allows for no difference between self and other—an assumption that communication theory suggests is usually inaccurate (after all, no two people have identical environments or learning experiences; see Berlo, 1960, p. 123). *Ethnocentrism* or *egocentrism* results.

At the other extreme, lack of any perceived similarity between self and perceived other offers little basis for seeking compromise or shared meaning. This state has been called *polarization*. Like its opposite, extremely low congruency can prove maladaptive (see Shils, 1956, p. 154).

"Breadth of perspective" also has relevance to two concepts—conflict and uncertainty—stressed in recent writings about public relations theory. Ehling (1981) has argued persuasively that conflict management is a central focus, if not the defining focus, of public relations as a coherent field of study. And conflict, by its nature, seems to imply some awareness and addressing of differing viewpoints, plans, goals, and perspectives.

"Breadth of perspective" also deals with such awareness. It helps provide a context for study of conflict at an intrapersonal or more molar level. Two view-points or perspectives can have any one of at least four relations to each other.

1. *Irrelevance*. Here, holding one view would have no bearing on the holding of another.

2. *Supplementarity*. Here, holding one view would support holding of another. At the inter-personal level, persons having supplementary viewpoints might oper-ate with what group dynamicists call promotive interdependence (where success by one person would promote success by the other) (see Deutsch, 1960, p. 415).

3. *Actual conflict*. Here, the two people who have conflicting views would operate in a condition of contrient interdependence (with validation of beliefs held by one leading to disconfirmation of beliefs held by the other, and vice versa) (see Deutsch, 1960, p. 415). Intrapersonally, this amounts to cognitive dissonance (see Festinger, 1957).

4. *Conflict based on misunderstanding*. Here, one or both parties perceive con-flict in viewpoints, but the perception is inaccurate.

Obviously, condition 3 poses intractable problems in that it requires change or accommodation in one or both personally held perspectives. Condition 4, on the other hand, may involve changing only the perception of one person or group by another. Such change may both add to and depend on breadth of perspective by the perceiver. Clearly, public relations (and conflict-management) strategies are going to differ from one condition to the next.

Breadth of perspective and conflict management also seem to share a concern for the notion of uncertainty. Handling conflict (or avoiding it) may often (al-though not always) lead to a concern for *uncertainty reduction* (the attainment of resolutions that varied parties agree with wholeheartedly and will support). How-ever, a focus on breadth of perspectives can lead one to ask if *uncertainty enhance-ment* is not sometimes a fruitful public relations goal leading to greater information-seeking and tolerance. Chaffee and Wilson (1977) implied as much in their innovative study of news-agenda diversity as indexed with the H-statistic in infor-mation theory. H has high values, in their conceptualization, where (a) a person or group attaches high importance to news items in a large number of topic categories, and (b) items and item assignments do not cluster largely in any one or a few of these categories.

Perhaps journalism in the libertarian tradition and public relations share a broad concern, usually implicit, for uncertainty enhancement in many (not all) circum-stances. Advertisers and marketers, on the other hand, may focus largely on uncer-tainty reduction as implied by the notion of brand loyalty (sticking with a given product unquestioningly over time). At least, this concept merits further discussion in defining various disciplines.

In summary, breadth of perspective is important to public relations practice and scholarship for at least three reasons.

First, its is in line with America's libertarian heritage. As long noted by press scholars, this view emphasizes the need for a free marketplace of ideas in which the important and trivial, the true and untrue can meet in open competition.

This position takes on added salience if one buys the widely held view that the truly professional practitioner must promote the welfare of society as well as the client. In this context, professionalism requires concern for truth of *overall impres-sion* as well as truth of fact (Culbertson, 1983b). The public seemingly is entitled to both types of truth—even where there are few competent media people to help insure that the libertarian's free marketplace of ideas will correct untruths or im-balances (Culbertson, 1973).

Second, apparently breadth of perspective can often lead to productive, flexible, innovative behavior and output as suggested by Hage (1980) and demonstrated by Pelz and Andrews (1967). In a related vein, former President Richard M. Nixon has suggested that schooling in, mastery of, and ability to integrate contrasting perspectives can contribute to progressive, successful leadership. For example, General Douglas MacArthur and Prime Minister Shigeru Yoshida formed a unique partnership in rebuilding Japan after World War II partly because both men had lived and studied in the West and the Orient, permitting them to form a blend of elements of the two contrasting worlds (see Nixon, 1982, pp. 88–92). Zhou Enlai of China was an effective leader partly because he subscribed to Communist orthodoxy as well as ancient Chinese customs and tradition (see Nixon, 1982, pp. 234–241). And Konrad Adenauer of West Germany was said to have balanced loyalty to his homeland with "an affection for things French" (Nixon, 1982, p. 155).

Third, the concept can help articulate and add substance to the two-way sym-metric model of public relations practice. Grunig and Hunt (1984) argued per-suasively that this model represents a real step forward in many contexts for the evolving public relations function.

In conclusion, it is worth noting that entertainment of varied perspectives is not presented as a universal good. There are doubtless times (as when one is caught in a burning theater) when action, not weighing of alternatives, is the key to success or survival. Too much weighing may leave little time for meaningful behavior.

It has also been argued persuasively that over-emphasis on breadth of perspective within a cultural or social group can destroy true diversity for an entire society by discouraging people, particularly the young, from fully accepting, developing, and carrying out unique aspects of their group's behavior and belief systems. For example, the Amish and Mennonite religious sects have rebelled against sending their children to American public schools on the grounds that exposure to the "outside world" and its temptations would lead to disintegration of such sects. In a 1972 decision, the U.S. Supreme Court concluded that there was some validity to such claims (see Keim, 1976, pp. 149–181).

However, Connor (1979) also suggested that excessive "closedness" can bring suffering, cruelty, and unquestioning followership even of leaders calling for mass suicide, such as that at Jonestown, Guyana in 1978.

Viewed in varied contexts, breadth of perspectives seems applicable in many social and public relations settings.

ACKNOWLEDGMENTS

The author expresses appreciation for comments and suggestions provided by Dr. James Grunig, Dr. Dennis Jeffers, and Joung-Soon Park, a doctoral student in mass communication-journalism at Ohio University.

REFERENCES

Adorno, T. W., Frenkel-Brunswik, E., Levinson D. J., & Sanford, R. N. (1950). *The authoritarian personality*. New York: Wiley.

Argyris, C. (1973). Interpersonal barriers to decision making. In W. G. Bennis, D. E. Berlew, E. H. Schein, & F. I. Steele (Eds.), *Interpersonal dynamics*. (pp. 447–467). Homewood, IL: The Dorsey Press.

Argyris, C. (1974). *Behind the front page*. San Francisco: Jossey-Bass.

Berlo, D. K. (1960). *The process of communication*. New York: Holt, Rinehart & Winston.

Blood, R. W., Becker, L. B., & Carey, C. M. (1984, August). *Electoral knowledge and uncertainty*. Paper presented to Communication Theory and Methodology Division, Association for Education in Journalism and Mass Communication, Gainesville, FL.

Blumer, H. (1953). The mass, the public and public opinion. In B. Berelson & M. Janowitz, (Eds.), *Reader in public opinion and communication*. (pp. 43–50). Glencoe, IL: The Free Press.

Blumler, J. G., & McQuail, D. (1969). *Television in politics: Its uses and influences*. Chicago: University of Chicago Press.

Boorstin, D. J. (1971). From news-gathering to news-making: A flood of pseudo-events. In W. Schramm & D. F. Roberts (Eds.), *The process and effects of mass communication*. (pp. 116–150). Urbana, IL: University of Illinois Press.

Bowes, J. E., & Stamm, K. R. (1975). Evaluating communication with public agencies. *Public Relations Review, 1,*23–37.

Brown, J. D., Becker, L. B., & McLeod, J. M. (1976, August). *Causal analysis of coorientation variables using a non-experimental, longitudinal design.* Paper presented to Theory and Methodology Division, Association for Education in Journalism, College Park, MD.

Bucher, R., & Stelling, J. G. (1977). *Becoming professional* Beverly Hills, CA: Sage.

Chaffee, S. H., & McLeod, J. M. (1968). Sensitization in panel design: A coorientational experiment. *Journalism Quarterly, 45,* 661–669.

Chaffee, S. H., & Wilson, D. G. (1977). Media rich, media poor: Two studies of diversity in agenda-holding. *Journalism Quarterly, 54,* 466–476.

Charnley, M. V. (1966). *Reporting.* New York: Holt, Rinehart & Winston.

Connor, R. (1979). *Walled in: The true story of a cult.* New York: Signet.

Culbertson, H. M. (1973). Public relations ethics: A new look. *Public Relations Quarterly, 17,* 15–17, 23.

Culbertson, H. M. (1983a). Three perspectives on American journalism. *Journalism Monographs, 83.*

Culbertson, H. M. (1983b). How public relations textbooks handle honesty and lying. *Public Relations Review, 9,* 65–73.

Culbertson, H. M., & Stempel, G. H. III (1982). *A study of the public relations posture of osteopathic medicine in Ohio.* Columbus, Ohio: Ohio Osteopathic Association.

Culbertson, H. M., & Stempel, G. H. III. (1986). How media use and reliance affect knowledge level. *Communication Research, 13,* 579–602.

Deutsch, M. (1960). The effects of cooperation and competition upon group process. In D. Cartwright & A. Zander (Eds.), *Group dynamics* (pp. 414–448). New York: Harper & Row.

Edelstein, A. S. (1973). Decision-making and mass communication: A conceptual and methodological approach to public opinion. In P. Clarke (Ed.), *New models for mass communication research.* (pp. 81–118). Beverly Hills, CA: Sage Publications.

Ehling, W. P. (1981, August). *A theory of public relations management: Applications of decision, conflict, interorganizational and communication conceptual schemes to public relations practice.* Paper presented to Public Relations Division, Association for Education in Journalism and Mass Communication, East Lansing, MI.

Epstein, E. J. (1975). *Between fact and fiction: The problem of journalism.* New York: Random House Vintage Books.

Festinger, L. (1957). *A theory of cognitive dissonance.* Evanston, IL: Row, Peterson.

Goffman, E. (1959). *The presentation of self in everyday life.* Garden City, NY: Doubleday Anchor Books.

Grunig, J. E. (1976). Organizations and publics: Testing a communication theory. *Journalism Monographs,* No. 46.

Grunig, J. E. (1982). The message-attitude-behavior relationship. *Communication Research, 9,* 163–200.

Grunig, J. E. (1984). Organizations, environments and models of public relations. *Public Relations Research and Education, 1,* 6–29.

Grunig, J. E., & Hunt, T. (1984). *Managing public relations.* New York: Holt, Rinehart & Winston.

Grunig, J. E., & Stamm, K. R. (1979). Cognitive strategies and the resolution of environmental issues: A second study. *Journalism Quarterly, 56,* 715–726.

Hage, J. (1980). *Theories of organizations: Form, process and transformation.* New York: Wiley Interscience.

Hampden-Turner, C. (1971). *Radical man.* Garden City, NY: Anchor Books.

Henry, J. (1965). *Culture against man.* New York: Vintage Books.

Johnson, M. L. (1971). *The new journalism.* Lawrence, KS: University of Kansas Press.

Johnstone, J. W. C., Slawski, E. J., & Bowman, W. W. (1976). *The news people.* Urbana, IL: University of Illinois Press.

Keim, A. N. (Ed.). (1976). *Compulsory education and the Amish: The right not to be modern.* Boston: Beacon Press.

Klapper, J. T. (1964). *The effects of mass communication.* Glencoe, IL: The Free Press.

Likert, R. (1961). *New patterns of management.* New York: McGraw-Hill.

Lipset, S. M. (1960). *Political man.* Garden City, NY: Doubleday.

Matthews, S. H. (1979). *The social world of old women.* Beverly Hills, CA: Sage.

McCombs, M., & Poindexter, P. (1983). The duty to keep informed: News exposure and civic obligation. *Journal of Communication, 33,* 88–96.

Mead, G. H. (1955). *Mind, self and society.* Chicago: University of Chicago Press.

Meyer, P. (1973). *Precision journalism.* Bloomington, IN: Indiana University Press.

Nixon, R. M. (1982). *Leaders.* New York: Warner Books.

Patterson, T. E. (1980). *The mass media election: How Americans choose their president.* New York: Praeger.

Pelz, D. C. (1975). Problem solvers vs. decision makers. In D. C. Pelz, H. Mayer, & S. W. Gellerman (Eds.), *Organizing the organization for better r and d* (pp. 7–22). New York: Amacom.

Pelz, D. C., & Andrews, F. M. (1967). *Scientists in organizations: Productive climates for research and development.* New York: Wiley.

Rivers, W. L., & Schramm, W. (1969). *Responsibility in mass communication.* New York: Harper & Row.

Robinson, J. P. (1978). Daily news habit of the American public. *American Newspaper Publisher's Association News* (Research Report No. 15). Reston, VA: American Newspaper Publisher's Association.

Rokeach, M. (1960). *The open and closed mind.* New York: Basic Books.

Rubin, B. D. (1977). Overview. In B. Rubin (Ed.), *Communication Yearbook I* (pp. 3–4). New Brunswick, NJ: Transaction Books.

Ryan, M. & Tankard J. W. Jr. (1977). *Basic news reporting.* Palo Alto, CA: Mayfield Publishing.

Scheff, T. (1964). The role of the mentally ill and the dynamics of mental disorder: A research framework. *Sociometry, 26,* 436–453.

Schramm, W. (1967). Communication development and the development process. In L. Pye (Ed.), *Communications and political development* (pp. 30–57). Princeton, NJ: Princeton University Press.

Shils, E. A. (1956). *The torment of society.* Glencoe, IL: The Free Press.

Simon, R. (1980). *Public relations: Concepts and practices.* Columbus, OH: Grid.

Stamm, K. R., & Pearce, W. B. (1971). Communication behavior and coorientational relations. *Journal of Communication, 21,* 208–220.

Stewart, D., & Hoult, T. (1956). A social-psychological theory of the authoritarian personality. *American Journal of Sociology, 61,* 316–328.

Strauss, A. L., & Rainwater, L. (1962). *The professional scientist: A study of American chemists.* Chicago: Aldine.

Thayer, L. (1968). *Communication and communication systems.* Homewood, IL: Richard D. Irwin.

Turner, R. H. (1956). Role-taking, role standpoint and reference group behavior. *American Journal of Sociology, 61,* 316–328.

Warshay, L. (1962). Breadth of perspective. In A. Rose (Ed.), *Human nature and social processes.* Boston: Houghton Mifflin.

Weaver, D., & Fielder, V. D. (1983). Civic attitudes and newspaper readership in Chicago. *Newspaper Research Journal, 4,* 11–18.

Woelfel, J., Cody, M., Gillham, J., & Holmes, R. (1980). Premises of multidimensional attitude change theory: An experimental analysis. *Human Communication Research, 6,* 153–167.

Toward a Theory of the Public Relations Behavior of Organizations: Review of a Program of Research

James E. Grunig
Larissa Schneider Grunig
University of Maryland

Public relations as a form of organizational communication has been practiced for centuries, although it was not defined as a unique form of communication until the late 19th century. Public relations has emerged only recently as a domain of communication research, however, and much of that research has been applied. That is, the purpose of the research has been to help practitioners plan and evaluate specific public relations programs or campaigns. To our knowledge, few—if any—researchers have conducted theoretical research to describe systematically how organizations practice public relations and to explain why they practice it as they do.

In this chapter, we describe a program of research that systematically has attempted to explain why different kinds of organizations practice public relations in different ways. We have identified theoretical parameters of public relations behavior and searched for variables that explain the variation in that behavior. We have borrowed many of our variables from theories of organizational sociology and mass communication, but the end product is a theory unique to and of special value for explaining public relations.

ORGANIZATIONAL THEORY
AS AN ORGANIZING
FRAMEWORK

Construction of a theory of public relations behavior must begin with a definition of public relations and a classification of the range of organizational activities included within the rubric of "public relations." Definitions abound in textbooks, but few of them are rigorous enough to produce a set of variables that describe public relations. We begin with the assumption that public relations is organizational communication, but we use the term in a broader sense than that which is usually attached to "organizational communication" by communication scholars (J. Grunig, 1975).

Scholars of organizational communication usually use that term to describe communication behaviors that occur naturally within an organization (i.e., without the intervention of a communication professional). Public relations differs from "organizational communication" in that it is managed communication (J. Grunig & Hunt, 1984). That is, professional communicators in a public relations department or in a department with a name such as public affairs, corporate communication, or employee relations set up and manage systems of communication both inside and outside the organization.

Admittedly, defining public relations as managed organizational communication would not exclude the marketing communication activities of organizations from the definition. In many organizations, the distinction between marketing and public relations is a blurred one. In general, however, public relations departments deal with the "public affairs" of an organization—the interdependencies that organizations have with other systems in their external and internal environments, whereas marketing departments use communication to develop and dispose of products. Whereas marketing communicators deal only with the consumer public, public relations practitioners deal with all other publics that affect or are affected by an organization.

Public relations departments, however, often do supply marketing departments with the necessary technical skills to communicate about products through means other than paid advertising. Thus, as we show later in this chapter, public relations programs generally provide two functions for organizations: public affairs and marketing support. At some point, it may be fruitful to extend the theory of public relations that we develop in this chapter to explain both public relations and marketing as managed communication activities of organizations. At this point, however, we limit our theories to the activities defined as public relations by most organizations.

Scholars of both public relations and organizational communication often have confused two kinds of theories about the way organizations or the people in them communicate. A positive theory, on the one hand, is a descriptive, explanatory theory. It explains how people or organizations behave and searches for variables that cause the behavior. Nearly all theories in the physical and biological sciences are positive theories, as are the majority of theories in the social and behavioral sciences. Our purpose from the beginning of this program of research has been to construct a positive theory of the public relations behavior of organizations.

Most "theories" in public relations textbooks, in contrast, are normative. They describe how an organization should practice public relations. Some textbooks also contrast this ideal practice of public relations with case study descriptions of how organizations actually have practiced it. Many textbooks in organizational communication similarly are normative. They prescribe communication as a solution to a multitude of organizational problems. Normative theories are not bad, however; many sophisticated normative theories can be found in economics, management science, and philosophy. In public relations, a sophisticated normative theory would be a contingency theory, a theory that specifies the most appropriate communication systems for different kinds of organizations based on a well-developed set of theoretical premises.

In our program of research, we have attempted primarily to develop a descriptive (positive) theory of public relations—a theory that explains how and why public relations is practiced as it is in the real world. We have assumed, however, that such a positive theory would also provide normative prescriptions. In other words, we believed we would find that organizations practice the most appropriate type of public relations for their environments. Once we had described the environment of an organization, therefore, we could prescribe the best form of public relations for that organization. If we could develop a theory of how organizations do and should adapt to the environment, we could then save them a great deal of the trial and error that would be necessary for them to arrive at the ideal form of public relations on their own.

As we show as this article develops, however, we have found consistently that organizations do not practice the kind of public relations that our theories argue, logically, would be best in their environments. Thus, we have had to conclude that our first attempts at developing a positive theory instead produced a normative theory. We have gone on, however, to develop a positive theory to explain why organizations practice public relations as they do. That theory, in turn, specifies the conditions that would have to be changed before an organization could practice the form of public relations that the original, now normative, theory specified as best.

To develop an organizational theory of public relations, we have searched for variables that should or do correlate with different kinds of public relations behavior. We have found most of those variables in the field of organizational sociology, especially in structural and systems theories of organizations. Systems and structural theories pay particular attention to the relationship between organizations and their environments (Aldrich, 1971; Aldrich & Pfeffer, 1976; Campbell, 1969; Hannan & Freeman, 1974; Katz & Kahn, 1966). As Kuhn (1979) pointed out, the organization only can respond to the parts of the environment of which it is aware. Public relations departments, therefore, contribute to organizational success through systematic monitoring of relevant external constituencies, those that can affect or are affected by the organization.

Systems theories maintain that the environment affects the structure of the organization. We entered this program of research, therefore, believing that both environment and structure have a mediating effect on the public relations behavior of the organization. Our task has been to search for organizational and environmental variables that interact meaningfully with public relations variables.

Public Relations Variables

The first step in a research program such as this one is to develop meaningful concepts to describe and classify the dependent variables in the theoretical system, in this case public relations behaviors. We began our search for a classification system for public relations in J. Grunig (1976) and continued it in J. Grunig (1984) and Schneider (1985a).

In the first study by J. Grunig (1976), 216 public relations practitioners in the Washington-Baltimore area estimated the frequency with which their organiza-tions used 16 common public relations procedures, such as writing press releases, conducting informal and formal research, holding open houses, and preparing publications. We used Thayer's (1968) concepts of synchronic and diachronic communication to group these 16 procedures into two theoretical patterns of public relations behavior. The purpose of synchronic communication is to "syn-chronize" the behavior of publics to benefit the organization. The purpose of diachronic communication is to negotiate a "state of affairs" that benefits both organization and publics. Factor analysis of the 16 public relations procedures produced two factors that approximated these two theoretical patterns of public relations behavior.

J. Grunig (1976) then correlated these two public relations factors with several organizational structural variables that characterize two types of organizations, organic and mechanical (Burns & Stalker, 1961). Schneider (1985a) later corre-lated the 16 public relations activities with four types of organizations developed by Hage and Hull (1981): traditional, mechanical, organic, and mixed mechan-ical/organic. In both cases, correlation of the public relations behaviors with types of organizations produced some explanation of the reasons that organizations practice public relations differently. However, we concluded that the synchronic-diachronic conceptualization did not capture enough of the variation in public relations behavior to produce a deep theory.

Thus, J. Grunig (1984) introduced four models of public relations behavior based on J. Grunig and Hunt's (1984) discussion of the historical development of public relations. These four models are representations of the values, goals, and behaviors held or used by organizations when they practice public relations— simplified in the same way that a perfect vacuum or perfect competition are simplified representations in other sciences. The models are produced from the combinations of two dichotomous dimensions: direction (one-way vs. two-way) and balance of intended effect (asymmetrical vs. symmetrical). (By 1984, J. Grunig considered the concepts of "asymmetrical" and "symmetrical" to be more precise than "synchronic" and "diachronic.")

Thus, J. Grunig's four models include press agentry/publicity (one-way asym-r-etrical), public information (one-way symmetrical), two-way asymmetrical, and two-way symmetrical. Detailed descriptions of these models can be found in J. Grunig (1984) and J. Grunig and Hunt (1984). Briefly, however, "press agen-try/publicity" describes propagandistic public relations that seeks media attention in almost any way possible. Public relations programs described by the public information model employ "journalists-in-residence" to provide truthful and accurate information about an organization but not to volunteer negative information. "Two-way asymmetrical" public relations programs use research (methods of scientific persuasion) to identify the messages most likely to produce the support of publics without having to change the behavior of the organization. "Two-way symmetrical" public relations departments use bargaining, negotiating, and conflict–resolution strategies to bring symbiotic changes in the ideas, attitudes, and behaviors of both the organization and its publics.

These four models, therefore, have served as a second-stage typology to explain the variance in the way organizations practice public relations. In organizational sociology, typologies have long played a dominant role in theorizing. Thus, the four models of public relations fit into that research tradition. As a typology, the four models have served a valuable role in the middle stage of our research program; but our goal has been to refine them and eventually to isolate keys variables from the typology that characterize public relations behavior. As we show later in this article, our research on the four models gradually has revealed their limitations and suggested more powerful concepts to replace them.

Up to this point, however, the four models have provided an extremely useful framework for our research. Our research has followed the route that philosopher-of-science Shapere (1977) has described as typical of a domain of scientific research. At the beginning of a research program, theories are vague, general hunches that stimulate research to test and improve on those hunches. With research, the initial hunches become better-specified theories. In the meantime, the models as hunches have captured much of what public relations is like in the real world and have stimulated even better conceptualizations of that behavior. We turn next, therefore, to the variables that we have used in our attempts to explain the occurrence of the four models.

Explanatory Variables

Throughout our research, we have identified concepts that seem to explain public relations behavior within the framework of an organization interacting with its environment in an attempt to produce a moving equilibrium with that environment. As a result, we have identified environmental and structural variables that define types of organizations—types that organizational theory suggests might explain the variations in public relations behavior described by the four models. We describe these types of organizations hereafter as we review the research reported in seven theses and two dissertations.

Our research, however, has shown only a weak relationship between types of organizations and the four models of public relations. As a result, we have come to realize that our conceptualization of the relationship between types of organizations and the models of public relations is a normative rather than a descriptive theory.

We want a theory that does more than prescribe public relations behavior, how-ever. Thus, we have turned to other variables to develop a reconceptualized de-scriptive theory, including education of the public relations practitioner, manage-ment support of and understanding of public relations, whether the public relations director is a part of the organization's "dominant coalition," the extent to which the organization is open or closed to its environment, the technology of the organiza-tion, and the amount of conflict experienced by the organization.

We describe, in turn, each of the studies that we and our students have con-ducted in this search for an organizational theory of public relations. We begin the review of our recent research with an examination of the reliability and validity of the models.

RELIABILITY AND VALIDITY
OF THE FOUR MODELS
OF PUBLIC RELATIONS

After identifying the four models of public relations conceptually, one of our first steps in this research program was to develop indices to measure each model. We then tested the reliability of each of these indices and correlated them with other, related public relations variables as a test of their validity. The results have sup-ported the models as a conceptual device but also have revealed their limitations.

Reliability

J. Grunig originally developed an index of eight items for each of the four models based on a table of characteristics of the models introduced in J. Grunig and Hunt (1984) and slightly revised in J. Grunig (1984). One or two items were developed for six dimensions describing the models: the purpose of public relations, the organizational goal for which the models are a means (control or adaptation), the public relations role (advocacy, dissemination, or mediation), one-way versus two-way communication, media relations as an application of the models, and the role of research.

If these indices are reliable measures of the four models, they should "yield the same results on repeated trials" (Carmines & Zeller, 1979, p. 11). J. Grunig (1984) calculated Cronbach's alpha as an estimate of the reliability of the models and found that some items had to be deleted to bring alpha to an acceptable level. Alpha can be interpreted as a correlation of the index with an alternative measure that could be constructed (Carmines & Zeller, 1979).

Six other studies (Fabiszak, 1985; Lauzen, 1986; McMillan, 1984; E. Pollack, 1984; R. Pollack, 1986; Schneider, 1985b) used these four indices as measures of the four models. Several items were rewritten during the course of the research to improve the indices, and Cronbach's alpha was calculated in each study. In the first six studies, respondents (usually the public relations director of a sampled organization) were asked to use a 5-point Likert-type scale to estimate the extent to which they agreed or disagreed that each item described the public relations program of their organization. In Lauzen (1986), respondents estimated the percentage of time that each item described the public relations activities of their organizations. For the research questions, respondents estimated the number of times that their organizations had conducted the types of public relations research described by the four models in the previous year.

Table 2.1 shows Cronbach's alpha as calculated for each scale in each of six studies. In two studies, items were deleted from two scales to improve their reliability. Table 2.1 shows that alpha has generally been about .60 for three of the four indices. The public-information index has been less reliable than the other three indices, although in three studies it has been .60, .64, and .67. The public information index probably has been least reliable because several of its items related to information dissemination describe public relations activities that are conducted by all public relations practitioners and that are not exclusive to that one model.

There is no universally accepted standard for how high Cronbach's alpha should be. Carmines and Zeller (1979) said that they believe reliability should not fall below .80 for "widely used scales" (p. 51). However, the kinds of scales to

TABLE 2.1
Cronbach's Alpha Calculated for Indices of Four Public Relations Models
in Seven Studies

	N	Press Agentry	Public Information	Two-way Asymmetrical	Two-way Symmetrical
Purposive sample J. Grunig (1984)	52	.74	.67**(.36)	.57	.63*(.53)
Federal government agencies, E. Pollack (1984)	310	.66	.49	.56	.65
Associations, McMillan (1984)	116	.58	.44	.57	.56
Hospitals, Fabiszak (1985)	180	.56	.64*(.52)	.31**(.16)	.64
Scientific organizations, R. Pollack (1986)	178	.65	.42	.56	.50
Purposive sample, Schneider (1985b)	75	.56	.44	.52	.53
Franchises, Lauzen (1986)	273	.61	.60	.64	.64

*One item deleted, alpha before item was deleted in parentheses.
**Three items deleted, alphas before items were deleted in parentheses.

which they refer are generally attitude scales that consist of items carefully constructed to differ only slightly from one another in meaning. Our indices consist of
questions that range widely over the purpose and practice of public relations. In
the real world, few organizations practice public relations in precisely the same
fashion as specified by the four models.

In addition, one should realistically expect a relatively large amount of measurement error on scales such as these. Scores for an organization are based on the
impressions of one person or a small number of people. These people must rely on
their subjective impressions and imperfect memories when they respond to a
questionniaire. Thus, one would expect the reliability of these indices to fall below
those of attitude scales; and in this context, the modal reliability of about .60 found
in our research is quite high.

One also could argue that the theoretical consistency of the indices is at least as
important, and perhaps more important, than their empirical reliability. That is, the
items in an index should follow the logic of the theory they measure. We believe
our indices follow the theoretical logic of the four models well. The moderate levels
of the alphas, therefore, show that, in the real world, public relations behavior is
reasonably close to that described by the models, but that it sometimes deviates
from these models. We interpret the moderate levels of reliability as showing that
the four models function best as normative models specifying how public relations
should function in different organizations, but that they are less accurate as positive
models because organizations deviate from the theoretical norm. Later, we return
to the question of whether the models can serve as both normative and positive
concepts to describe public relations.

Theoretical Accuracy and Validity

In two studies (J. Grunig, 1984; Lauzen, 1986), factor analyses were done on all
of the items in the four indices to determine the accuracy of the four models. Factor
analysis allowed us to ask whether the four models describe public relations
empirically or whether some other configuration of items would describe actual
public relations practice more accurately than one based on the conceptualized four
models. In both studies, factor analysis produced several factors with a small
number of items loading on each. Generally, each factor represented one of the
dimensions of each model, such as research activities, purpose, or direction of
communication. We concluded, therefore, that another configuration of items
would not describe public relations behavior more accurately than the four indices
constructed for each of the models.

We then asked whether our indices are valid: Do they measure the four theoretical models that they are supposed to measure? In several studies, we have
been able to test the concurrent validity of the four models (Carmines & Zeller,
1979; Stamm, 1981; Wimmer & Dominick, 1983). Concurrent validity is the
extent to which variables such as the four models correlate with criterion variables—measured at the same time—that should have a logical relationship to the

four models. We have measured several such concurrent variables: a list of typical public relations techniques taken from J. Grunig (1976), public relations roles (Broom & Dozier, 1986), correlations among the models themselves, and predictions by reporters of models practiced by governmental science agencies (Habbersett, 1983).

Correlations with Public Relations Techniques. E. Pollack (1984), Fabiszak (1985), and McMillan (1984) correlated J. Grunig's (1984) list of 16 public relations techniques with the indices of the four public relations models for practitioners in federal government agencies, hospitals, and associations, respectively. Fabiszak (1985) and McMillan (1984) also added techniques typical of hospital and association public relations to the list.

Table 2.2 shows that the technical components of public relations—such as writing press releases, making contacts with journalists, preparing publications, or holding press conferences—did not correlate strongly or consistently across studies

TABLE 2.2

Correlations of Public Relations Techniques with the Four Public Relations Models in Three Studies

	Press Agentry	Public Information	Two-way Asymmetrical	Two-way Symmetrical
Writing press releases				
Federal government	−.01	.03	.03	.03
Hospitals	.09	.09	.07	−.03
Associations	−.05	−.05	.02	−.12
Preparing house organs, magazines, newsletters, publications				
Federal government	.07	.13	.07	.13*
Hospitals	−.02	−.01	.07	−.08
Associations	−.04	.16*	.06	−.06
Making informal contacts with journalists				
Federal government	−.02	.05	−.06	.12
Hospitals	.04	−.12*	.19**	.16*
Associations	−.10	−.01	.11	−.01
Press conferences and formal contacts with journalists				
Federal government	.02	.02	.04	.06
Hospitals	.08	−.07	.19**	.14*
Associations	−.08	−.04	.11	.03
Making informal contacts with the public				
Federal government	−.19**	−.15*	−.04	.20**
Hospitals	−.09	−.21**	.03	.01
Associations	−.07	−.13*	.11	.05

(Continued)

TABLE 2.2

(*continued*)

	Press Agentry	Public Information	Two-way Asymmetrical	Two-way Symmetrical
Making contact with thought leaders				
Federal government	−.21**	−.31**	.17*	.29**
Hospitals	−.21**	−.35**	.30**	.33**
Associations	−.27**	−.16*	.09	.14*
Staging events, tours, open houses				
Federal government	−.14*	−.23**	.08	.19**
Preparing tapes, films, and AV materials				
Federal government	−.05	−.12	.11	.11
Hospitals	−.03	−.05	.13*	.14*
Associations	.01	.01	.30**	.11
Preparing institutional advertisements				
Federal government	.09	−.10	.08	.05
Hospitals	.13*	−.02	.32**	.10
Contacting government officials				
Federal government	−.11	−.02	−.06	.21**
Hospitals	−.22**	−.28**	.01	.17**
Associations	−.12	−.11	.25**	.16*
Writing speeches				
Federal government	.03	−.07	.05	−.06
Hospitals	−.11	−.21**	.20**	.19**
Associations	−.21**	−.10	.19**	.13
Fundraising				
Hospitals	.00	−.06	.15*	.05
Associations	−.14	−.02	.06	.11
Marketing				
Hospitals	−.09	−.19**	.29**	.22**
Product/service promotions				
Associations	.08	.06	.14*	.03
Coordinating volunteers				
Hospitals	.05	.05	.05	−.02
Holding conventions, meetings, workshops				
Associations	.08	.08	.00	−.06
Promoting trade exhibits and shows				
Associations	.13*	.06	.11	−.09
Building membership				
Associations	.18**	.02	.04	.04
Furnishing advertising materials to members				
Associations	.18**	.10	.17*	.06

Conducting public service campaigns				
Associations	−.19**	−.19**	.14	.22**
Counseling management on public opinion				
Federal government	−.04	−.12	.22**	.34**
Hospitals	−.26**	−.43**	.20**	.43**
Associations	−.06	.04	.26**	.25**
Conducting formal surveys before a project				
Federal government	−.13	−.13	.18**	.27**
Hospitals	−.37**	−.48**	.38**	.45**
Associations	−.06	.04	.26**	.25**
Conducting formal surveys to evaluate a project				
Federal government	−.10	−.17*	.22**	.27**
Hospitals	−.37**	−.47**	.37**	.19**
Associations	.01	−.02	.33**	.30**
Conducting informal research before a project				
Federal government	−.09	−.18**	.26**	.32**
Hospitals	−.39**	−.50**	.36**	.51**
Associations	−.16*	−.10	.14*	.22**
Conducting informal research to evaluate a project				
Federal government	−.11	−.12	.19**	.30**
Hospitals	−.34**	−.52**	.36**	.51**
Associations	−.04	−.04	.18*	.26**

Note: From: Federal government: E. Pollack (1984), n = 310; Hospitals: Fabiszak (1985), n = 180; Associations: McMillan (1984), n = 116;

with any of the models, although there are some exceptions. For example, the public information model correlated positively with preparing house organs, magazines, publications, and newsletters and negatively with making informal contact with the public. Tours, events, and open houses correlated positively with the two-way symmetrical model in the federal government and negatively with the public information and press agentry models. Marketing in hospitals correlated positively with the two-way asymmetrical and two-way symmetrical models and negatively with the public information model. Fundraising correlated with two-way asymmetrical public relations in hospitals. In associations, press agentry correlated positively with promoting trade shows and exhibits, building membership, and furnishing advertising materials to members.

These positive correlations support the validity of the four models; but the generally low correlations with techniques suggests that many of the techniques are not unique to any one model. Instead, they are tools used by practitioners following any or all of the models.

In contrast, however, strong positive correlations occurred between several research methods and the two two-way models and negative correlations with the press agentry and public information models. Formative research (before a project) was most typical of the two-way symmetrical model and evaluative research (after a project) of the two-way asymmetrical model. Informal research was most typical of the two-way symmetrical model and formal surveys of the two-way asymmetrical model. In addition, counseling management on public opinion correlated positively with the two-way models and negatively with the one-way models. It correlated most highly with the two-way symmetrical model. Contacting govern-ment officials and making contact with thought leaders were also most typical of the two-way symmetrical model.

Overall, then, these patterns of correlations provide evidence of the concurrent validity of the four models of public relations.

Correlations with Public Relations Roles.   Broom and Smith (1979) studied the literature on roles played by consultants, and they isolated four possible roles that public relations practitioners might fill. They called these roles (a) the expert prescriber, (b) communication facilitator, (c) problem-solving facilitator, and (d) communication technician. In a national study of PRSA members, Broom (1982) found strong correlations among all but the technician roles. Dozier (1983) factor analyzed the items used in Broom's survey of PRSA members and from two other data sets and isolated two major and two minor public relations roles (see also Broom & Dozier, 1986).

The two major roles were the communication manager and the communication technician. The communication manager role subsumed the expert prescriber and problem-solving process facilitator roles. The communication liaison role was a variation on the manager role: It represented a manager without much power in the organization. The media relations role was a variation on the technician role. The communication liaison and media relations roles were less stable than the manager and technician roles across the different data sets, however; and Dozier (in prep.) has argued that the manager and technician roles represent the most frequent roles of public relations practitioners.

E. Pollack (1984), Fabiszak (1985), McMillan (1984), and R. Pollack (1986) measured the four roles identified by Dozier (1983) and correlated them with the models of public relations. Because the two-way symmetrical and asymmetrical models require research and management skills, we expected them to correlate with the communication manager and liaison roles. Because the press-agentry and public-information models essentially involve the dissemination of information and its placement in the media, we expected them to correlate with the communication technician and media relations roles.

E. Pollack (1984), Fabiszak (1985), and McMillan (1984) measured these four roles in two ways: the role that describes the top public relations person in the organization and the percentage of public relations practitioners filling each role.

The communication manager and technician roles of the top public relations person correlated strongly with the four models (Table 2.3), but the percentage of practitioners in each role did not. The majority of practitioners in any organization appears to be in the technician role, which seems to explain the lack of correlation between the percentage of people in each role and the models. R. Pollack (1986) measured the four roles by the percentage of time an organization's public relations department devoted to each role, rather than by measuring the percentage of practitioners, and found correlations like those with the role of the top person.

The media relations and communication liaison roles did not correlate con-sistently with the models; but, as Broom and Dozier (1986) pointed out, these are two minor public relations roles.

These results, therefore, also support the validity of the four models by showing

TABLE 2.3

Correlations of Four Public Relations Roles of the Top Public Relations Person in an Organization with the Four Public Relations Models in Four Studies

	Press Agentry	Public Information	Two-way Asymmetrical	Two-way Symmetrical
Communication Manager				
Federal government[a]	−.17**	−.11*	−.03	.07
Hospitals	−.25**	−.29**	.10	.27**
Associations	−.18*	−.27**	.20**	.26**
Scientific organ's[b]	−.18**	−.32**	.22**	.14*
Communication techni-cian				
Federal government[a]	.10*	.14*	.06	.02
Hospitals	.26**	.36**	−.11	−.32**
Associations	.16*	.28**	−.09	−.06
Scientific organ's[b]	.13*	.22**	−.02	−.10
Media relations				
Federal government[a]	.06	.14*	−.10	−.06
Hospitals	.12	.20**	−.09	−.18**
Associations	.02	.10	−.03	−.29**
Scientific organ's[b]	.10	−.21**	−.28**	−.14*
Communication liaison				
Federal government[a]	.00	−.10	.00	.04
Hospitals	−.15*	−.32**	.12	.24**
Associations	−.02	−.11	−.07	.07
Scientific organ's[b]	−.08	−.16*	.14*	.15*

Note: Federal government: E. Pollack (1984), $n = 310$ Hospitals: Fabiszak (1985), $n = 180$ Associations: McMillan (1984), $n = 116$ Scientific organizations: R. Pollack (1986), $n = 178$

[a] Kendall's Tau, as role was measured as a dichotomous variable; for other studies role was measured as the percentage of time practitioner spent in each role.

[b] Percentage of time in each role for the entire department

*p < .05

**p < .01

that public relations departments with a manager rather than a technician at the head practice models that require a manager as well as communication technicians.

Correlations Among the Four Models. Because the four models of public relations were constructed from the interaction of two dimensions, direction and intended effect, positive correlations should be expected between models that share one of the two dimensions. Negative correlations should be expected between the models that do not share a common dimension.

Table 2.4 shows consistently strong and positive correlations between the one-

TABLE 2.4
Correlations Among Four Models of Public Relations in Six Studies

	Press Agentry	Public Information	Two-way Asymmetrical	Two-way Symmetrical
Press agentry				
J. Grunig purposive sample	—	.66**	.14	−.34**
Hospitals	—	.63**	.08	−.41**
Associations	—	.62**	.37**	.06
Scientific Organ's	—	.55**	−.03	−.19**
Schneider purposive sample	—	.60**	.12*	−.15*
Franchises	—	.47**	.72**	.52**
Public information				
J. Grunig purposive sample	.66**	—	−.21*	−.38**
Hospitals	.63**	—	−.23**	−.52**
Associations	.62**	—	.17*	.10
Scientific Organ's	.55**	—	−.28**	−.08
Schneider purposive sample	.60**	—	.10*	−.01
Franchises	.47**	—	.56**	−.23**
Two-way asymmetrical				
J. Grunig purposive sample	.14	−.21*	—	.44**
Hospitals	.08	−.23**	—	.37**
Associations	.37**	.17*	—	.43**
Scientific Organ's	−.03	−.28**	—	.61**
Schneider purposive sample	.12*	−.10*	—	.30**
Franchises	.72**	.56**	—	.31**
Two-way symmetrical				
J. Grunig purposive sample	−.34**	−.38**	.44**	—
Hospitals	−.41**	−.52**	.37**	—
Associations	.06	.10	.43**	—
Scientific Organ's	−.19**	−.08	.61**	—
Schneider purposive sample	−.15*	−.01	.30**	—
Franchises	.52**	−.23**	.31**	—

Note: From: Grunig purposive sample: J. Grunig (1984), n = 52 Hospitals: Fabiszak (1985), n = 180 Associations: McMillan (1984), n = 116 Scientific organizations: R. Pollack (1986), n = 178 Schneider purposive sample: Schneider (1985b), n = 75 Franchises: Lauzen (1986), n = 273
*p < .05
**p < .01

way models (press agentry and public information) and between the two-way models (two-way asymmetrical and two-way symmetrical). There are some positive correlations between the asymmetrical models (press agentry and two-way asymmetrical), but the pattern is mixed. Correlations are generally negative between the two symmetrical models (public information and two-way asymmetrical). As expected, there are mostly negative correlations between models that do not share a dimension (public information and two-way asymmetrical and press agentry and two-way symmetrical).

The distinction between the one-way and two-way models, therefore, seems to describe the actual practice of public relations better than the symmetrical–asymmetrical distinction. In addition, public relations of franchises with their franchise holders differs from other forms of public relations. Franchisors used all models of public relations together, although they did not use the public information and two-way asymmetrical models concurrently. In summary, the correlations among models provide moderate support for the validity of the models; although they also show that the models are not so distinct in practice as they are in theory.

Reporters' Perceptions of Government Public Relations.   J. Grunig and Hunt (1984) predicted that the public information model was the most common form of public relations practiced in government, and both E. Pollack (1984) and Habbersett (1983) confirmed this prediction. E. Pollack (1984) found that the overall means for 166 federal government agencies on a 1–5 scale was 3.01 for public information, 2.95 for press agentry, 2.73 for two-way symmetrical, and 2.65 for two-way asymmetrical.

Habbersett (1983) used a similar scale to measure how science reporters perceived the media relations programs of the federal agencies that they covered. Her results also showed that the public information model predominates in the federal government. On a 1–5 scale, the reporters rated government media relations as 4.00 on public information, 3.69 on press agentry, 3.40 on two-way asymmetrical, and 2.66 on two-way symmetrical. J. Grunig and Hunt (1984) also argued that two-way symmetrical techniques would improve media relations; when Habbersett asked science reporters to evaluate a number of two-way symmetrical media relations techniques, they expressed a strong preference for nearly all of them.

These two studies, therefore, further support the validity of the models of public relations. J. Grunig and Hunt (1984) predicted that public information would be most common in government, and two studies showed that it was. They also argued, normatively, that the two-way symmetrical model would improve media relations; and reporters agreed that it would.

In total, then, the data reported here do seem to provide evidence supporting the concurrent validity and empirical accuracy of the four models. They do exist in the real world, and they do seem to capture variations in public relations behavior better than any competing theory. The correlations are modest because many of the concurrent indicators could be expected to covary with the models, but the indicators are not theoretical components of the models.

The evidence presented in this section suggests, however, that there is room for improving the conceptualization of the models. In particular, the data show that organizations combine some of the models in practice more than anticipated by the theory, which (as we see later) seems to suggest that an organization may use different models when they are most relevant strategically to a public relations problem rather than using a single model as an overarching framework for all public relations programs.

Our next step, then, is to look at our research on the relationship between the models and variables that should, theoretically, explain their occurrence.

ENVIRONMENTS, ORGANIZATIONAL TYPES, AND THE FOUR MODELS OF PUBLIC RELATIONS

Organizational sociologists, for many years, have described two types of organizations. One type was essentially a closed system, the other an open system. Burns and Stalker (1961) called these organizations *mechanical* and *organic*, names that sociologists use most often for the two types of organizations. Other sociologists used similar names: *dynamic* versus *static* systems (Hage & Aiken, 1970), *monocratic* versus *innovative* organizations (V. Thompson, 1961), and the *systems model* (reaction to problems) versus the *goal model* (seeking a predetermined end) (Etzioni, 1964).

We used these two types of organizations as the key variables to explain public relations behavior in our early research. J. Grunig (1976), for example, factor analyzed a number of organizational attributes and found two factors with variable loadings resembling these two kinds of organizations, which he called *problemsolving* and *fatalistic* organizations. He also found support for the hypothesis that problem-solving organizations practiced diachronic public relations and fatalistic organizations practiced synchronic public relations, as these terms were just defined.

Hage and Hull (1981) expanded this dichotomous typology of organizations into four kinds of organizations. In their recent theory, each of the four types of organizations occupied a different environmental niche and, as a result, developed technology and structure appropriate for that niche. They identified the four niches from the combinations of two variables, scale and complexity.

Scale is related both to an organization's size and to the size of demand for its products and services. But scale goes beyond size; it is the "repetitiveness of events." The more repetitive the demand for products and services the more repetitive the organization's technology must be to produce products and services to meet the demand. Environmental complexity is based on the complexity of the knowledge base that is relevant to an organization. The more complex the knowl edge in an organization's environment, the more specialists the organization must employ (which is the basis of Hage's, 1980, definition of the structural complexity of an organization.)

Hage and Hull placed Burns and Stalker's mechanical organization in the environmental niche defined by low complexity and large scale. The organic organization occupies the high-complexity, small-scale niche. Hage and Hull also identified the traditional organization, which occupies the niche of low complexity and small scale; and the mixed mechanical/organic organization, which has an environment with high complexity and large scale.

The Hage–Hull typology provided us with a natural extension of J. Grunig's (1976) attempt to link problem-solving and fatalistic organizations with diachronic and synchronic public relations. Thus, the typology has been the focus of our recent attempts to construct an organizational theory of public relations (J. Grunig, 1984; Schneider, 1985a, 1985b).

The Product/Service Environment

Schneider (1985a) found that the mixed mechanical/organic organization had the most extensive and powerful public relations department of the four organizations. J. Grunig (1984) then used the Hage–Hull typology to describe what he called the *product/service* environment of the organization, which he distinguished from the organization's *political/regulatory* environment. He believed that the product/service environment would explain which model of public relations the organization uses in support of its marketing function and that the political/regulatory environment would explain the model used in the public affairs component of public relations.

J. Grunig (1984) hypothesized that there would be a relationship between the type of organization that Hage and Hull predicted would occupy each environmental niche in the product/service environment and the model or models of public relations that it practices. He then presented case-study evidence that supported his theory.

J. Grunig theorized that traditional organizations would practice press agentry: Public relations would be restricted mostly to publicity or marketing support to make products or services known to consumers. Because the products or services are not complex, the traditional organization would have little reason to seek information from consumers or to do research—essential parts of the two-way models. Because the product is simple, the information provided could be simplistic as is more typical with press agentry than with the public-information model.

J. Grunig (1984) predicted that mechanical organizations would practice the public-information model "because their markets are large and stable . . . and they have little need to seek information from consumers. They use the public-information model to give consumers or users factual information about products or services" (p. 22). He predicted that organic organizations would practice two-way symmetrical public relations because of their need to "adapt to their complex, changing product-service environment" (p. 22).

Finally, Grunig predicted that mixed organizations would practice a combination of two-way symmetrical and two-way asymmetrical public relations:

> These firms must hire the most "marketing, advertising, and sales personnel to merchandise a diversified array of products" (Hage & Hull, 1981: 26). Thus, they probably use the two-way asymmetrical model for their marketing public relations, although many will also use the two-way symmetrical model to help them keep in touch with consumers in complex and changing markets. (p. 22)

Five studies tested the relationship between the four models of public relations and the Hage-and-Hull typology (Fabiszak, 1985; McMillan, 1984; E. Pollack, 1984; R. Pollack, 1986; Schneider, 1985b). The first four studies gathered data from samples of 116 to 310 organizations. As a result, the researchers could administer only one questionnaire per organization; it was administered by mail to the top public relations person whenever possible. The single respondents provided estimates of the scale and complexity of their organizations, which the researchers used to construct dummy variables to place organizations into one of the four Hage–Hull types of organizations. Although we realized the limitation of a single-person measure, we believed that the public relations director was in as good a position as any single person in the organization to assess the nature of its environment.

E. Pollack (1984), Fabiszak (1985), McMillan (1984), and R. Pollack (1986) each correlated the types of organizations with the four models of public relations. The correlation coefficients were consistently small and nonsignificant.

The lack of correlation between the types of organizations and models of public relations could have resulted from an incorrectly specified theory or from an invalid measure of the types of organizations. Schneider (1985b), therefore, studied a smaller group of 48 organizations in greater depth. She examined "global" characteristics of the 48 organizations rather than the individual characteristics of one of its members (Pavlik & Salmon, 1983). She chose 12 organizations that fit each of the Hage–Hull types in the Maryland–District of Columbia–Virginia area after interviewing experts and examining the organizations' internal media and the mass media. She then interviewed one or two public relations practitioners in each organization in depth and combined that information with qualitative observations of the organization.

Her classification of organizations into one of the Hage–Hull types, therefore, was based on much more information than were the classifications in the previous studies. As a comparison, however, she asked interviewees the same questions to measure scale and complexity as had the previous four researchers. Crosstabulation of her globally and qualitatively determined types with the quantitatively deter-

mined types, however, produced little overlap in the classifications. The quantitative types, as in the previous studies, did not correlate significantly or meaningfully with the models of public relations. Although the correlations were still
modest, the qualitative types did correlate with the four models of public relations
in a way that supported our theoretical predictions (Table 2.5).

Table 2.5 shows that three of the four types of organizations had their highest
positive correlation with the predicted model of public relations. The organic type
provided the exception, because it did not correlate significantly with any of the
models. In addition, we had predicted that the mixed organization would correlate
with both two-way models, but it correlated significantly only with the two-way
symmetrical model.

Schneider's (1985b) extensive qualitative analysis provided additional information about public relations in the four types of organizations. Traditional organizations, Schneider found, practice press agentry as expected. They also employ
practitioners with little training in public relations and with the lowest level of
overall education. They have the smallest public relations budget and hire few
outside consultants. Practitioners typically plan special events and write speeches
but do no research and seldom have an internal communication program. They
rarely counsel top managers, but they have a good deal of autonomy in conducting
their promotional activities.

Schneider found that mechanical organizations practice the public information
model, as we expected, but that they also practice press agentry nearly as often.
These organizations have moderately sized public relations departments, but they
also rely on free-lancers and public relations firms more than does any other
organizational type. Budgets for public relations are relatively large. However,

TABLE 2.5

Kendall's Tau Correlations of Hage and Hull's Four Types of Organizations
with the Four Public Relations Models

Type of Organization & Predicted Model	Press Agentry	Public Information	Two-way Asymmetrical	Two-way Symmetrical
Traditional (Press agentry)	.13*	.01	−.01	.04
Mechanical (Public information)	.21**	.22**	.02	−.18**
Organic (Two-way symmetrical)	.03	−.08	−.02	−.01
Mixed mechanical/organic (Two-way asymmetrical & two-way symmetrical)	−.36**	−.14*	.00	.16**

Note: From Schneider (1985b); $n = 75$.
*$p < .05$
**$p < .01$

senior managers of mechanical organizations have little understanding of public relations, and they use the department mostly as a means of helping to dispose of products and services in their large-scale, but not complex, environment. Practitioners—in spite of being highly professional—rarely counsel management. Public relations activities are journalistic, and internal publications are important for these organizations. As the public information model suggests, these practitioners make more contact with the media than do practitioners in any of the other types. They make less contact with government officials, however, than practitioners in the other types. As the emphasis on disposing of products suggests, public relations is more closely aligned with advertising and marketing in mechanical organizations than in any other organizational type.

The correlations in Table 2.5 showed no significant correlations between the organic organizational type and any of the four models of public relations, although these organizations had the highest mean score on the two-way symmetrical model of any of the four types—the predicted model for the type. Organic organizations are small, and they also have the smallest public relations departments proportionately of any of the types. Top management supports public relations strongly, however, and frequently hires outside consultants. Public relations activities are not journalistic. Organic organizations concentrate on internal publics and publications more than any other type, probably because of their high-tech nature and the frequent raids on their specialized personnel by competitors (see also Rogers & Larsen, 1984). They have a dynamic, unstable environment, however, and thus seem to have a public relations department that does not help the organization maintain a moving equilibrium with the environment because it does not contribute to two-way communication with that environment.

Schneider's (1985b) analysis of the mixed mechanical/organic organization confirmed her previous finding (Schneider, 1985a) that these organizations have the best developed and most sophisticated public relations programs. Table 2.5 shows a significant correlation of this type with the two-way symmetrical model, although mean scores showed the two-way asymmetrical model to be common there too, as we had predicted. These organizations have a large public relations budget, and top management is intimately involved in public relations. Public relations managers, in addition, have more autonomy than in the other types of organizations. Top management apparently gives these practitioners free rein because of respect for their training and knowledge in public relations: They have a high level of education and specialized training in public relations. Practitioners in mixed organizations also counsel top management more than in any other type of organization. Finally, because of the complex nature of their environments, practitioners in mixed organizations communicate with more outside publics than do practitioners in any other Hage–Hull type.

Schneider's complete quantitative and qualitative analysis, therefore, provided evidence that organizations do practice public relations in a way that is reasonably close to the kinds of public relations needed in their environmental niche. However, she concluded that the Hage–Hull typology can explain only a small portion of the variation in public relations behavior and that other variables must be added to our theory to explain public relations more completely.

The results based on the Hage–Hull typology suggest, therefore, that our theory provides a normative set of suggestions for how organizations should prac tice public relations in order to interact with their environments more effectively. The results also suggest that organizations actually have a tendency to practice the most appropriate model, but that the tendency is not a strong one. We have concluded that the theoretical linkages between an organization's product/service environment as defined by the Hage–Hull typology and the models of public relations provide more of a normative, prescriptive theory than a positive, descrip tive theory. Thus, we have continued to search for concepts that describe why organizations so often depart from the public relations model that our theory says should be most effective for them.

The Political/Regulatory Environment

J. Grunig (1984) theorized that the Hage–Hull typology of organizations, which he said described the product/service environment, would explain the marketing support component of public relations. As we saw in the last section, Schneider's (1985b) analysis of the mechanical organization, in particular, supported the rele vance of the typology to marketing support. J. Grunig also described a politi cal/regulatory environment that he said would describe the public affairs compo nent of public relations. He described six niches in the political/regulatory environment, based on two variables—environmental constraints and environmen tal uncertainty.

J. Grunig reasoned that when uncertainty is low in the political/regulatory environment, organizations would use a one-way model of public relations. When uncertainty is high, they would use a two-way model. J. Grunig also reasoned that the relationship between environmental constraints and the asym metrical/symmetrical dimension of the public relations models would be cur vilinear. At a low level of constraint, organizations would use asymmetrical com munication to try to dominate their environment; at a high level, they would use it to try to eliminate the constraints. At a medium level of constraint, which is characterized by pressure from activist publics and the threat of government regula tion, organizations would use symmetrical communication in an attempt to be responsive to publics that could create greater constraint. Figure 2.1 displays Grunig's predictions for the political/regulatory environment.

In four studies (Fabiszak, 1985; McMillan, 1984; E. Pollack, 1984; R. Pol lack, 1986), researchers measured environmental constraints and uncertainty and developed dummy variables for each of the six environmental niches. With only a few exceptions, the correlations were low and nonsignificant. Fabiszak (1985)

| Environmental | Extent of Environmental Constraint | | |
Uncertainty	Low	Medium	High
Low	Press Agentry	Public Information	Press Agentry
High	Two-way Asymmetrical	Two-way Symmetrical	Two-way Asymmetrical

FIG. 2.1.   Predicted models of public relations in six niches of the political/regulatory environment (Grunig, 1984).

found an expected significant correlation between the low uncertainty/medium constraint niche and the public information model (Tau = .16), and McMillan (1984) found the expected significant correlation (Tau = .14) between the high uncertainty/high constraint niche and the two-way asymmetrical model. A few other significant negative correlations were found between niches and one or more models that were not hypothesized for them. Overall, however, these results were disappointing.

One could argue that these nonsignificant results provide reason to reject the theory. But two methodological problems may have produced the negative results. These researchers, as they had for variables of the product/service environment, measured constraints and uncertainty in a questionnaire mailed to one member of each organization. In addition, the models were not measured separately for the marketing support and public affairs components of public relations. Thirdly, public affairs is a more common component of public relations in corporations than in government agencies, hospitals, and associations—which were the subjects of three of these four studies.

In 1984, graduate students in the University of Maryland's Seminar in Public Relations Management conducted case studies of 13 corporations and measured the models separately for public affairs and marketing support components of public relations. Their results suggested that the models fit the typology better when measured in this way and when the theory was applied to corporations. R. Pollack (1986) also included corporations in her sample of scientific organizations and found evidence that the two two-way models are used most often in corporations. Before abandoning the political/regulatory typology, therefore, we plan to do further research on corporations and to measure the models individually for different public relations programs.

OTHER VARIABLES RELATED
TO THE MODELS
OF PUBLIC RELATIONS

At early stages of our research program, we included several variables in our analysis that organizational theory and our research in J. Grunig (1976) and Schneider (1985a) suggested might be associated with public relations behavior.

These included technology, organizational structure, education in public relations, and the support and understanding of top management for public relations. As the research progressed, however, we used several additional variables in an attempt to develop a descriptive explanation of public relations behavior that deviates from the normative theory of organizations and environments we just reviewed. These included representation of public relations in the organization's dominant coalition, values of the organization, openness of the organizational system, and specific public relations situations. In this section, then, we review the research on all of these variables.

Technology

J. Thompson (1967) introduced a theory of technology that has been employed extensively in organizational sociology. As he defined it, *long-linked* technology, such as is used with an assembly line, employs techniques that are linked serially to one another, so that one stage of work cannot begin until the previous one is completed. *Mediating* technology, such as that used by banks or insurance companies, links clients who are otherwise independent. With *intensive* technology, organizations focus several techniques on accomplishing a major goal.

On the surface, these technologies seem to be logical determinants of public relations behavior. After reviewing the literature on the three technologies, for example, Bales (1984) concluded that organizations with long-linked and intensive technologies would try to buffer their units and roles from the environment. Thus, the press agentry and two-way asymmetrical models, and, to a lesser extent, the public information model, would seem most relevant to an organization with these technologies. Bales also argued that organizations with mediating technology would have the greatest need for boundary spanners to link the organization with clients; thus, we predicted that they would have the greatest need for two-way symmetrical public relations.

Schneider (1985a) found a correlation of .30 between long-linked technology and size of the public relations department. Later, she (Schneider, 1985b) found a correlation of .25 between long-linked technology and size of the PR department and of .25 with the two-way asymmetrical model in mixed mechanical/organic organizations. These correlations suggest that the long-linked technology variable essentially serves as a surrogate measure for an organization that is a major corporation. Corporations probably have the largest public relations departments and probably use the two-way asymmetrical model most often.

In contrast to the predictions we have drawn from Bales' (1984) discussion of boundary spanning, Schneider (1985b) found significant correlations between intensive technology and two-way symmetrical public relations in all organizational types except the mixed mechanical/organic. Although we are speculating, a possible explanation for that finding is that organizations with intensive technology (meaning they focus on a single, major goal) have learned that it is too risky to try to buffer themselves from the environment with asymmetrical communication.

Symmetrical public relations buffers these organizations better because it produces compromise rather than tenuous persuasion or manipulation. Mixed organizations differ, however, because they tend to be corporations in which the historical precedence of asymmetrical public relations overwhelms the logic of practicing the two-way symmetrical model.

In summary, therefore, we have found technology to be an inconsistent explanatory variable for public relations behavior, and we no longer attempt to incorporate it into our theory.

Organizational Structure

J. Grunig (1976) measured a number of variables describing organizational structure and used them to identify the problem-solving and fatalistic types of organizations. These variables include complexity (measured by the number of specialists who must have a college degree), centralization of decision-making in the hands of a few top managers, stratification of employees who work at different levels of the hierarchy from each other, and formalization (number of rules and regulations). Formalization has not correlated with any of the four models of public relations, but the other three variables have (Table 2.6).

Table 2.6 shows a fairly consistent pattern of relationships between centralization and the four models. The one-way models are used in centralized organizations, the two-way models in decentralized organizations. Complex organizations (those with more specialists who must have higher education) also tend not to use

TABLE 2.6
Correlations of Three Structural Variables with the Four Public Relations Models
in Three Studies

	Press Agentry	Public Information	Two-way Asymmetrical	Two-way Symmetrical
Complexity (education)				
Federal government	−.15*	−.04	−.13*	−.01
Associations	−.16*	−.03	−.25**	.03
Centralization				
Federal government	.07	.23**	−.15*	−.23**
Hospitals	.22**	.32**	−.16*	−.19**
Associations	.03	.09	−.11	−.17*
Stratification (status differences)				
Federal government	.09	.07	.07	−.22**
Hospitals	.08	.13*	−.16**	−.20**
Associations	−.15*	−.01	.01	−.01

Note: From: Federal government: E. Pollack (1984),$n = 310$; Hospitals: Fabiszak (1985), $n = 180$; Associationns: McMillan (1984), $n = 116$.
*$p < .05$
**$p < .01$

TABLE 2.7
Correlations of the Education in Public Relations of the Top Public Relations Official
with the Four Public Relations Models

	Press Agentry	Public Information	Two-way Asymmetrical	Two-way Symmetrical
Federal government	−.06	−.19**	.14**	.13**
Hospitals	−.15*	−.07	.06	.14*
Associations	−.01	−.10	.23**	.16*
Scientific organizations	.09	.03	.01	−.05

Note: From: Federal government: E. Pollack (1984), $n = 310$; Hospitals: Fabiszak (1985), $n = 180$; Associations: McMillan (1984); $n = 116$; Scientific organizations: R. Pollack (1986), $n = 178$.
*$p < .05$
**$p < .01$

the asymmetric models (press agentry and two-way asymmetrical). Finally, stratified organizations tend not to use the two-way symmetrical model.

These relationships are logical, but we believe that both structure and public relations behavior are a function of the organization's environment or of some other variable. Thus, we have not assigned these structural variables a central role in our theory. We have found them to be most useful in developing a theory of internal public relations, which is reviewed elsewhere (J. Grunig, 1985).

Education in Public Relations

In most of our studies, we have measured the education of the top public relations official in public relations. We theorized that the two-way symmetrical and asymmetrical models are sophisticated means of practicing public relations that require specialized training, whereas practitioners working within the press agentry or public information models could succeed with journalistic training or no training at all. Table 2.7 generally confirms our logic, although the correlations are small.

Top Management Support and Understanding of Public Relations

The public relations function does not exist in isolation in an organization. Unless top management understands and supports that function, we reasoned, the organization probably would not practice the more sophisticated two-way models of public relations. Table 2.8 supports our reasoning, although the correlations are not always significant in every study. In general, though, management support and understanding correlate positively with the two-way asymmetrical and two-way symmetrical models and negatively with the press agentry and public information models.

TABLE 2.8
Correlations of Management Support and Understanding
of the Public Relations Function with the Four Public Relations Models

	Press Agentry	Public Information	Two-way Asymmetrical	Two-way Symmetrical
Management support				
Federal government	−.19**	−.20**	.05	.18**
Hospitals	−.18**	−.36**	.19**	.31**
Associations	.04	−.05	.10	.07
Management understanding				
Federal government	−.04	−.04	.00	.15*
Hospitals	−.17*	−.42**	.14*	.24**

Note: From: Federal government: E. Pollack (1984), n = 310; Hospitals: Fabiszak (1985), n = 180; Associations: McMillan (1984), n = 116.
*p < .05
**p < .01

Representation in the Dominant Coalition

In a study of scientific organizations, R. Pollack (1986) looked more in depth at top management support of public relations. She increased the number of related variables to include, in addition to top-management support, involvement of the public relations director in major decisions, whether PR decisions are made by the PR director or top management, influence of the PR department in organizational decision-making, authority level of the PR department, percentage of recommendations made by the PR department that were implemented by the organization in the last three years, and how important the dominant coalition believes public relations is to organizational success.

Factor analysis of these variables produced two highly correlated factors. One factor described the extent to which public relations is represented in the dominant coalition. The second factor described the autonomy of the public relations department. The percentage of PR decisions implemented by the organization and the extent to which the PR department alone makes public relations decisions loaded more highly on the second factor. The other variables loaded more highly or equally on the first factor.

Table 2.9 shows that these factors are important determinants of the model of public relations practiced, especially the "representation in the dominant coalition" factor. Two interpretations are possible: (a) public relations departments represented in the dominant coalition are able to practice a two-way model of public relations, or (b) public relations practitioners with the knowledge or experience to practice a two-way model are more likely to be represented in the dominant coalition.

TABLE 2.9
Correlations of the Two Management Support Factors
with the Four Public Relations Models

	Press Agentry	Public Information	Two-way Asymmetrical	Two-way Symmetrical
Representation of PR in the dominant coalition	$-.28^{**}$	$-.33^{**}$	$.34^{**}$	$.19^{*}$
Autonomy of PR	$-.18^{*}$	$-.11$	$.17^{*}$	$.12$

Note: From R. Pollack (1986), $n = 178$
$^{*}p < .05$
$^{**}p < .01$

We think the second explanation is more accurate, for several reasons. The greater the percentage of practitioners in the public relations department with a bachelor's degree in public relations, the greater the likelihood of representation in the dominant coalition ($r = .15$). The more years in public relations of the public relations director, the greater the likelihood of representation in the dominant coalition ($r = .25$). And public relations directors with a science background were also more likely to be represented in the dominant coalition ($r = .25$). These correlations suggest that more knowledgeable sophisticated public relations managers are more likely to be represented in the dominant coalition.

R. Pollack's (1986) data also suggested that these more sophisticated practitioners and departments are most likely to be found in corporations. A breakdown of mean scores on the dominant coalition factor by corporate, nonprofit, and government organizations showed that corporate public relations directors are most likely to be represented in the dominant coalition, and government directors are least likely to. In addition, the highest positive correlation in Table 2.9 is between "representation in the dominant coalition" and the two-way asymmetrical model, which Pollack's data also showed as the most common model in corporations. These correlations suggest that researchers should look closely at corporations for examples of where public relations is practiced according to our normative theory of the most appropriate model of public relations for a given environment (although corporations may practice the two-way asymmetrical model because they are unaware of the two-way symmetrical model).

Organizational Power, Values, and Codes

A systems approach assumes that organizations and environments adapt to each other and that organizational structure and behavior can be predicted from characteristics of the environment. The research we have discussed thus far, however, shows that environmental variables explain only a small part of the variation in public relations behavior.

R. Pollack's (1986) finding that organizations are more likely to practice the two-way models of public relations when the top public relations manager is represented in the dominant coalition suggests that an alternative theory of organizations, the political-value approach, may provide the explanation of why organizations practice the different models of public relations. The political-value approach maintains that the power elite in an organization—the dominant coalition—sets organizational policy and makes decisions that may not be the most likely to put the organization in equilibrium with its environment (e.g., Cyert & March, 1973; Hage & Dewar, 1973; Jackson & Morgan, 1982; Mintzberg, 1983).

Organizations could have the structures and public relations models that they do simply because the dominant coalition chooses them (Robbins, 1983). What, then, explains why the dominant coalition makes the choices that it does? Organizational sociology (Hage, 1980) suggests that values could explain those decisions. Hage (1980) listed several values that seem to be logically related to the four models: liberal versus conservative political values, external versus internal values, and efficiency versus innovativeness. We reasoned that dominant coalitions with liberal, external, and innovation values would choose a symmetrical public relations model, and that coalitions with conservative, internal, and efficiency values would choose an asymmetrical model.

McMillan (1984) found a small, significant correlation ($r = .14$) between the item "most executives of this association are politically conservative" and the two-way asymmetrical model. But Likert-type items about the desirability and benefits of government regulation did not correlate with any of the models. R. Pollack (1986) also found a small correlation ($r = .16$) between a conservatism factor and the two-way asymmetrical model; but she found no correlations between the models and efficiency and innovation factors. Similarly, Lauzen (1986) found no significant correlations between efficiency and innovation as values and the four models. R. Pollack (1986) did find positive correlations between a factor measuring strong central authority as a value in managing an organization and the press agentry ($r = .27$) and public-information ($r = .20$) models.

The political and innovativeness values, therefore, had only a weak relationship with public relations; but R. Pollack (1986) found stronger relationships with internal and external values. Because she examined public relations in scientific organizations, she developed several questionnaire items to measure internal and external values based on Donohue, Tichenor, and Olien's (1973) distinction between "knowledge of" and "knowledge about" science.

"Knowledge of" science is produced from within the science system and reinforces that system. "Knowledge about" science is produced from outside the system and is more critical of that system. The distinction is similar to Katz and Kahn's (1966) concept of system codes, which are reflected in the intelligibility to an outsider of language used in an organization. System codes restrict the input of information into an organization. The more rigid these codes, the less "knowledge about" a system will flow into the organization and the more system members will be restricted to "knowledge of" the system. Thus, dominant coalitions with rigid system codes should not be open to the environment and should not value the environment. Dominant coalitions with flexible codes should be open to and value the environment.

Table 2.10 shows that R. Pollack's (1986) "knowledge of" factor correlated positively with both press agentry and public information and her "knowledge about" factor with the two two-way models of public relations. These results and the correlations between conservatism and the two-way asymmetrical model suggest that liberalism and flexible system codes and conservatism and rigid codes are similar mindsets and that internal and external values are components of those two mindsets.

At this point, our theorizing goes beyond the research we have conducted thus far and begins to take us into our plans for future research. We think that rigid and flexible mindsets are related to an ideology that is a component of organizational culture. Theories of organizational culture, of course, are in vogue among organizational scholars, especially after several popular books (e.g., Deal & Kennedy, 1982; Peters & Waterman, 1982) identified culture as a key component of successful organizations.

The concepts of organizational ideology and culture suggest that the models of public relations may operate at two levels. First, they may function as a component of the ideology that frames the dominant coalition's choice of public relations strategies. Second, they may function as a set of strategies that public relations departments apply in specific situations. Strategies may depart from ideology, however, which would explain why the measures of the models we have used thus far show that organizations frequently mix the models in their public relations activities.

Culture and ideology help to explain who comes to power in an organization and how those people use their power (Mintzberg, 1983). Managers with certain values and expertise are most likely to acquire power in a given organizational culture; and, once in power, these managers can use cultural myths, rites, and

TABLE 2.10
Correlations of Two System Code Factors with the Four Public Relations Models

	Press Agentry	Public Information	Two-way Asymmetrical	Two-way Symmetrical
"Knowledge of" Factor	.31**	.28**	−.16*	−.13
"Knowledge about" Factor	−.02	−.01	.13	.20*

Note: From R. Pollack (1986); $n = 178$.
$^*p < .05$
$^{**}p < .01$

rituals to exercise that power (Deal & Kennedy, 1982). The crucial question for our research, therefore, is how public relations managers gain the power they need to affect the public relations ideologies that, in turn, frame public relations strat-egies.

R. Pollack's (1986) study suggested that public relations managers gain power in the organization when they possess the knowledge or experience needed to practice either the two-way asymmetrical or two-way symmetrical model. L. Grunig (1987) found that public relations managers are involved extensively with the dominant coalition but mostly in an advisory, rather than policy-making, role. Like Pollack, she found that the public relations managers who did have more than an advisory role in the dominant coalition had a high level of education and, especially, specialized training in public relations. Most often, they were found in the mixed mechanical–organic organizations of the Hage–Hull typology. They also worked in organizations whose dominant coalitions valued public relations.

In short, public relations managers appear to gain power when they possess the expertise needed to practice one of the two-way models and are in an organization whose dominant coalition values that expertise. Such expertise is rare among public relations practitioners, however. As a result, few organizations can practice the normative models that would be most appropriate in their environments, even when the dominant coalition has external values. That conclusion, finally, explains the low level of correlation that we have found between the models and environ-mental variables.

With this knowledge of when the four models function as part of organizational ideology, we turn next to two studies that suggest that the models also function at a lower level of abstraction in an organization—as public relations strategies used in specific situations.

Situationality of the Models as Strategies

In all of the studies reported in this chapter, we have measured each model only once for an organization. For many organizations, the scores were similar on all models, and we encountered much evidence that organizations used more than one model in their public relations programs. These results suggest that organizations use different models as strategies for dealing with different publics or different public relations problems.

Cupp (1985) found support for the idea that the models are used situationally. She conducted case studies of nine chemical companies in West Virginia to determine how they use public relations in crises. She measured the four models of public relations in three ways: for the company's overall public relations program, as a model for planning crisis public relations programs, and as public relations practitioners said they would respond in two hypothetical crisis situations. She found that the overall model did not predict the crisis model nor the models used in the hypothetical situations. The same organizations also employed different models in the two hypothetical situations.

Nelson (1986) conducted case studies of a bank and a large telecommunications company to determine the extent to which the dominant coalitions of the two companies dictated the public relations ideology of the companies and the extent to which the top public relations managers had enough power to affect that ideology. She found that the dominant coalition did indeed choose the organization's public relations policy but in a way that was both strategic and ideological. Nelson found that the dominant coalitions in the two companies provided the public relations department with what might be called a definition of or paradigm for public relations. That definition reflected the organization's concern with key publics in its environment.

The dominant coalition of the telecommunications company defined public relations as media relations because it wanted to use the media to affect government policy and to make potential customers aware of its services. The dominant coalition of the bank defined public relations as community relations because it was heavily affected by local community groups and wanted to be considered a good neighbor.

The choice of a model of public relations for these two kinds of programs was both strategic and ideological. Strategically, one could argue that either the two-way symmetrical or two-way asymmetrical model would be effective for the telecommunication company's media relations. The company chose the two-way asymmetrical model because that model fit best with its ideology. At the bank, strategy won out over ideology. The bank's values favored an asymmetrical model; but the dominant coalition chose the two-way symmetrical model because, strategically, it would seem to work best for dealing with community groups.

These recent studies suggest a more advanced theory of public relations behavior, which we will use to guide our future research. Before discussing that theory, however, we discuss a line of research that is particularly relevant to the practice of the two-way symmetrical model.

PUBLIC RELATIONS
AND CONFLICT

The public relations profession developed through historical stages that resemble, in turn, the press agentry, public information, and two-way asymmetrical models of public relations (Grunig & Hunt, 1984). Only recently have practitioners begun to employ the two-way symmetrical model, and relatively few actually use it. In practice, the asymmetrical models of public relations seem to dominate the ideology and practice of public relations. In contrast, Ehling (1985) has argued, in essence, that managed organizational communication is not public relations unless it follows the two-way symmetrical model. Whereas the more relevant body of

theory for the asymmetrical models of public relations is persuasion and attitude
theory, the most relevant body of theory for the symmetrical models is related to the
management of conflict (e.g., Fisher & Ury, 1981). Ehling (1985), for example,
has argued that the purpose of public relations is to help organizations deal with
conflict.

We believe that managed organizational communication using all of the four
models can be described as public relations. Like Ehling, however, we believe that
the two-way symmetrical model will be most effective for organizations with complex environments and that are the most socially responsible. Thus, our research
program also has begun to address the question of how public relations contributes
to the management of conflict within and among organizations and publics. We do
not assume that conflict is always bad for an organization. In fact, the more
innovative an organization, the more likely it will be to produce conflict. Conflict,
therefore, can be good for an organization because it stimulates change. But
organizations must deal with that conflict, and symmetrical public relations seems
ideal for conflict management.

In the first study of conflict resolution, Lauzen (1986) studied the relationship
of the four models to conflict within franchises. She hypothesized that environmental constraints would produce conflict for an organization. She then hypothesized
that an organization would respond to the conflict by trying to dominate the
environment, using an asymmetrical model of public relations, or cooperating with
the environment, using a symmetrical model. She also hypothesized that asymmetrical public relations would increase (and symmetrical public relations would
decrease) the amount, intensity, and duration of the conflict.

A correlational analysis showed a positive relationship between the occurrence
of conflict and the press agentry, two-way asymmetric, and two-way symmetrical
models. These three models, in turn, had negative correlations with the frequency,
intensity, and duration of conflict. Franchises, in other words, turned to public
relations when they experienced conflict; and three of the four models of public
relations seemed to reduce that conflict.

This finding seems to contradict our hypothesis that the two-way symmetrical
model will reduce conflict more effectively than the other models. Unfortunately,
the Lauzen (1986) study did not allow us to test the effect of the models separately.
Franchises differed from other organizations that we have studied in that they
reported using all of the models except public information simultaneously. Lauzen
found that most franchises did not have a formal public relations program, and the
blurring of the models seem to reflect an unmanaged approach to public relations.
We will have to develop field or laboratory experiments that isolate the effects of
the models if we are to test their effectiveness in managing conflict.

Evidence of the ineffectiveness of the press agentry, public information, and
two-way asymmetrical models in reducing conflict came from L. Grunig's (1986)
case studies of how 31 organizations responded to pressure from activist groups.
She measured the model that best described the public relations programs of the

organizations and the model that they used with an activist group when that group pressured the organization.

Very few of the organizations used the two-way symmetrical model in their overall programs. In every case, however, the organizations relied on one of the other models when activist groups created a crisis situation. But none of these organizations resolved the conflict effectively using the other models. Thus, L. Grunig's research supports the value of the two-way symmetrical model in an oblique way by showing that none of the other models effectively reduces conflict. Of course, much more research is needed to test the relationship between the two-way symmetrical model and conflict resolution.

CONCLUSIONS

In this chapter, we have summarized a 3-year program of research in which we have attempted to build an organizational theory of public relations. We identified four theoretical models of public relations and tried to explain when and why organizations employ the models. We began that program with a set of theoretical concepts that, using Shapere's (1977) characterization of early stages of theorizing, can best be described as vague, general hunches. We have followed those hunches in a systematic fashion, using correlational statistics and case studies to isolate the key variables and to search for relationships among those variables. Now we believe that we have identified the components of a deep, general theory than can be specified and tested in more elegant ways.

Originally, we believed that the models would describe a single public relations policy and a set of programs that follows that policy for each organization. We found adequate but not strong levels of reliability and validity for that notion. We found some evidence that four types of organizations defined by Hage and Hull explain some of the variance in the models. We concluded, however, that the logical relationship between the models and the environment of an organization functions as more of a normative than a positive theory of public relations.

In particular, we have concluded that organizations do and should use different models strategically to deal with different public relations problems and different sources of conflict in their environments. At the meso level of the public relations department, the models function as situational strategies for dealing with different publics and different public relations problems. A single organization, therefore, employs different models as the situation changes.

We then pursued other variables to construct a positive theory that could explain why organizations actually practice the models that they do. That research identified organizational ideology and power of the public relations department vis-à-vis the dominant coalition as central concepts in the positive theory.

The research suggested, first, that the models are a part of the organization's ideology, which is a component of organizational culture. Ideology seems to determine the openness of the system's codes. System codes, in turn, define the organization's relationship to the environment and the model of public relations valued most by the dominant coalition.

Strategic use of the public relations models by the public relations department reflects choices made by the dominant coalition. The dominant coalition chooses a public relations strategy that it believes will be useful for dealing with the publics that are most troublesome or constraining in its environment. And it chooses a strategy that fits with the organization's ideology.

We found, secondly, that public relations practitioners with the knowledge, training, and experience to practice a two-way model of public relations are more likely to be included in the organization's dominant coalition. They also are more likely to have power in that coalition rather than to serve it in an advisory role. When public relations managers have power in the dominant coalition, they can influence organizational ideology and the choice of publics in the environment for which strategic public relations programs are planned. At that point, public relations practitioners can fulfill a communication counseling and management role— and truly practice the profession defined for them in public relations textbooks but seldom fulfilled in the real world.

Finally, we have studied the relationship of the models of public relations to conflict management. We have some evidence that the two-way symmetrical model is most effective in resolving conflict, but we have no cases in which that model was used alone and in which its main effect could be isolated. In the future, we hope to find evidence that this newest model of public relations, when used strategically, will produce greater benefits for the organization than will the other models. But we also will have to determine how the public relations manager can influence organizational culture so that it is open to the practice of the two-way symmetrical model.

As our research progresses, we will develop a causal model to describe the interrelationships among the variables that we have isolated. We and four colleagues at other universities have been awarded a 6-year grant from the International Association of Business Communicators Foundation (IABC) that will allow us to test this model on many kinds of organizations in the United States, Canada, and Great Britain. The causal model and a literature review supporting it will be presented in J. Grunig (in preparation).

At present, our research has been limited by the fact that it has been conducted on organizations that have been available to us and of interest to our students— such as hospitals, government agencies, and associations. We have done some research on corporations, but we intend to include a larger proportion of corporations in our international sample (about 50%). Thus far, we have also studied only public relations departments within organizations because we have been testing an organizational theory of public relations. In the future, we plan to study how public relations firms use these models—in particular, how different organizations select firms to employ the models in their organizational communication programs.

ACKNOWLEDGMENT

The authors express their appreciation to the Computer Science Center of the University of Maryland, which funded all of the data analyses reported in this article.

REFERENCES

Aldrich, H. E. (1971). Organizational boundaries and inter-organizational conflict. *Human Relations, 24,* 279–287.

Aldrich, H. E., & Pfeffer, J. (1976). Environments of organizations. *Annual Review of Sociology, 2,* 79–105.

Bales, R. W. (1984, May). *Organizational interface: An open systems, contingency approach to boundary-spanning activities.* Paper presented to the International Communication Assoc., San Francisco.

Broom, G. M. (1982). A comparison of sex roles in public relations. *Public Relations Review, 8*(3), 17–22.

Broom, G. M., & Dozier, D. M. (1986). Advancement for public relations role models. *Public Relations Review, 12*(1), 37–56.

Broom, G. M., & Smith, G. D. (1979). Testing the practitioner's impact on clients. *Public Relations Review, 5, Fall,* 47–59.

Burns, T., & Stalker, G. M. (1961). *The Management of Innovation.* London: Tavistock.

Campbell, D. (1969). Variation and selective retention in sociocultural evolution. *General Systems, 16,* 69–85.

Carmines, E. G., & Zeller, R. A. (1979). *Reliability and validity assessment.* Beverly Hills: Sage.

Cupp, R. L. (1985). *A study of public relations crisis management in West Virginia chemical companies.* Unpublished master's thesis, University of Maryland, College Park, MD.

Cyert, R., & March, J. G. (1973). *A behavioral theory of the firm.* New York: McGraw-Hill.

Deal, T. E., & Kennedy, A. A. (1982). *Corporate cultures.* Reading, MA: Addison Wesley.

Donohue, G. A., Tichenor, P. J., & Olien, C. (1973). Mass media functions, knowledge, and social control. *Journalism Quarterly, 50,* 652–659.

Dozier, D. M. (1983, November). *Toward a reconciliation of "role conflict" in public relations research.* Paper presented to the Western Communications Educators Conference, Fullerton, CA.

Dozier, D. M. (in prep). The organizational roles of communication and public relations practitioners. In J. E. Grunig (Ed.), *Excellence in public relations and communication management: Contributions to effective organizations.* Hillsdale, NJ: Lawrence Erlbaum Associates.

Ehling, W. P. (1985). Application of decision theory in the construction of a theory of public relations management, II. *Public relations research & education, 2*(3), 4–22.

Etzioni, A. (1964). *Modern organizations.* Englewood Cliffs, NJ: Prentice-Hall.

Fabiszak, D. L. (1985). *Public relations in hospitals: Testing the Grunig theory of organizations, environments and models of public relations.* Unpublished master's thesis, University of Maryland, College Park.

Fisher, R., & Ury, W. (1981). *Getting to yes: Negotiating agreement without giving in.* New York: Penguin Books.

Grunig, J. E. (1975). A multi-systems theory of organizational communication. *Communication Research, 2,* 99–136.

Grunig, J. E. (1976). Organizations and public relations: Testing a communication theory. *Journalism Monographs, 46.*

Grunig, J. E. (1984). Organizations, environments, and models of public relations. *Public Relations Research & Education, 1*(4), 6–29.

Grunig, J. E. (1985, May). *A structural reconceptualization of the organizational communication audit, with application to a state department of education.* Paper presented to the International Communication Assoc, Honolulu.

Grunig, J. E. (Ed.). (in prep). *Excellence in public relations and communication management: Contributions to effective organizations.* Hillsdale, NJ: Lawrence Erlbaum Associate.

Grunig, J. E., & Hunt, T. (1984). *Managing public relations.* New York: Holt, Rinehart and Winston.

Grunig, L. S. (1986, August). *Activism and organizational response: Contemporary cases of collective behavior.* Paper presented to the Association for Education in Journalism and Mass Communication, Norman, OK.

Grunig, L. S. (1987, February). *Power in the public relations department as a function of values, professionalism, and organizational structure.* Paper presented at the 16th annual communication conference, Howard University, Washington, DC.

Habbersett, C. A. (1983). *An exploratory study of media relations: The science journalist and the public relations practitioner.* Unpublished master's thesis, University of Maryland, College Park, MD.

Hage, J. (1980). *Theories of organizations.* New York: Wiley.

Hage, J., & Aiken, M. A. (1970). *Social change in complex organizations.* New York: Random House.

Hage, J., & Dewar, R. A. (1973). Elite values versus organizational structure in predicting innovation. *Administrative Science Quarterly, 18,* 279–290.

Hage, J., & Hull, F. (1981). *A typology of environmental niches based on knowledge technology and scale: The implications for innovation and productivity.* Working Paper 1, University of Maryland: Center for the Study of Innovation, Entrepreneurship, and Organization Strategy, College Park, MD.

Hannan, M. T., & Freeman, J. H. (1974, August). *Environment and the structure of organizations: A population ecology perspective.* Paper presented to the American Sociological Association, Montreal.

Jackson, J. H., & Morgan, C. P. (1982). *Organization theory: A macro perspective for management.* Englewood Cliffs, NJ: Prentice-Hall.

Katz, D., & Kahn, R. L. (1966). *The social psychology of organizations.* New York: Wiley.

Kuhn, A. (1979). *Unified social science.* Homewood, IL: Dorsey.

Lauzen, M. (1986). *Public relations and conflict within the franchise system.* Unpublished doctoral dissertation, University of Maryland, College Park, MD.

McMillan, S. J. (1984). *Public relations in trade and professional associations: Location,* model, structure, environment and values. Unpublished master's thesis, University of Maryland, College Park, MD.

Mintzberg, H. (1983). Power in and around organizations. Englewood Cliffs, NJ: Prentice-Hall.

Nelson, D. G. (1986). The effect of management values on the role and practice of public relations within the organization. Unpublished master's thesis, University of Maryland, College Park, MD.

Pavlik, J. V., & Salmon, C. T. (1983). Theoretic approaches in public relations research. Public Relations Research & Education, 1(2), 39–49.

Peters, T. J., & Waterman, R. H. (1982). In search of excellence: Lessons from America's best-run companies. New York: Harper & Row.

Pollack, E. J. (1984). An organizational analysis of four public relations models in the federal government. Unpublished master's thesis, University of Maryland, College Park, MD.

Pollack, R. A. (1986). Testing the Grunig organizational theory in scientific organizations: Public relations and the values of the dominant coalition. Unpublished master's thesis, University of Maryland, College Park, MD.

Robbins, S. P. (1983). Organization theory: The structure and design of organizations. Englewood Cliffs, NJ: Prentice-Hall.

Rogers, E. M., & Larsen, J. K. (1984). Silicon valley fever. New York: Basic Books.

Schneider, L. A. (1985a). The role of public relations in four organizational types. Journalism Quarterly, 62, 567–576, 594.

Schneider, L. A. (1985b). Organizational structure, environmental niches, and public relations: The Hage-Hull typology of organizations as predictor of communication behavior. Unpublished doctoral dissertation, University of Maryland, College Park, MD.

Shapere, D. (1977). Scientific theories and their domains. In F. Suppe (Ed.), The structure of scientific theories (pp. 518–565). Urbana: University of Illinois Press.

Stamm, K. R. (1981). Measurement decisions. In G. H. Stempel, III & B. H. Westley (Eds.), Research methods in mass communication (pp. 87–104). Englewood Cliffs, NJ: Prentice-Hall.

Thayer, L. (1968). Communication and communication systems. Homewood, IL: Irwin.

Thompson, J. (1967). Organizations in action. New York: McGraw-Hill.

Thompson, V. A. (1961). Modern organization. New York: Knopf.

Wimmer, R. D., & Dominick, J. R. (1983). Mass media research. Belmont, CA: Wadsworth.

PART II

REPORTS OF ORIGINAL RESEARCH

Beyond Ethical Relativism in Public Relations: Coorientation, Rules, and the Idea of Communication Symmetry

Ron Pearson
Mount Saint Vincent University, Canada

The idea of balanced, two-way communication is an important concept in public relations theory because of the implications it has for public relations ethics. The concept nicely indicates the site of moral tension in public relations, the tension that exists at the boundary between client interests and public or audience interests. Sullivan (1965) described this as a tension between partisan and mutual values. Similarly, Culbertson (1973) discussed the interplay among partisan and nonpartisan interests. Robinson (1966) also introduced questions of ethics in public relations in terms of a model in which client benefits need to be balanced against mutual benefits. Public relations practice is situated at precisely that point where competing interests collide. Indeed, public relations problems can be defined in terms of the collision, or potential collision, of these interests. Serving client and public interests simultaneously is the seemingly impossible mission of the public relations practitioner.

INTRODUCTION: PUBLIC RELATIONS AND ETHICAL RELATIVISM

One indication that the tension between partisan and nonpartisan interests is difficult for many practitioners to overcome is empirical evidence suggesting that ethical relativism is a common moral stance among practitioners. Ethical relativism is the view that objective moral standards are unknowable or do not exist, and that, as a result, no way exists to mediate among competing interests. Ryan and Martinson (1984) suggested that practitioners are unable to discover unambiguous, objective standards for ethical decision making:

> Although some scholars have attempted to establish moral anchors in public relations . . . widespread agreement on substantive principles has not yet been achieved. . . . If public relations has adopted any underlying principle, it is possibly the subjectivism (or individual relativism) theory that each individual must establish his or her own moral base lines. (p. 27)

Finn (1965) also noted that different organizations have their own thresholds of what is considered ethical behavior. Wright (1985a) suggested that some absolute standards are coming to be accepted by many public relations practitioners and that all Americans do view the world through ethical and moral screens (Wright, 1985b). Yet Wright (1985b) described a tension between this general ethical orientation and the fact that different views are often impossible to reconcile. He wrote:

> The American business and communication environments are characterized by an enormous value-diversity which is neither consistent nor integrated. We lack neatly defined standards of moral judgement and for decades our entire culture has been marked by an assortment of change in ethical values. . . . Individuals and groups holding different and sometimes incompatible moral values often interact with public relations' assistance. (p. 51)

Delattre (1984) attempted to skirt the specter of relativism in public relations by arguing that the impossibility of agreement means merely that people who disagree can't both be right. Yet, this view provides scant consolation for the practitioner who wants to do "the right thing" and searches, therefore, for over-arching ethical standards.

The argument that ethical relativism accurately describes the moral stance of much public relations practice is also supported by interview data reported by Olasky (1985). Practitioners in his study have apparently despaired of discovering objective standards of truth and are unable to see beyond a moral relativism that breeds considerable cynicism. Olasky reported this telling admission of one senior public relations practitioner: "Does the word 'lie' actually mean anything anymore? In one sense, everyone lies, but in another no one does, because no one knows what is true" (p. 43). Another practitioner said bluntly: "There is no such thing as truth. You judge actions depending on whether they're done by someone above you or someone below you" (p. 43). Finally, a third practitioner predicted: "to talk of lying is to live in the past. I doubt if the word will even be in our everyday vocabularies in a couple of decades. There are no lies anymore, just interests waiting to be served" (p. 44). Clearly, these three practitioners are aware of nothing objective, stable, and abiding in the realm of moral maxims. They confront a mad cacaphony of competing interests with no way to decide among them except self-interest. Center and Walsh (1985) similarly acknowledged that "ethical standards [in public relations] have tended to be reflections of the employers or clients served" (p. 345).

These public relations practitioners are not alone in their descriptions of their moral environment. The moral philosopher MacIntyre (1981) has drawn similar conclusions about contemporary times: "The most striking feature of contemporary moral utterance is that so much of it is used to express disagreements; and the most striking feature of the debates in which these disagreements are expressed is their interminable character. . . . There seems to be no rational way of securing moral agreement in our culture" (p. 7). MacIntyre discussed a variety of characteristics of contemporary moral arguments. One of these is the "conceptual incommensurability" of rival arguments, the idea that basic premises of opposing arguments are radically incompatible and that no way exists to decide between them. Interest groups who protest the killing of seals off the northeast coast of Canada argue from premises that are incommensurable with the basic premises of the Newfoundland seal hunter who, for decades, has harvested the fruits of the seas to make a living. Likewise, members of the antinuclear lobby speak a language that is quite different from that of big utilities. Public relations practitioners are often called on to solve the problems arising from this collision of incompatible languages, premises, and ideas. MacIntyre suggested that it is overly complacent to appeal to the rhetoric of moral pluralism to describe this state of affairs; rather, he thinks it is more accurate to talk about moral disorder.

Using the language of systems theory and contemporary public affairs management, Gollner (1983) suggested a reason for the state of affairs described by MacIntyre that links it directly to the genesis of public relations. Gollner attributed the increasing importance of public relations and public affairs management to the "crowding in" of external issues on organizational decision-making. He described a shrinking world in which the mutual dependence among organizations and institutions (systems) is increasing rapidly. One result of this burgeoning complexity is that often incompatible value systems, which hitherto had been isolated from one another, are now forced to interact. Public relations' raison d'etre is the resulting conflict.

But do ethical questions in public relations practice have to founder in the debate between objectivism and relativism? If objective standards appear wanting or impossible, is relativism, along with a growing sense of cynicism, the only alternative? Perhaps the task of mediating among conflicting interests does not have to be envisioned in terms of an absolute opposition between interests. Instead, it can be asked what type of communication system can most likely mediate among these interests. This refocuses the practitioner's challenge. The important question becomes, not what action or policy is more right than another, but what kind of communication system maximizes the chances that competing interests can be transformed. This question shifts the emphasis from an area in which practitioners do not have special expertise—ethical theory—to areas in which they do have expertise—communication theory and practice. This shift, however, is not meant to suggest that communication theory and practice are amoral, and that ethical questions can be avoided or made irrelevant. Rather, ethical questions are raised in the context of how organizations and publics communicate (Pearson, 1987). Ethical communication is now the focus, not the question of whether the policies communicated about are themselves right or wrong in a moral sense. The core thesis of this argument is that some ways of communicating are more ethical than others and that this is a question of the structural constraints on communicative interaction. Thus, it can be asked: What are the structural characteristics of a communication system that promotes communication, negotiation, and compromise (Grunig & Hunt, 1984)? What are the structural characteristics of a communication system that promotes what Ehling (1984, 1985) called *message-exchange* or *communication-as-conversation*, or what Ackerman (1980) called *neutral dialogue*, or what Habermas (1970, 1984) called *communication symmetry*. How can these characteristics be evaluated or measured?

The purpose of this chapter is to suggest answers to these questions. First, the problem is stated as a question of unpacking the general concept of communication symmetry, a project that is initiated by introducing and developing the concept of dialogue and the closely related metaphor of conversation. Relevant ideas in Ehling (1984, 1985), Grunig (1987), and Grunig and Hunt (1984) begin this section, and a discussion of Ackerman's idea of neutral dialogue and Harbermas' description of the ideal speech situation follow. This part of the chapter concludes by indicating the kind of arguments that support the claim that dialogic or symmetrical modes of communication are presupposed by monologic or asymmetrical modes. The next part of the chapter suggests that the structure of communicative interaction can be approached as a question of the kinds of rules that both constrain and enable that interaction. Here, the focus is on how "dialogue" might be operationally defined and the possibility that a combination of communication rules theory and coorientation theory may provide useful insights into questions about communication symmetry and ethics. These two theories suggest empirically testable hypotheses relevant to the assessment of the structural and ethical characteristics of public relations communication systems. A selective review of literature that appeals to rules and/or coorientation theory supports this view. The chapter concludes by examining theoretical and practical implications of joining coorientation and rules theory to focus on the structure of interorganizational interaction. Having begun by unpacking the concepts of communication symmetry and dialogue and building theoretical definitions for them, the chapter now attempts to specify some of the variable dimensions of these concepts. Some tentative prescriptions for ethical public relations practice are suggested as well.

COMMUNICATION SYMMETRY, DIALOGUE, AND THE CONVERSATION METAPHOR

A circular way of answering the questions raised in the foregoing paragraphs asserts that systems that promote balanced, two-way communication must be characterized by symmetry. To break out of this circularity, it is necessary to unpack the idea of symmetry: What is symmetrical communication? A fruitful way to begin looking inside the idea of symmetrical communication is to introduce a word with a long history as a value in communication—*dialogue*. Plato was perhaps the first thinker to connect the idea of dialogue to certain desireable and ethically preferable styles of communication. Johannesen (1974) has suggested that dialogue is intimately connected with such notions as honesty, concern for the audience, genuineness, open-mindedness, empathy, lack of pretense, nonmanipulative intent, and encouragement of free expression. In contrast, monologue is characterized by deception, exploitation, dogmatism, insincerity, pretense, coercion, distrust, and self-defensiveness (p. 96). Some of these contrasts are also implied in discussions of ethical communication in public relations. Grunig and Hunt (1984) envisioned partisan interests submerged or transcended by mutual interests when symmetrical communication occurs. A symmetrical communication relationship for them is characterized by source and receiver who cannot be distinguished as such, but are equal participants in a communication process that seeks mutual understanding and balanced, two-way effects. Grunig (1987) added to this theory of symmetrical communication by spelling out a number of presuppositions implied in the concept. These include ideas such as equality and autonomy of communicators. Similar ideas are captured by Ehling's (1984, 1985) contrast between message dissemination and message exchange. Ehling also called this latter notion *communication-as-conversation*. It is usually during the dialogue of a conversation that communicators experience a sense that they are source and receiver simultaneously. Grunig's *symmetry* and Ehling's *message exchange* are both similar concepts, and both can be linked to the conversation metaphor.

Ackerman (1980) also appealed to this idea of conversation as a way of refurbishing liberal political theory when he suggested that we should think of liberalism as a way of talking about power. He built a theory of liberalism out of a theory of communication, rather than out of a theory of natural rights or social contract. Ackerman began by acknowledging a fundamental and significant fact of life, namely, that we live in a world where total demand for resources outstrips supply. He then posed the question of how anyone can justify his or her claim to power and control over resources. The answer he provided is that, for this claim to be rational, reasons for it must be given. Thus, Ackerman (1980) suggested this principle or rule of dialogue, which he calls *the rationality principle:* "Whenever anybody questions the legitimacy of another's power, the power holder must respond not by suppressing the questioner but by giving a reason that explains why he is more entitled to the resource than the questioner is" (p. 4). Thus, all claims, including those to inalienable natural rights, presuppose dialogue as their foundation. But not any reasons will do. Ackerman suggested, for instance, a consistency principle that requires that reasons given on one occasion must not be inconsistent with other reasons given to support claims to power. The most important rule, however, is one that Ackerman called *the neutrality principle*. This rule places a significant constraint on power talk by designating as illegitimate a power structure that can only be justified in a conversation in which a power holder claims privileged moral authority. Ackerman (1980) argued: "No reason is a good reason if it requires the power holder to assert a) that his conception of the good is better than that asserted by any of his fellow citizens, or b) that, regardless of his conceptions of the good, he is intrinsically superior to one or more of his fellow citizens" (p. 11). The upshot of this final rule is that an illegitimate claimant to power over scarce resources will be reduced to silence, because he or she will not be able to provide reasons, only unsupportable claims of superior moral insight.

What Ackerman called *neutral dialogue* is similar to what Habermas (1970, 1984) has described as an *ideal communication* situation. Moreover, Habermas' description of dialogue can also be interpreted as suggestions for the kind of communication rules that must obtain before undistorted, dialogical communication can take place. While acknowledging that this ideal is not empirically achievable, he suggested that rational discourse unavoidably posits or "anticipates" the ideal as a precondition for rational discourse. Habermas' insights seem highly relevant for public relations theory (Pearson, 1986). For instance, Habermas' (1970) formulation of the ideal communication situation is couched in the language of symmetrical communication, as is Grunig's theory. For Habermas (1970), an ideal communication situation occurs "when there is complete symmetry in the distribution of assertion and dispute, revelation and concealment, prescription and conformity, among partners of communication" (p. 371).

Habermas (1984) suggested another definition of dialogue: Dialogue occurs when participants are able to move freely from one level of abstraction to another. Moving to higher levels of abstraction during a public relations transaction allows participants to raise questions that, in day-to-day communication, are part of a background consensus shared within a community of discourse. For Habermas, this would include the opportunity to question the basic assumptions of capitalism. For most public relations transactions, these values would likely go unquestioned, but participants might well interpret these values differently and question one another on how they can best be reflected in the behavior of an organization or its publics.

McCarthy (1982) offered this useful summary of Habermas' view of dialogue:

The aim of practical [ethical] discourse is to come to a rationally motivated agreement about problematic rightness claims, an agreement that is not a product of external or internal constraints on discussion but soley of the weight of evidence and argument. . . . (T)he absence of constraints built into the very structure of communica' tion . . . can be characterized formally in terms of a freedom to move from level to level of discourse. The conditions of practical discourse must allow for a progressive radicalization of the argument. (p. 312)

For Habermas, the general structural requirement of communication within which it is possible to achieve a "progressive radicalization" of the argument is a symmetrical and balanced relationship between or among participants. This means equal freedom among participants to initiate and maintain discourse, to challenge or explain, freedom from manipulation, and equality with respect to power. A way of conceptualizing these relationships involves using the language of speech acts (see Burleson & Kline, 1979). Freedom to initiate and maintain communication means equal opportunity to use *communicatives*—speech acts that involve saying, speaking, asking; freedom to challenge and explain means equal opportunity to use *constatives*—speech acts that involve asserting, describing, explaining; freedom from manipulation means equal opportunity to use *representatives*—speech acts that involve admitting, confessing, concealing, denying; equality vis-à-vis power means equal opoortunity to use *regulatives*—speech acts that involve command' ing, forbidding, allowing, warning.

Using this taxonomy, one can envision ethical communication between an organization and its publics as communication in which spokespersons for each have equal opportunity to use all four categories of speech acts. Such communica' tion would also involve a situation in which communicators recognize an obliga' tion to make good on what Habermas (1976/1979) called the "validity claims" implied in speech acts. Thus, a speech act that makes an assertion (a constative) implies an obligation on the part of the speaker to furnish evidence for the claim should a listener request it. For Habermas, this means an implied offer to return to the experiential ground of the speaker's certainty. Similarly, a speech act that makes a rightness claim (a regulative) implies an obligation on the part of a speaker to provide justification by referring to the norms on which he or she bases his or her convictions about rightness. If, in both of these cases, a listener remains unsatisfied, speaker and listener would engage in discourse to probe the more basic epistemological or normative claims implied in the speaker's utterance.

Habermas' theory also provides other arguments that are extremely important for a theory of public relations that stresses the ideas of dialogue and two-way symmetrical communication. These arguments suggest that monological commu' nication styles presuppose dialogical communication such that dialogic interaction, or intersubjectivity, is the more basic category. Habermas (1984) distinguished two fundamentally different kinds of rationality. One he called *cognitive instrumental rationality*. This kind of reason, said Habermas, has, as a result of empiricism, marked deeply the way in which the modern era understands itself. Its goal is *instrumental mastery*. "On this model rational actions basically have the character of goal-directed, feedback-controlled interventions in the world of existing states of affairs" (p. 11). Approaches to public relations that stress environmental control are concerned with the instrumental mastery of that environment.

The second type of reason Habermas (1984) called *communicative rationality*, a concept that carries with it "connotations based ultimately on the central experience of the unconstrained, unifying, consensus-bringing force of argumentative speech" (p. 10). This view, according to Habermas, takes a phenomenological approach that the first view of reason, what Habermas called the *realistic* view, does not take. The realistic view starts from the assumption that the world exists, whereas the latter view "gives a phenomenological twist to the question and reflects on the fact that those who behave rationally must themselves presuppose an objective world" (1984, p. 11). Instead of embarking on problem-solving action in a world that is presupposed, the phenomenologist asks how this world is constituted; he or she wonders how it is even possible for instrumental reason to identify problems, set goals for itself, implement strategies, and monitor results. For Habermas, that world is constituted through intersubjective, communicative action. Presupposed by one-way, monological (instrumental) rationality is two-way, dialogical (communicative) rationality.

The idea that monologue presupposes dialogue is a powerful one. Although a real objective world probably exists independently of observers, what the world means does not. These meanings, the meanings according to which humans engage in social action, or institutions engage in public relations campaigns, are generated in and through human interaction. The core idea here is that truth, whether empirical or social, scientific or moral, theoretical or practical, is never the product of a single inquiring mind, but of at least two. The core problematic of public relations ethics is how far the interaction that produces this meaning is dialogic.

Habermas' distinction between monological and dialogical rationality nicely articulates the tension between two approaches to public relations theory—the tension between asymmetric and symmetric approaches (Grunig, 1987). Emphasis on social scientific methodologies and management by objectives techniques suggests an instrumental rationality. Emphasis on symmetry, dialogue, conversation, and mutual understanding implies a communicative rationality. Habermas' distinction parallels distinctions made in Grunig's four-part typology of public relations models. Only the two-way symmetric model is a dialogical model. And applying Habermas' insights, one can argue that it is presupposed by the other models, all of which are examples of instrumental, monological rationality. What Grunig and Hunt call scientific persuasion is the apex of instrumental rationality. Habermas is concerned to articulate an alternative kind of rationality that would act as a bulwark against an instrumental rationality bolstered by advances in social science. Like other critical theorists, he is worried about the dehumanizing effects wrought by instrumental reason, of the specter of life administered according to monological rationality. For this reason he would be concerned about an allegience between public relations theory and asymmetric social scientific technique. He would be concerned that such a relationship would lead to the flourishing of two-way asymmetric public relations at the expense of two-way symmetrical public relations.

DIALOGUE
AND COMMUNICATION RULES

For the purposes of this chapter, Habermas' and Ackerman's theories are important for at least three reasons. One, they build on the dialogue/conversation idea, an idea that is present in one form or another in at least two extant public relations theories—that of Ehling and that of Grunig. Second, in Habermas particularly, dialogical communication relationships are not merely seen as desired styles of communication, but also as the pre-condition or ground for monological styles. Thus, the idea of two-way, symmetrical dialogue takes on important epistemological and ontological implications. Third, these theories introduce the idea that legitimate and ethical conversations about power—or about any policy issues relevant to an organization and its publics—is constrained by certain kinds of rules. Ackerman made three such rules explicit and provided justification for them. Habermas did not discuss rules specifically, but it seems reasonable to interpret him using the language of rules. Thus, one way of approaching a key research question of this chapter—the question of assessing the structure of inter-organizational communication systems—is to think of structural constraints on communication in terms of communication rules and then to raise questions both about actors' perceptions of these rules and about the perceptions of observer/researchers. The following paragraphs outline the theoretical support for this move.

Cushman and Whiting (1972) argued that certain kinds of rules must be consensually held among communicators before communication can occur at all. It follows, perhaps more obviously, that certain kinds of rules must be similarly held if communication is to have a prescribed structure. Cushman and Whiting distinguished two kinds of rules: content and procedural rules. Content rules are rules about what words can mean; these can be called semantic rules. Procedural rules prescribe the ways in which people interact. These are rules about the pragmatic aspect of language use or the use of speech acts; Habermas describes his theory of communication as one concerned with pragmatics. According to Cushman and Whiting (1972), "procedural rules will govern and guide the organization of symbols and the organization of participants in the (communication) system" (p. 230). Some of these rules are implicitly and unknowingly held by communicators like the rules guiding conversation in a hospital waiting room; others can be highly explicit and codified like the rules of parliamentary procedure. A formal set of communication rules for public relations practitioners would also be highly codified. They might be more like the rules of parliamentary procedure or debate.

Shimanoff (1980) differentiated types of rule-behavior relationships along a continuum from least to most rule-conscious behavior. For instance, one may conform to a communication rule by accident without even tacit knowledge of it. Shimanoff called this *rule-fulfilling behavior*. *Rule-conforming behavior* implies tacit knowledge but excluded an actor's referring to the rule. *Rule-following behavior* implies conscious knowledge of a communication rule and conscious comparison of communication behavior to the rule. *Rule-reflective behavior* involves critical assessment of the rule itself; the actor inquires "whether the rule is a valuable rule . . . does it encourage ethical, just, or elevated (communication) behavior" (p. 123). One can imagine communication technicians involved in rule-conforming and rule-following communication behavior. Public relations managers and executives, together with members of an organization's public(s), should more often be involved in rule-reflective behavior. Indeed, according to Ehling (1985), this type of joint, rule-reflective behavior is part of the definition of public relations. He wrote: ". . . public relations activities are organized, purposeful action schemes entailing decision-making and problem-solving with reference to *design and implementation of an agreed-to, co-sponsored communication system*" (p. 20, italics added).

The organizational communication theorists Farace, Monge, and Russell (1977) have studied the communication relationships between supervisor and subordinates from a perspective that focuses on conversational rules. These authors suggested the following rule-related topics, all of which are of potential relevance for the quality of organization/public interaction and all of which are procedural rules:

1. Who initiates interaction? Who terminates interaction?;

2. How are delays treated? How frequent is contact?;

3. Who selects the topics of discussion?;

4. How are topic changes handled?;

5. How are outside interruptions handled?; and

6. How satisfied are communicators with these "communication rules"?

Because satisfaction with rules may be misguided, or the result of misinformation or manipulation, it could also prove valuable to ask how often communication rules themselves become topics of discussion. The same questions just listed could be asked with respect to discussion of the rules themselves. Thus, it could be asked: Who initiates and/or terminates discussion about communication rules? Who decides what rules can be discussed? When rule changes are agreed on, how soon are they implemented? How soon are they re-evaluated? How satisfied are communicators with the procedures for discussing the rules themselves? These topics are examples of Shimanoff's rule-reflective behavior. They are also questions posed at the level of what Ehling (1985) called *reflectiveness*. It's interesting that both Shimanoff and Ehling should use the same word to describe this behavior.

Farace, Monge, and Russell were concerned with the structure of interaction between individuals in organizations (supervisors and subordinates specifically), but there is no reason why similar questions cannot be raised about communication relationships between organizations, the key area of interest for public relations. Indeed, these types of questions could be asked of spokespersons representing an organization and its publics. As a minimum, it seems reasonable to assume that a communication environment that promotes dialogue may be marked by mutual agreement among communicators about communication rules, and mutual satisfaction with these rules. More importantly, however, one would expect it to be marked by agreement on and satisfaction with the mechanisms for criticizing and changing rules. Coorientation theory provides a perspective for testing these hypotheses. The following paragraphs summarize the basic tenets of coorientation theory and review a handful of coorientation studies that can be interpreted from the rules perspective.

COORIENTATION THEORY
AND COMMUNICATION RULES

Coorientation theory (Newcomb, 1953) asks questions about the mutual orientation of two individuals or organizations to some object; in the context of this chapter, the object is communication rules. Of interest is how each person regards the rules, and how each perceives that the other regards the same rules. How similar are their beliefs and evaluations of the rules? What is the degree of similarity or congruence that each communicator perceives that the other has with his or her own beliefs and evaluations? How accurate are these perceptions of the other's beliefs and evaluations? A number of combinations is possible, and each one can be expected to have different implications for communication symmetry and dialogue.

1. Communicators can have similar understandings of the communication rules and accurately perceive that this is the case. This can be called *monolithic consensus* (Scheff, 1967).
2. They can have similar understandings but perceive that they do not. Scheff called this *pluralistic ignorance*.

3. Communicators can have dissimilar understandings of what the communication rules are, and accurately perceive that this is the case. This
is Scheff's *dissensus*.

4. They can have dissimilar understandings of the rules but believe that
they do not. This is Scheff's *false consensus*.

These four categories might be repeated for the question of how satisfied
communicators are with the communication rules. Similarly, they could be repeated at the level of rule-reflectiveness with respect to the questions about what the
rules are for talking about and changing the rules, and with respect to the question
of how satisfactory these rules are. A number of combinations is possible, because
both questions of agreement and satisfaction are asked at two levels. On the face of
it, the most desireable state would seem to be one in which communicators have
high agreement and accuracy about how to raise and discuss questions about
communication rules and are satisfied with these procedures. To the degree that
communicators have these perceptions, one might hypothesize that they would
describe their communication interactions as more like dialogue and, hence, more
ethical. Similarly, a communicator who is dissatisfied with communication rules
but perceives that satisfactory mechanisms exist for dealing with this problem is
likely to perceive a more ethical, dialogical, or symmetrical communication environment. At the opposite extreme, communicators who are dissatisfied with
communication rules but perceive no way of solving the problem are likely to
perceive a non-dialogic (or monologic) and unethical communication environment.

But the perceptions of communicators are not the only interesting measures. A
researcher may discover cases of false consensus in which communicator satisfaction is misguided. A communicator could perceive a communication situation as
dialogical and ethical, whereas the researcher would be aware that it was not. For
instance, one communicator might believe that it is possible to raise questions
about communication rules themselves, whereas the other communicator may have
a rule that says such topics are inappropriate. This disagreement about an important communication rule would lead the researcher/observer to describe the communication environment as non-dialogic and unethical.

Few empirical studies using coorientation theory have been explicit studies of
communication rules. This seems to be especially true in the public relations
literature, where discussion of coorientation theory is usually introduced as a tool
for measuring coorientation on public issues (Broom, 1977), although a coorientational study by Hesse (1976), in the area of political public relations, raised issues
related to the dialogue/monologue distinction. Some studies in the literature on
reporter–source interaction can be interpreted using the language of rules, dialogue, and ethics introduced previously (Carter, 1958; Ryan 1979). Culbertson's
(1983) study of different perspectives on American journalism can also be interpreted from a rules perspective; indeed, the author acknowledges that this
perspective is relevant to the study. In the organizational communication literature,

empirical studies do exist where the object of study has been communication rules (Russell, 1972; Schall, 1983).

Carter (1958) found high agreement between physicians and newspaper report-ers on the question of the relative importance of journalistic values in stories reporting science news. Both groups agreed accuracy was most important, fol-lowed by reader interest, usefulness, prompt publication, and completeness. These five values can be envisioned as communication rules. Both physicians and report-ers, therefore, agree on the relative importance of the communication rules govern-ing the production of science news stories. But perceived congruence was higher for reporters than for physicians. Reporters thought physicians would be more like them than physicians thought reporters would be like them. This is an example of what Scheff called *pluralistic ignorance*. Because physicians thought that reporters used different communication rules than the reporters actually used, one can imagine physicians approaching interview situations with more trepidation and caution than a reporter might. Perhaps they would also view their communication interactions with reporters as less dialogical and less ethical than they would prefer. This would be especially true if physicians also felt that they could not discuss these rules with the reporter.

Ryan's (1979) study used a coorientation approach and found that scientists and journalists agreed on many communication rules, but not on some others. Examples of rules about which disagreement existed were (a) science writers should rely on scientists to point out the important facts; (b) scientists should refuse to talk to inadequately trained reporters; and (c) a reporter should use the word "breakthrough" or "cure" only if the scientist approves. At issue here, to recall Habermas' distinctions, is the kind of speech acts that scientists should be able to employ during an interview. Ryan (1979) concluded that "in these areas of disagreement serious barriers to effective science news communication are most likely to occur" (p. 26). Disagreement about communication rules is thus likely to have an impact on interaction. In the Carter study, perceived disagreement about rules was inaccurate. In the Ryan study, however, disagreement actually existed. Moreover, Ryan reported that scientists and reporters were aware of this disagree-ment. To the extent that they saw no room for negotiation on these rules, it is likely that a scientist would be cautious during an interview, and the reporter suspicious. On the other hand, if both scientists and reporters perceived a possibility of discussing these rules and how they might be modified, given situational exigen-cies, both might perceive the interview situation as more fruitful, dialogical, and ethical.

Hesse (1976) studied the accuracy of a Wisconsin senator's perceptions of constituent's opinions. He found this accuracy to be higher among senators who practiced dialogic communication than among those who practiced monologic communication. The latter group included more urban senators whose commu-nication strategies included dependence on the mass media, use of press releases, and speeches. Although communication rules were not the object of study for

Hesse, it seems reasonable to infer that each group of senators saw different kinds of communication rules as being appropriate for senator–constituent communication relationships. Hesse's results suggest that communication rules that emphasize listening behavior are more appropriate where accuracy of understanding is the goal of communication. An interesting research question is whether constituents of rural senators in Hesse's study would characterize senatorial communication as more ethical than would constituents of urban senators.

Culbertson's (1983) study of journalistic perspectives also raised questions about communication rules in the context of coorientation theory. He studied the beliefs about contemporary newspaper journalism of 258 news personnel from 17 newspapers and found support for the view that there are three distinct clusters of such beliefs—traditional, interpretive, and activist. Each of these groups believes different communication rules to be appropriate for journalistic communication in newspapers. The traditionalist, for instance, appeals to rules dictating use of inverted pyramid style and summary lead. An interpretivist appeals to rules emphasizing in-depth reporting and clear explication of context. The activist is concerned to challenge and circumvent communication rules dictated by perceived front office collusion with established power structures. In Culbertson's study, only the traditionalist perceived high congruence with readers. Perhaps readers who do in fact share and approve of the traditional journalistic values and communication rules would be more likely to view the traditional approach as ethical. The reader of a traditional newspaper who shares an interpreter's communication rules would probably say that the paper was less ethical.

Schall (1983) studied communication rules for gaining power and influence in two different groups in an organization. She found that one group placed a high value on seeking and sharing information, whereas the other was more secretive and shared information only with trusted colleagues. Clearly, different communication rules applied in the different groups. Schall's study was not a coorientation study, but the author noted that each group had an accurate understanding of the rules in the other group. High disagreement about communication rules existed and congruency and accuracy were also high. As a result, communication relationships between the groups were strained and cautious. Neither group would likely consider inter-group communication relationships as either dialogial or ethical. Russell (1972) also studied communication rules in an organization and focused on coorientation between supervisors and subordinates on procedural communication rules. A questionnaire was used to discover how both supervisors and subordinates viewed their current communication, what they thought was ideal, and how each predicted that the other would answer these questions. One finding of this study was that supervisors perceived that communication was less frequent than did subordinates and that it was less satisfactory for this reason. Russell also discovered that higher levels of understanding and satisfaction with communication rules were positively associated with other aspects of supervisor–subordinate relationships. Where high mutual understanding of rules was discovered, subordinates also had higher morale and had higher evaluations from supervisors. Both supervisor and subordinate saw their relationship in a more social and informal way than supervisor/subordinate pairs with lower understanding of communication rules. Perhaps they would also see it as more dialogical and more ethical.

CONCLUSION: THEORETICAL
AND PRACTICAL IMPLICATIONS

The foregoing review of literature supports the idea that coorientation about communication rules would afford a useful way of answering questions about communication symmetry. In public relations, the degree of symmetry of interaction between an organization and its publics is an important question. The importance of this question is related to its relevance for public relations ethics in general and to the problem of ethical relativism in particular. The objectivism–relativism debate can be avoided by a focus on the structure of organizational–public interaction and this structure can be conceptualized in terms of communication rules. Coorientation theory affords a way of testing hypotheses about the relationship between communicators' perceptions of the dialogical or ethicial nature of communication and their perceptions about communication rules. Empirical research using coorientation theory would also allow observers to note relationships of which situated communicators are unaware. A critical observer could make judgments about how ethical such relationships are by appealing to models like that of Habermas, or to rules like those suggested by Ackerman. The public relations practitioner concerned with ethics could use coorientation theory as an element of program evaluation where the focus is communication rules as well as the relevant public issues. Indeed, a key public relations goal is the establishment of symmetrical, dialogical, or ethical communication relationships. Coorientational methods furnish tools for formative and summative research efforts in support of achieving these goals. Overall, envisioning communication structures in terms of rules and using coorientational methods to assess perceptions of these rules holds some promise for measuring ethics, a domain that is often held to be unmeasurable.

Using communication rules, a researcher could suggest a number of variable dimensions in the general concept of dialogic or symmetric communication. In general, each rule would describe a separate dimension of this concept. Rules could be deduced from theories such as those described in this chapter. As well, content analysis of interviews with representatives of organizations and their publics would reveal other rules. However, they are determined, an ethical theory for public relations would include a list of these dimensions and theoretical justification for them. Variance along each dimension would be an empirical question that could be assessed by using coorientation theory. The important ethical questions are whether there is deviance from either mutually agreed-to prescriptions for communication or from prescriptions deduced from a theory of communication ethics. To sum up and unify the ideas presented in this chapter, the following paragraphs recap the core assumptions of the theory discussed, and specify some tentative prescriptions for ethical practice that can be deduced from this theory. Five variable dimensions of dialogic communication are outlined, and each of these is discussed.

OUTLINE OF AN ETHICAL
THEORY FOR PUBLIC RELATIONS

Basic Premise

Ethics in public relations is not fundamentally a question of whether it is right or wrong to tell the truth, steal clients from one another, accept free lunches or bribes, or provide information for insider trading, and so on. Rather, ethical public rela- tions practice is more fundamentally a question of implementing and maintaining interorganizational communication systems that question, discuss, and validate these and other substantive ethical claims.

Suggested Prescriptions for Ethical
Communication

Necessary conditions for ethical public relations practice consist in the following.

1. Communication Relationships

Implementation and maintenance of dialogical communication relationships between an organization and its public. This means following certain agreed-on communication rules that apply equally to the organization and to its publics. Additionally, it is a question of adherence to rules for dialogue deduced from a theory of communication ethics. Rules describe variable dimensions of the general concept of dialogue or communication symmetry in public relations.

Dimension 1. Degree of Communicator Understanding of and Satisfaction With Rules Governing the Opportunity for Beginning and Ending Communicative In- teraction. This dimension refers to rules about the the use of speech acts called communicatives. At its simplest, this dimension may imply that an organization or public make known its phone numbers or mailing address. At a more complex level it may involve metacommunication (rule-reflectiveness) about the conditions under which a communicant can terminate communication. Ehling (1985) has observed that interorganizational communication systems need to have longevity to promote satisfactory conflict management. Required longevity would vary situationally and would be an issue for metacommunication.

Dimension 2. Degree of Communicator Understanding of and Satisfaction With the Rules Governing the Length of Time Separating Messages, or a Question From its Answer. Acceptable lengths of time will vary from situation to situation and general rules can be adduced for different situations. Crisis situations may require shorter delays than more routine interorganizational communication. Ideally, this issue would be a topic of rule-reflective communication or metacommunication.

Dimension 3. Degree of Communicator Understanding of and Satisfaction With Rules Governing Opportunity for Suggesting Topics and Initiating Topic Changes. This dimension can be understood in terms of constative speech acts, those that make assertions and raise questions of fact. This dimension reflects Habermas' definition of dialogue as the opportunity to make arguments progressively more radical, that is by asking questions that get at premises and assumptions that are not always or usually topics of discussion. This dimension also measures the relative power that participants have or perceive they have vis-à-vis communication.

Dimension 4. Degree of Communicator Satisfaction That a Partner in Communication has Provided a Response That Counts as a Response. The rule referred to here is Ackerman's neutrality principle. This is not a question of whether a communicator likes the answer or not, but of whether a substantive response is given at all. Low satisfaction on this dimension would likely obtain in situations where communicators claimed some kind of privileged moral insight. This dimension also taps satisfaction with issues related to the use of the speech acts called regulatives, speech acts that command, demand, or order.

Dimension 5. Degree of Communicator Understanding of and Satisfaction With Rules for Channel Selection. This dimension is meant to tap insights implied in the conversation metaphor that can be identified, either implicitly or explicitly, in some of the theories examined heretofore. A perhaps controversial prescription related to this issue would exhort practitioners to use mass-mediated channels only as a last resort and/or to maintain good relations with mass media representatives. To promote interaction that is more like dialogue, practitioners might prefer specialized publications with fast feedback loops along with mediating structures (Berger & Neuhaus, 1977) or small, "in-between" organizations, membership in which is equally available to representatives of organizations and publics.

2. Audit

Implement and carry out regular audits to assess organization/public coorientation regarding rules and level of satisfaction with rules. An argument might be made that this audit should be conducted either by an independent agent or by a joint research team with representatives from both focal organization and public.

3. Metacommunication Systems

Implement, maintain, and promote metacommunication systems for addressing communication problems and consider all parts of number 1 to apply to interaction at the metacommunication level. It's important that none of the substantive policy issues under discussion constrain metacommunication about communication rules.

General Expectations About Relationships Involving Aforementioned Dimensions

A communication environment that promotes dialogue will be marked by mutual understanding among communicators about the actual communication rules in place and mutual satisfaction with these rules. Most importantly, however, one would expect a dialogic communication environment to be marked by accurate understanding of and satisfaction with mechanisms for criticizing and changing rules. Overall, communicator perceptions of an ethical communication environ- ment would be expected to vary postively with levels of satisfaction along dimen- sions such as those just described.

An independent observer would judge the communication environment as di- alogical, symmetrical, or ethical on two levels. The first would be the degree to which actual communication practice conformed to rules agreed o and validated by metacommunication among situated communicators. The second level would be the degree to which actual practice conformed to communication rules deduced from a communication ethics theory used by the researcher.

REFERENCES

Ackerman, B. (1980). *Social justice in the liberal state.* New Haven, CT: Yale University Press.
Berger, P. L., & Neuhaus, R. (1977). *To empower people: The role of mediating structures in social policy.* Washington, DC: American Enterprise Institute.
Broom, G. M. (1977). Coorientational measurement of public issues. *Public Relations Review, 3*(1), 110–119.
Burleson, B. R., & Kline, S. L. (1979). Harbermas' theory of communication. A critical explication. *Quarterly Journal of Speech, 65,* 412–428.
Carter, R., Jr. (1958). Newspaper "gatekeepers" and the sources of news. *Public Opinion Quarterly, 22*(2), 133–144.
Center, A. H., & Walsh, F. E. (1985). *Public relations practices: Managerial case studies and problems.* Englewood Cliffs, NJ: Prentice-Hall.

Culbertson, H. M. (1973). Public relations ethics: A new look. *Public Relations Quarterly,* *17,* 15–17, 23–25.

Culbertson, H. M. (1983). Three perspectives on American journalism. *Journalism Mono-graphs, 83.*

Cushman, D. C., & Whiting, G. C. (1972). An approach to communication theory: Toward consensus on rules. *Journal of Communication, 22,* 217–238.

Delattre, E. J. (1984). Ethics in the information age. *Public Relations Journal, 40*(6), 12–14.

Ehling, W. P. (1984). Application of decision theory in the construction of a theory of public relations I. *Public Relations Research and Education, 1*(2), 25–39.

Ehling, W. P. (1985). Application of decision theory in the construction of a theory of public relations II. *Public Relations Research and Education, 2*(1), 4–22.

Farace, R. V., Monge, P. R., & Russell, H. M. (1977). *Communicating and organizing.* New York: Random House.

Finn, D. (1965). The struggle for ethics. In O. Lerbinger & A. J. Sullivan (Eds.), *Informa-tion, influence and communication* (pp. 467–479). New York: Basic Books.

Gollner, A. B. (1983). *Social change and corporate strategy: The expanding role of public affairs.* Stamford, CT: Issue Action Press.

Grunig, J. (1987, May). *Symmetrical presuppositions as a framework for public relations theory.* Paper presented to the Conference on the Applications of Communication Theo-ry: Public Relations, Normal, IL.

Grunig, J., & Hunt, T. (1984). *Managing public relations.* New York: Holt, Rinehart & Winston.

Habermas, J. (1970). Towards a theory of communication competence. *Inquiry, 13,* 360–375.

Habermas, J. (1979). What is universal pragmatics? In (T. McCarthy Ed. & Trans.) *Communication and the evolution of society* (pp. 69–94). Boston: Beacon Press. (Origi-nal work published 1976).

Habermas, J. (1984). *The theory of communicative action.* Vol 1 (T. McCarthy, Trans.). Boston: Beacon Press.

Hesse, M. B. (1976). A coorientation study of Wisconsin state senators and their con-stitiuencies. *Journalism Quarterly, 53*(4), 626–633, 660.

Johannesen, R. L. (1974). Attitude of speaker toward audience: A significant perspective for contemporary rhetorical theory and criticism. *Central States Speech Journal, 25,* 95–104.

MacIntyre, A. (1981). *After virtue: A study in moral theory.* Notre Dame: University of Notre Dame Press.

McCarthy, T. (1982). *The critical theory of Jürgen Habermas.* Cambridge: MA: MIT Press.

Newcomb, T. M. (1953). An approach to the study of communicative acts. *Psychological Review, 60*(6), 393–404.

Olasky, M. (1985). Inside the amoral world of public relations: Truth molded for corpo-rate gain. *Business and Society Review, 53,* 41–44.

Pearson, R. A. (1986, August). *The ideal public relations situation: Alternative criteria for program evaluation.* Paper presented to the Public Relations Division, Association for Education in Journalism and Mass Communication, Norman, OK.

Pearson, R. A. (1987, May). *Business ethics as communication ethics: The role of public*

relations in moral corporate conduct. Paper presented to the conference on the Applications of Communication Theory: Public Relations, Normal, IL.

Robinson, E. J. (1966). *Communication and public relations.* Columbus, OH: Charles E.
Merrill.

Russell, H. M. (1972). *Coorientational similarity toward procedural aspects of communication: A study of communication between extension agents and their supervisors.* Unpublished doctoral dissertation, Department of Communication, Michigan State University, East Lansing.

Ryan, M. (1979). Attitudes toward coverage of science news. *Journalism Quarterly, 56*(2),
18–26.

Ryan, M., & Martinson, D. L. (1984). Ethical values, the flow of journalistic information
and public relations persons. *Journalism Quarterly, 61,* 27–34.

Schall, M. S. (1983). A communication-rules approach to organizational culture. *Administrative Science Quarterly, 28,* 557–581.

Scheff, T. (1967). Toward a sociological model of consensus. *American Sociological Review, 32,* 32–46.

Shimanoff, S. B. (1980). *Communication rules: Theory and research.* Beverly Hills: SAGE
Publications.

Sullivan, A. J. (1965). Values in public relations. In O. Lerbinger & A. J. Sullivan (Eds.),
Information, influence and communication (pp. 412–439). New York: Basic Books.

Wright, D. (1985a). Age and the moral values of practitioners. *Public Relations Review,
11*(1), 51–60.

Wright, D. (1985b). Individual ethics determine public relations practice. *Public Relations
Journal, 41*(4), 38–39.

Chapter 4

The Aborted Debate
Within Public Relations:
An Approach Through Kuhn's
Paradigm

Marvin N. Olasky
The University of Texas

> Public Relations Quarterly *survey question addressed to public relations* *practitioners:* "The word 'image' . . . does it leave you with a bad taste, or do *you believe it is an accurate description of the end product of your efforts?"* *One answer:* "Creating images causes no problem for me. The image of PR *people does. It stinks."*
> —Public Relations Quarterly (1973, pp. 12, 24)

> *Public relations counselor J. Carroll Bateman:* "All too frequently, we appear *to suffer from the delusion that we can really play God with people. We* *would do much better to lay off this kind of nonsense . . ."*
> —Bateman (1958, p. 17)

Why have public relations practitioners generally been depicted as low-life liars? Why has a comment such as this been so common: "PR is dangerous. Publicists do not often lie, but telling half the truth is an integral part of their business, and stretching the truth is not uncommon" (Sandman, Rubin, & Sachsman, 1976, p. 367)? Or this: "Public relations works behind the scenes; occasionally the hand of the PR man can be seen shifting some bulky fact out of sight, but usually the public relations practitioner stands at the other end of a long rope which winds around several pulleys before it reaches the object of his invisible tugging" (Mayer, 1958, p. 123). Why have practitioners regularly been labeled "high-paid errand boys and buffers for management," "tools of the top brass," "hucksters," "parrots," "awed by the majesty of their organization charts," "desperate," "impotent, eva-sive, egomaniacal, and lying" (Henry, 1972, pp. 89–90)? (And those are just the comments from the fans of public relations!)

　　Some public relations practitioners have argued that the root cause of such complaints is financial envy, particularly that of lower-paid newspaper folk. There is undoubtedly some truth in that defense, yet contempt for public relations goes far beyond the ranks of potentially jealous journalists. Other practitioners have cited ignorance on the part of the public as to what public relations men and women actually do all day. There may be some truth in that claim too, yet the Supreme Court, which operates with as much secrecy as some public relations departments, is generally revered, while the "PR man" has been equated ethically with that lowly cousin of the chief justice, the local ambulance-chaser.

One good place to go for an explanation of why a trade is in trouble, conceivably, might be the textbooks that attempt to communicate methodology, while insinuating philosophy, to future generations. The nine public relations textbooks that were surveyed for this chapter, to their credit, did not entirely avoid the question of public relations disgrace. Their authors tried to come up with reasons to explain why the very words "public relations" bring sneers and tears. Their common failing, though, was an embrace of what could be called "the doctrine of selective depravity," otherwise known as "Don't blame us, it's them, the immoral outsiders, who cause trouble" (Aronoff & Baskin, 1983; Cutlip & Center, 1978; Lovell, 1982; Marston, 1979; Newsom & Scott, 1981; Nolte, 1974; Reilly, 1981; Seitel, 1984; Simon, 1983).

The most widely used textbook, Cutlip and Center's (1978) *Effective Public Relations*, noted in the first chapter of its revised fifth edition that "The labeling of public relations effort as frivolous or shallow, or as the synonym for a false front, has a long history" (p. 15). Examples were provided:

> An editor tells his readers, "If you want to get plausible disguises for unworthy causes, hire a public relations expert." A columnist speaks of the "perversion of the language by public relations . . . an accepted form of lying to the public to manipulate it as the promoters wish." A newspaper labels public relations "a parasite on the press." (p. 15)

But Cutlip and Center then provided 500 pages of "how-to" techniques; they returned to the central problem only in the final chapter. There, they concluded lamely that all practitioners should "face the fact that they are special pleaders" (p. 576). The problems of public relations, they suggested, are caused not by the nature of such special pleading, but by some particularly unfortunate practices. For instance, public relations "was given a black eye in the mind of the public by Richard Nixon's preoccupation with his misshapen concept of the function . . . Nixon's typical response to each new revelation of wrongdoing in his administration was 'Let's PR it'" (p. 576).

The eight other textbooks analyzed all contended or implied that the problems of public relations were similarly at the periphery: that were it not for some corrupt practitioners, or for Richard Nixon, or for some others who falsely use the title "public relations counsel," or for certain mildly troublesome practices, public relations would be clothed in such magnificent robes that even insouciant children would not be able to detect nakedness triumphant. There were complaints about those who "usurp the title" of public relations practitioner, such as the Chicago prostitute arrested for soliciting after she passed out business cards with her name, phone number, address, and the two words, "Public Relations." But there was avoidance of key trouble spots. For instance, Fraser Seitel, director of public affairs at Chase Manhattan Bank and author of *The Practice of Public Relations* (1984), minimized the problems at large institutions but complained that, "There is noth-ing to prevent someone with little or no formal training from 'hanging out a shingle' as a public relations specialist. Such frauds embarrass professionals in the field" (p. 4). Lawrence Nolte (1974), in *Fundamentals of Public Relations*, noted that some "use the designation as a respectable cover for activities which are not public relations at all" (p. 9). But blaming the periphery does not come to grips with the corruption that can be found at the center of the public relations trade. Nor does it explain why public relations' progress over the past 30 years has been so small that the apologies offered now are virtual repetitions of those made then.

Examination of a fascinating monograph from 1951, J. A. R. Pimlott's *Public Relations and American Democracy*, showed that history does not repeat itself, but excuses do. Practitioners then, according to Pimlott, said

> . . . that their indifferent reputation is due to the incompetence and dishonesty of a minority of their number—to 'the lunatic fringe of the profession, the headline wheedlers, the something-for-nothing boys,' to 'the antics of the quacks and char-latans who cling to the fringe of our profession,' to 'the snide, weasel-minded, smart, conscienceless lads." (p. 202)

Pimlott observed:

> There is something in the argument. As an explanation of the persistently poor reputation of the group it is, however, neither probable nor in accordance with the facts. Other professions carry lunatic and even dishonorable fringes without suffering much loss of esteem; and the truth is that public distrust arises less from tyros and quacks on the fringe than from the more widely publicized activities of some of the leading figures. (p. 203)

A third of a century after Pimlott's book, defense of "special pleading" and crit-icism of "the fringe" continues.

There was one promising moment during the late 1950s and early 1960s, though, when basic questions about public relations purpose were being asked. One leading public relations agency, Ruder and Finn, held seminars designed to examine "PR philosophy," and an interest in reassessment was revealed even in the pages of *Public Relations Journal*. For instance, J. Carroll Bateman (1957) argued that basic goals of practitioners would have to change if they were ever to win greater public acceptance. Bateman wrote that,

To ourselves and to others we have too long—and perhaps wrongly—held ourselves out as 'molders of public opinion,' or to put it more bluntly, as professional persuaders. Persuasion is a means rather than an end. . . . The worst thing that can happen to us in public relations is to continue to be tagged as manipulators of people or of public opinion. As manipulators we shall not win friends, nor find a lasting place in society. Nor shall we even be comfortable with ourselves. (p. 8)

Bateman (1958) raised other pertinent questions in a *Public Relations Journal* article the following year entitled, "A New Moral Dimension for Communication." He noted that "Many of the messages that are written or spoken today have been so carefully phrased to achieve a certain effect upon the intended audience that they mean nothing at all; or they serve as veils to meaning and may really mean the opposite of what they appear to say" (p. 17). He criticized the trade philosophy revealed in the popular credo, "Sell the sizzle, not the steak," by asking:

How long will it continue to work? Haven't we already perceived a deterioration of public confidence in communication that deals with sizzles instead of steaks? If those of us who are professionally engaged in the art of communication will not devise messages that inform and educate our audiences, are we not helping to degrade them? (p. 17)

As late as 1962, other *Public Relations Journal* writers were going back to basics also. For instance, W. Howard Chase (1962) argued in November of that year that the philosophy behind the popular term coined by Edward Bernays, the "engineering of consent," should be opposed because the term:

implies the use of all the mechanics of persuasion and communication to bend others, either with their will or against their will, to some prearranged conclusion. . . I can't help but think that carrying the "engineering of consent" line to a logical conclusion is the pistol at the back of the neck, reminiscent of Nazi times and not unknown behind the Iron Curtain. (p. 5)

Chase also criticized another mainstream definition of public relations, having good deeds and performances publicly acknowledged, because "It sounds Pharisaical, so similar to the Pharisee on the street corner 'thanking God that I am not as other men. . .'" (p. 5).

While this debate was percolating, though, there was an uprising in the ranks. Mainstream practitioners complained that a time when public relations was getting bigger and perhaps "badder," but certainly more powerful and profitable, was no time to get self-critical. For instance, publicity supervisor John L. Normoyle (1958) tried to cut off incipient introspection at the knees by writing in *Public Relations Journal* that "Public relations, after a long struggle for recognition, has reached that point in its development which calls for a pause to evaluate its accomplishments and chart a course for the future. Unfortunately, it is also a time when unrealistic pipe-dreams can inhibit the objective reasoning necessary at this stage" (p. 23). The bit of questioning that was going on was turned by Normoyle into an orgy of self-examination and dreamy speculation.

By 1963, crossness at attacks on crassness was dominant in the *Public Relations Journal*. Copywriter Dennis Altman (1963), for instance, urged public relations practitioners to dump any concern about "intangibles" and instead create a new, improved "image of smartness, Machiavellian smartness" which would get them "to the front of the bus. . . Of course, your lives may not be happier up front. We get more ulcers, and more insomnia up there. But at least, after riding in front for a while, if you decide you don't like it, you'll be able to afford to get off and take a cab" (p. 7). The more discerning practitioners knew that getting off was not that easy, not that easy at all. But the era of debate was put to bed, finally, with a 1963 article on public relations goals by counselor Andrew Lazarus. Lazarus (1963) used a true point, the real grounding of public relations (like all business) in financial calculation, to deride thought about the ethical grounding, which is at least as essential. The goal of practitioners, he wrote, should be simply "to make money—for their management, their clients and themselves" (p. 6). "This may be a reductio ad absurdum," he continued, "but the absurd would pay off more than "defending our profession, contemplating our navels, and needlessly worrying about our status" (p. 6).

The debate in *Public Relations Journal*, and to a large extent in public relations as a whole, just died after that. There were still occasional articles of mild criticism, including one by Georgetown University public relations director Arthur Cuervo (1975). He wrote that the real problem of public relations was that "mainstream practitioners engage in the engineering of consent that helps to mold public opin- ion to the profitable interest of the client at the expense of the public good," and take pride in doing so. Cuervo described the tendency "to blame the quacks in the field" and to say, "throw the rascals out and all will be right with the world of public relations." He noted that such a convenient placing of blame did not get to the core of the problem, for "*At the top of the PR enemies list should be the practitioners themselves*" (pp. 11–12). But Cuervo's article apparently provoked little redrawing of the enemies list; *Public Relations Journal* articles from 1977 through 1983 made it appear that the slightly open door to reevaluation was slammed shut.

Why did the public relations debate abort some 25 years ago? We can begin to answer that question through a brief restatement and application of the major argument developed in Thomas Kuhn's (1962) seminal book, *The Structure of Scientific Revolutions*. Kuhn's work was a trumpet blast directed at scholars who want so much to get on with the work of empirical investigation that they blithely accept faulty theoretical foundations. Although most applications of his theory have been in academic disciplines, Kuhn's work would appear to be applicable as well to a "practical" field such as public relations where the tendency to run toward clients, without first walking through presuppositions, is very strong.

Kuhn's basic building block was the paradigm, a particular theory that domi-nates a scientific or occupational field. Paradigms are "universally recognized scientific achievements that for a time provide model problems and solutions to a community of practitioners" (1962, p. x). A paradigm explains to practitioners which problems are important and indicates how they are to be solved. Knowledge within the paradigm grows because of what Kuhn called *normal science*, the incremental advances that are made possible when practitioners, confident in their methodology, see little need for additional theorizing or criticism and instead make small but significant contributions to the growth of knowledge within their profession.

The existence of a paradigm is extremely useful for a profession; all fields or endeavors need presuppositions and frameworks to organize data. "Normal sci-ence" does allow for significant linear progress or growth within a particular discipline. As Kuhn noted, within an established paradigm the practitioner can get on with his work without being forced to spend time defending the fundamental principles of the paradigm or the world view that is its base. An academic or occupational community tends to be happiest when novelty is far from its mind and when work unencumbered by epistemological worry can proceed.

Although something is gained through such organization, something also is lost: The normal scientist (or historian, or public relations practitioner) tends to screen out data that do not fit in the paradigm. He ignores such information, terms it *peripheral*, and points to the positive growth of the field. Problems, though, arise with the development of what Kuhn called *anomalies*, those results of normal practice that cannot be reconciled with the paradigm, even when efforts are made to adjust or stretch it slightly. "There are always some discrepancies" between theory and practice, Kuhn noted, and effective practice can continue despite "per-sistent and recognized anomaly," but particular anomalies may "call into question explicit and fundamental generalizations of the paradigm" (1962, pp. 81–82). Anomalies may reach the stage of "crisis" and produce profound repercussions for practitioners, who feel not only insecure but deeply puzzled as to why their activities are not producing expected results.

No theory provides a perfect fit with the facts, but when practitioners begin to understand that the most pressing problems they face have no solution within the old paradigm, halting questioning of that paradigm begins. The few practitioners who dare to question are eventually joined by others who begin working outside the bounds of "normal science" in an attempt to resolve the crisis. Normal science even gives way to "extraordinary" science, which is typified by an enthusiastic reexamination of a profession or discipline's boundaries, uncowed by the deep shadows of the old paradigm. Alternative suggestions begin to blossom.

Kuhn (1962) emphasized the resistance that such new paradigm proposals are likely to encounter, noting that rigidity within a profession may stifle challenges from inside, and suggesting that younger people who have received training in some other field are more likely to be able to see forests and not just trees: "In each case a novel theory emerged only after a pronounced failure in the normal problem-solving activity" (pp. 74–75). Because the emergence of a new theory breaks with one tradition of scientific practice and introduces a new one conducted under different rules and within a different universe of discourse, it is likely to occur only when the first tradition is felt to have gone badly astray (see Kuhn, 1962, p. 85). New proposals are generally ridiculed as unprofessional, immature works of young, ignorant folk, but the new paradigm(s) eventually capture(s) the more flexible and thoughtful minds of the younger generation, and changes do come.

What does all this have to do with public relations? As historian David Hollinger (1980) has put it, "*The Structure of Scientific Revolutions* excites the imagination of working historians chiefly because much of what it says about scientific communities seems to apply so strikingly to other kinds of communities" (p. 196). One such community is public relations, which is unquestionably a set of activities defined and controlled by a tradition of "special pleading." Those who receive formal public relations education often read Cutlip and Center's (1978) defense of special pleading and their observation that, "*Presenting all sides of an issue and providing an objective, balanced appraisal of the merits of conflicting views is a responsibility of the news media, not the practitioners*" (p. 579). Similarly, textbook writer Raymond Simon (1983) told aspirants to public relations that "your primary obligation is to the organization for which you work" (p. 271). Interviewing during 1983 showed that the many practitioners who enter public relations without academic training receive the same message in ways hardly more subtle; many interviewees at one major corporate public relations department reported being told, with only small variations in language, "It's not your business to care what's right" (Olasky, 1987, p. 144).

Many veteran practitioners and educators do not understand that the justifications of special pleading, primary responsibility to employer, and lack of concern for objectivity, *are all part of a paradigm* initially developed by Edward Bernays during the 1920s (see Olasky, 1987). As Kuhn pointed out, for those within the paradigm, their way of conducting research and doing business is seen not as a product of their philosophies, but as the only truly professional or scientific way to act. Yet there have been modes of public relations that involved neither special pleading nor a sense of primary responsibility to anything other than objective truth as best perceived (see Olasky, 1987).

This is not to say that recently there have been *no* discussions of philosophy within the citadels of public relations practice. A Public Relations Society of America task force that in 1981 attempted to provide a succinct definition of the trade settled for not one sentence but two: "Public relations helps an organization and its publics adapt mutually to each other [sic]," and "Public relations is an organization's efforts to win the cooperation of groups of people" (Public Relations Journal, 1981, p. 16). Those two definitions reflected a debate within public relations on whether "two-way" communication (the former definition) or "one-way" communication, from the organization outward (the latter definition) should predominate. But, in practice, both camps emphasized subjective feelings of adaptation and communication rather than objective concepts of attempting to arrive at

a "balanced appraisal of the merits of conflicting views." Even honest communication is not worth much if the activities on which it is based are dishonest.

What *public* discussion there is has gone on almost entirely within the boundaries of the current paradigm of special pleading. There has been an awareness of
anomalies—chiefly the public's growing resistance to attempts at manipulation—
but they are not subjects for polite conversation. Those few individuals who have
tried to bring up questions of objective truth at the beginning of public relations
strategy sessions generally have been told that such considerations may be interesting but are outside the tradition—and the sessions inevitably have lurched into the
planning of manipulation. The advocacy of both one-way and two-way styles of
communication have been subsets of a desire to use mass psychology to gain
organizational goals. That is why public relations practitioners of both persuasions
have been regarded as low-life liars. That is why those who do not like public
relations' image but see no problem with the goal of image-building are their own
worst enemies.

After walking through Kuhn's paradigm we can better perceive what happened
to the public relations debate of the late 1950s and early 1960s. The anomalies
were perceived. A crisis was brewing. But the public relations occupation was too
profitable for its beneficiaries to accept the reformation and reconstruction that
paradigm changes require. There was resistance to the development of extraordinary science and an insistence on the continuation of normal science, even at the
cost of losing credibility for the public relations occupation as a whole. The trade
was made: acceptance of a low status for public relations in return for acceptance of
fat paychecks. Public relations practitioners would continue to pretend that they
could play God with people, as Bateman put it, even though through this pretense
they were producing more atheists all the time.

In short, the basic debate about public relations purpose was aborted some 25
years ago because public relations practitioners had developed a comfortable paradigm and did not want to give it up. Without the existence of multiple doses of
research on the actual effects of manipulative attempts—in the sciences, such
research is the medication used to reduce obstinate fevers—practitioners could
continue whistling in the dark, at least all the way to the bank.

Today, we need a debate that will be more productive than the debate of the late
1950s. If we realize that current public relations is the result of a paradigm that has
had destructive practical applications, then we may be open to the search for other
roads to professionalism. If we do not, any new discussions may be aborted like
those of years past, and public relations will speed up its descent into further
disrepute.

ACKNOWLEDGMENT

This chapter was presented to the Qualitative Studies Division of the Association
for Education in Journalism and Mass Communication, Gainesville, FL, August
1984.

REFERENCES

Altman, D. (1963). How to get off the back of the bus. *Public Relations Journal, February.*

Aronoff, C., & Baskin, O. (1983). *Public Relations: The Profession and the Practice.* St. Paul: West.

Bateman, J. C. (1957). The path to professionalism. *Public Relations Journal, March.*

Bateman, J. C. (1958). A new moral dimension for communication. *Public Relations Journal, August.*

Chase, W. H. (1962). Nothing just happens, somebody makes it happen. *Public Relations Journal, November.*

Cuervo, A. (1975). The poor image of the image makers. *Public Relations Journal, July.*

Cutlip, S., & Center, A. (1978). *Effective public relations,* (5th ed.). Englewood Cliffs, NJ: Prentice-Hall.

Henry, K. (1972). *Defenders and shapers of the corporate image.* New Haven: College and University Press.

Hollinger, D. (1980). T. S. Kuhn's theory of science and its implications for history. In G. Gutting (Ed.), *Paradigms and revolutions.* Notre Dame, IN: Notre Dame Press.

Kuhn, T. (1962). *The structure of scientific revolutions.* Chicago: University of Chicago Press.

Lazarus, A. (1963). Who says public relations is intangible? *Public Relations Journal, September.*

Lovell, R. (1982). *Inside Public Relations.* Boston: Allyn & Bacon.

Marston, J. (1979). *Modern Public Relations.* New York: McGraw-Hill.

Mayer, M. (1958). *Madison Avenue, U.S.A.* New York: Harper & Brothers.

Newsom, D., & Scott, A. (1981). *This is PR: The realities of public relations.* Belmont, CA: Wadsworth.

Nolte, L. (1974). *Fundamentals of public relations.* New York: Pergamon.

Normoyle, J. L. (1958). Let's stop kidding ourselves. *Public Relations Journal, June.*

Olasky, M. (1987). *Corporate public relations: A new historical perspective.* Hillsdale, NJ: Lawrence Erlbaum Associates.

Pimlott, J. A. R. (1951). *Public relations and american democracy.* Princeton, NJ: Princeton University Press.

PRJ (1981). *Public Relations Journal, June, p. 16.*

PRQ (1973). *Public Relations Quarterly, Fall, pp. 12, 24.*

Reilly, R. (1981). *Public Relations in action.* Englewood Cliffs, NJ: Prentice-Hall.

Sandman, P. M., Rubin, D. M., & Sachsman, D. B. (1976). *Media: An introductory analysis of American mass communications.* Englewood Cliffs, NJ: Prentice-Hall.

Seitel, F. (1984). The practice of public relations (2nd ed.). Columbus, OH: Chas. Merrill.

Simon, R. (1983). Publicity and public relations worktext (5th Ed.). Columbus, OH: Grid.

Chapter 5

Credibility of Public Relations at the NRC

Linda Childers
University of Maryland

Credibility is probably the most important attribute that a public relations practitioner can possess in the fulfillment of professional duties. But how does the practice, as a whole, contribute to organizational credibility? And is one model of public relations more effective than others?

The U.S. Nuclear Regulatory Commission (NRC) provides an illustrative example of an organization fraught with credibility problems for which its model of communication may be partly to blame. Based on separate interviews with the assistant to the director in the Office of Public Affairs and the Office of Congressional Affairs at the NRC, this study is an attempt to view aspects of public relations within a specific organization with the hope of providing insight into organizations with similar problems. The research presented in this chapter, discussed within the context of current public relations literature, should also further the understanding of ideas that are important to a general theory of how public relations is practiced.

Although this analysis looks specifically at one organization's communication practices, it is not so narrow as to exclude other organizations' benefitting from examination of the NRC. An argument can be made against the "world in a teacup" approach to analyzing a single case in depth (Geertz, 1973), but the concepts, theories, and issues addressed here serve all public relations situations; the NRC merely provides the backdrop for their presentation. It must be remembered, however, that the views presented here are not meant to be an empirical determination of the communication practices at the NRC, but rather, the perceptions of the interviewees and investigator.

Before moving to a discussion of the NRC's public relations practices, some background about the organization is needed to provide an understanding of the NRC's functioning as well as its many criticisms. Temples (1982) has documented that even before the nuclear accident at Three Mile Island, no shortage of suggestions existed for reform of the NRC, created under the 1974 Energy Reorganization Act to take over the Atomic Energy Commission's (AEC) responsibility for licensing and regulation of commercial nuclear power plants. Realizing the potential conflict of interest involved in vesting the AEC with both promotion and regulation of nuclear power, Congress hoped that the new agency would be able to make a fresh start and avoid the mistakes of its predecessor (*Congressional Quarterly Weekly Report*, 1974). However, Temples (1982) contended that in many ways the new NRC was not significantly different from the AEC in its structure or policies. Soon, the NRC commissioners and staff were accused of harboring permissive attitudes toward the nuclear industry (Rolph, 1979). Ralph Nader testified before Congress that the NRC had "adopted the rhetoric of reform," but was "continuing . . . to mislead the Congress and the American people on the hazards associated with nuclear power" (U.S. Congress, House, Committee on Interior and Insular Affairs, 1977, p. 326).

The accident at Three Mile Island resulted in a barrage of studies that were critical of the NRC's performance before and during the incident. *The Report of the President's Commission on the Accident at Three Mile Island* (President's Commission, 1979), chaired by Dr. John Kemeny, uncovered serious managerial and attitudinal problems with the NRC. Particularly interesting to communication practitioners, a staff report of the Kemeny Commission found that:

> The *strained communication system* within the NRC . . . combined with the lack of clearly defined management responsibilities, results in a commission that is insulated from the day-to-day operations of its staff . . . [T]he commissioners lack detailed knowledge of the NRC's licensing and regulatory activies, including some related to the safety of nuclear power plants. This raises serious questions about *the information flow* within the agency, *the structure* of the organization, and finally, the degree to which the NRC is managed effectively by commissioners, who are expected to be both managers and adjudicators. (Gorison, 1979, pp. 31–32, italics added)

The Kemeny Commission report concluded that under its existing organizational structure, the NRC was simply incapable of managing its regulatory duties effectively. Considering the report's findings regarding the NRC's communication problems, it is surprising that the structure of the NRC's public relations department (OPA)[1] has not changed at all since its inception, according to the assistant to the director.

---

[1]The NRC calls its *public relations* function, *public affairs*. The two terms are used interchangeably here.

Criticisms of the NRC have come from within its own ranks as well. In 1987 the *New York Times* reported that safety at nuclear reactors nationwide is so low that a meltdown in the next 10 to 20 years would not be a surprise, according to retiring Commissioner James Asselstine. "The failure to address some of the problems that now exist could well kill the nuclear option," he warned ("Retiring U.S. Official," 1987).

Looking specifically at the NRC's credibility problems, one finds that the literature is full of arguments that the nuclear industry was established and is maintained because of political motives[2]. Otis (1981) argued that the roots of nuclear power help one to understand much about the "formidable coalition that continues to advocate this energy form even in the face of drastically rising costs, risk to the safety of the public, and quickly attainable alternatives" (p. 145). He explained that this coalition is made up of giant energy corporations, electric power businesses, and the federal government. Otis asserted that "far from being arm's length overseers of the development of a new energy form, the federal government has been an eager advocate of nuclear power from its inception" (pp. 145–146). He further stated that "strong institutional resistance to a nonnuclear future persists within both the NRC and the Department of Energy" (p. 146).

In addition to the NRC's credibility problem with respect to its motives, the accident at Three Mile Island has had a pervasive negative effect on the credibility of public officials. Dohrenwend et al. (1981) found that "the accident at Three Mile Island has had a lasting impact on the population of the area in terms of their distrust of authorities with respect to nuclear power" (p. 174). These researchers discovered that the public's level of distrust 5 months after the accident exceeded that reported for national and regional samples immediately after the accident. Childers (1984) determined that a random sample of residents in the Three Mile Island area in 1980 did not believe information disseminated from local, state, or federal officials about the accident. The sample was reinterviewed in 1981, 1982, and 1983, but the credibility of public officials had not been restored.

The foregoing criticisms of the NRC demonstrate that its program of communication can and should be improved. A closer inspection of the NRC's communication system provides support for the argument that the NRC's *one-way, asymmetrical* model of communication, as well as the public relations department's exclusion from meaningful participation in management decision-making constrain the effectiveness of the organization's public relations practices. Although the public relations function at the NRC cannot include activities involving promotion of the nuclear industry, it can be improved by establishing two-way symmetrical communication between the NRC and its publics. And crucial to the very definition of public relations, communication practitioners at the NRC should be allowed to participate in management decision-making, bringing with them information gathered about the organization, its environment, and its publics. The

---

[2]See, for example, Del Sesto (1979), Mullenbach (1963), and Walker and Lonnroth (1983).

gathering of this information should be designed to help practitioners counsel the Commission so it can more effectively fulfill its mission—that of "protecting the health and safety of the public" (*U.S. Nuclear Regulatory Commission 1985 Annual Report,* p. 202)—and improve the strained communication system and unacceptable information flow that the Kemeny Commission criticized.

J. GRUNIG AND HUNT'S MODELS OF PUBLIC RELATIONS

To understand the one-way, asymmetrical model of public relations practiced by the NRC, a public information model, J. Grunig and Hunt's public relations models must be explored. In his 1976 monograph, J. Grunig conceptualized two kinds of public relations behavior and asked the question, "Why do some practitioners engage in informative, two-way communication and others in one-way, manipulative communication?" He then categorized these two kinds of public relations using Thayer's (1968) concepts of synchronic and diachronic communication. J. Grunig explained that synchronic communication is asymmetrical in that the organization uses public relations to synchronize the behavior of publics with its own behavior. Diachronic communication, according to him, is symmetrical; an organization and publics attempt to reach a state of affairs that is acceptable to all.

J. Grunig later realized that his conceptualizations were too simple to explain the public relations behaviors and organizational structures that exist in the real world. In particular, he suggested that there seem to be four, rather than two, models of public relations in practice, and single organizations appear to practice combinations of the four models (J. Grunig & Hunt, 1984, chapters 1 and 2). J. Grunig explained that public relations behavior seems to vary along two independent dimensions—one-way versus two-way and asymmetrical versus symmetrical. Therefore, four models arise that represent combinations of the two dimensions. The four models, explained in J. Grunig and Hunt (1984), are:

1. Press agentry/publicity (a one-way asymmetrical model). This model is typified by the wizardry of P. T. Barnum in the middle of the nineteenth century.
2. Public information (a one-way symmetrical model)[3]. This model arose in the beginning of the twentieth century from Ivy Lee's belief that public relations people were "journalists in residence" who should provide truthful and accurate information about their client organization.
3. Two-way asymmetrical. This model had its intellectual roots in the work of the Committee on Public Information, headed by George Creel, during World War I.

---

[3]J. Grunig (1987) reconceptualized this model as asymmetrical. According to him, practitioners following the public information model have the effect of manipulating publics, even though that may not be their intent.

Edward Bernays, who worked in a supporting role on the Creel Committee, later supplied most of the social science theory for the asymmetrical model.
4. Two-way symmetrical. The roots of this model cannot be as easily traced to the ideas of a single practitioner. Both Bernays and Lee had said that public relations should represent the client to the organization as well as the organization to the client . . . Public relations textbooks, especially those written by educators in the 1950s and later, have also called for the practice of the symmetrical model. (pp. 48–49)

J. Grunig and L. Grunig (1986) later realized that the J. Grunig and Hunt (1984) typology is better understood as a normative (prescriptive), rather than a positive (descriptive), theory of how public relations is practiced. Their most recent research shows that organizations use the models in two ways. First, the models function as situational strategies for different publics and public relations problems—not as single organizing frameworks. Second, the presuppositions of the models function as part of an organization's ideology (J. Grunig, 1987, p. 22).

The public relations function at the NRC, however, does appear to use the public information model as an organizing framework. The OPA's goal is to provide the public with factual information as well as to keep management informed of public affairs activities. Clearly, this model was chosen to eliminate the perceived conflict of interest present in the AEC—that of regulation while simultaneously engaging in research and development[4]. Thus, the OPA is designed to be limited in definition to the dissemination of public information, thus excluding activities that might be perceived as promotion. As discussed earlier, the NRC has often been charged with abandoning this limitation. And, if the OPA is charged with keeping management informed of public affairs activities, a crucial aspect of the definition of public relations, the department is disappointing. Practitioners appear to be merely the presenters of information about the organization to the public with little or no participation in the management of the public relations function at the NRC[5]. Although they have access to the chairman of the Commission and the commissioners, they have virtually no influence in policy-making, and are thus limited in management responsibilities. Indicative of the OPA's poor

---

[4]Interestingly, the assistant to the director at the OPA shrugged off the "conflict of interest" issue. He stated that this conflict never existed.

[5]Broom and Dozier's (1985) panel study of members of the Public Relations Society of America produced a profile of roles played by public relations practitioners. (See also Dayrit, 1986; Ferguson, 1979; and Sullivan, 1985.) Broom and Dozier (1985) identified two main roles, *public relations managers*, or those who engage in activities that involve "expert prescription, communication facilitation, and problem-solving process facilitation," (p. 6) and *public relations technicians*, practitioners who engage in "rather limited non-management roles related to their specialized skills in writing, editing, and working with the media" (p. 4). Following Broom and Dozier's conceptualizations of public relations roles, the practitioners at the OPA are largely functioning as technicians. Although the assistant to the director at the OCA described himself as a communication liaison, he and his staff appear to be primarily fulfilling a technical, as opposed to managerial, role. See Dozier (1987a) for an exhaustive summary of research in public relations roles.

stance in the NRC's hierarchy of power, the assistant to the director stated that practitioners' autonomy can be "overtaken by circumstance," and their authority can be "pre-empted" by upper levels in the organizational hierarchy.

PUBLIC RELATIONS
AND ORGANIZATIONAL POWER

The relationship between the public relations function and the power structure of the NRC (as well as any organization) is an important one. Organizational scholars have turned to organizational strategy, size, technology, and environment[6] in trying to understand determinants of organizational structure and functioning.[7] However, Robbins (1983) reported that at best, these four factors explain only 50 to 60 percent of the variability in structure. He theorized that the missing link lies outside in the "twilight zone" of organizational politics, power, and coalition formation (p. 166).

The power-control perspective, Robbins explained, states that at any given time, an organization's structure is the result of a power struggle by internal constituencies who are seeking to further their interests. For Bacharach and Lawler (1980), "organizations are emergent activities; that is, they are the result of the conscious political decisions of particular actors and interest groups" (p. 2). Pfeffer (1978) asserted that "organizations are political systems, coalitions of interest, and rationality is defined only with respect to unitary and consistent orderings of preferences" (pp. 11–12). Further, he argued that the power-control view of organizational behavior proposes that these coalitions wrestle in a power struggle to control the organization, and this power struggle arises because there is dissension concerning preferences or in definition of the situation.

If these researchers are correct in suggesting that the power-control perspective is crucial to understanding organizations, the distribution of power in organizations might be an important determinant of the structure and functioning of the public relations department.[8] J. Grunig and L. Grunig (1986) considered top management support and understanding as well as representation in the dominant coalition as independent variables in their systems model of public relations. This

---

[6]Schneider (1985) provided an in-depth exploration of the relationship between organizational environment and communication behavior. She hypothesized that an organization's environmental niche, based on Hage and Hull's typology of organizations—traditional/craft, mechanical, organic, mixed/mechanical-organic—would predict communication behavior. She discovered, however, only a weak relationship between an organization's environmental niche and its communication practices.

[7]See, for example, Child (1972), Ford and Slocum (1977), and Pugh (1973).

[8]L. Grunig (1987) presented a comparative analysis of 87 public relations practitioners in the Washington, D.C. area based on in-depth personal interviews. She determined that power comes to public relations practitioners as a result of the value that the dominant coalition attaches to the public relations function, the expertise of practitioners (leading to increased autonomy), and routinization and

model attempts "to explain why different kinds of organizations practice public relations in different ways" (p. 70). Specifically, they argued that public relations does not exist in isolation in organizations. Unless those with power in the organization understand and support the public relations function, practitioners are not unlikely to practice sophisticated techniques of public relations.

This argument is supported at the NRC. Practitioners do not appear to be part of the dominant coalition. Although top management may provide support and understanding to the OPA as public information disseminators functioning in a technical capacity, there seems to be no support for expanding the role of the department to include other public relations functions beyond those embraced by communication technicians. As the assistant to the director at the OPA stated, the department's current methods are archaic.

Interestingly, the OCA, the department that interacts frequently with congressional representatives and the NRC's commissioners, seems to enjoy more status than the OPA and also performs duties beyond those of the technician. Serving as communication liaisons, practitioners of the OCA provide meaningful input to those most likely to be part of the NRC's dominant coalition. Access to and the ability to counsel Congressional members and committees, as well as the Commission, seem crucial if one is to affect the organization or effect organizational outcomes—power, as defined by Mintzberg (1983).

Concurrent with research on the relationship between organizational power and public relations, Pollack (1986) looked in depth at top management support of public relations in scientific organizations. In addition to this variable, she examined (a) involvement of the public relations director in major decisions, (b) whether public relations decisions are made by the public relations director or top management, (c) influence of the public relations department in organizational decision-making, (d) authority level of the public relations department, (e) percentage of recommendations made by the public relations department that were implemented by the organization in the last 3 years, and (f) how important the dominant coalition believes public relations is to organizational success.

Pollack discovered that her variables provided further understanding of the relationship between power-related variables and the model of public relations practiced. Specifically, factor analysis of the variables produced two highly correlated factors; one described the extent to which public relations is represented in the dominant coalition, and the second factor described the autonomy of the public relations department. The factors proved to be important determinants of the model of public relations practiced, especially the "representation in the dominant coalition" factor (Grunig & Grunig, 1986, p. 37).

---

sophistication of technology in the public relations department. Evidence of power included involvement with the organization's dominant coalition, autonomy from the typical clearance process for news releases, support for and understanding of the public relations function by top management, and discretion for budgetary decisions. Practitioners reported a limited degree of organizational power that varied with the structure of the organization.

Two interpretations of Pollack's findings were then provided by Grunig and Grunig. Either public relations departments represented in the dominant coalition are able to practice a two-way model of public relations, or public relations practitioners with the knowledge or experience to practice a two-way model are more likely to be represented in the dominant coalition. They reasoned that the second explanation is more accurate for several reasons. First, the percentage of practitioners in the public relations department with a bachelor's degree was positively correlated with the likelihood of representation in the dominant coalition ($r = .15$). Next, the more years in public relations that the director had, the greater the likelihood of representation in the dominant coalition ($r = .25$). And, public relations directors with a science background were more likely to be represented in the dominant coalition ($r = .25$). Grunig and Grunig (1986) concluded that "more knowledgeable, experienced practitioners and more sophisticated departments are more likely to be represented in the dominant coalition" (p. 38).

Grunig and Grunig's reasoning appears accurate for the NRC. The complexity, or "the degree of differentiation" (Robbins, 1983, p. 47) among employees of the department is low. The department is also low in horizontal differentiation, the "degree of separation between units based upon orientation of members, the nature of the tasks they perform, and their education and training" (p. 47). Low differentiation among practitioners might explain the department's lack of sophisticated public relations activities, and thus, its exclusion from the dominant coalition.

J. Grunig and Hunt (1984) argued that practitioners should be part of the organization's dominant coalition—participating in or influencing decisions, and thus practicing symmetrical or adaptive public relations. Unfortunately, the assistant to the director at the OPA characterized his department as "reactive," a posture that seems inappropriate given the NRC's mission of protecting the health and safety of the public. For J. Grunig and Hunt, there is little justification for public relations in an organization unless practitioners are included in the dominant coalition.

Broom and Dozier (1985) stated that involvement of practitioners in organizational decision-making is "perhaps more important to the profession of public relations than any other measure of professional growth" (p. 8). Involvement in management decision-making is fundamental to the very definition of public relations, they argued. "Isolation of public relations from decision-making limits the practice to a low-level support function. If practitioners are relegated the role of explaining and justifying others' decisions made independent of the public relations implication, then professional status is unlikely" (pp. 8–9).

PRESUPPOSITIONS
OF COMMUNICATION MODELS

Broom and Dozier's casting of the practitioner in an isolated, support capacity may well describe the public relations function of the NRC and other one-way, asymmetrical programs. In trying to understand why organizations practice public relations in this way, the presuppositions of J. Grunig and Hunt's (1984) communication models must be explored.

J. Grunig (1987) argued that presuppositions become important when the ideology of the dominant coalition is a critical predictor of an organization's communication practices. Grunig and Grunig's[9] research has shown that the dominant coalition of an organization, its power elite, identifies strategic publics in the environment as the target for public relations. The dominant coalition then turns the problem over to the public relations director and dictates to the director which model would be an appropriate strategy. Thus, the members of the dominant coalition decide how public relations will be practiced in their organization. In making this decision, presuppositions emerge.

Asymmetrical Presuppositions

J. Grunig explained that when an organization, its dominant coalition, or its public relations practitioners hold an asymmetrical worldview, they presuppose that the organization knows best. This assumption is embodied in the statement made by the NRC's assistant to the director at the OCA. Activism and public disapproval "don't come into play" in the decision-making process at the NRC, according to him. Although the public has input at hearings, all final decisions are up to the NRC, instilling the Commission with "a tremendous amount of power" and "a lot of authority." These comments seem to represent the asymmetrical notion that wisdom is not the product of a free marketplace of ideas. Rather, wisdom flows from the organization's leaders who have more knowledge than members of publics.

Other presuppositions that J. Grunig (1987) cited as part of an asymmetrical world view that are relevant to the NRC's communication practices include:

"*Closed system.* Information flows out from the organization and not into it" (p. 25). The assistant to the director at the OPA identified no means for assessing the information needs of the public. If practitioners are conceptualized as boundary-spanners, directing and monitoring information from as well as to the organization, the NRC is lacking in the latter direction. The NRC's performance in its regulatory duties could only be enhanced by increased responsiveness to incoming communication from the public. Specifically, current methods for including public concerns in the execution of the NRC's responsibilities need to be improved.

"*Conservatism.* Change is undesirable. Outside efforts to change the organization should be resisted; pressure for change should be considered subversive" (p. 26). Although changes have occurred in the NRC, especially after Three Mile Island, the public relations practices and structure of the OPA have not been responsive to innovation. Subscribing to a limited technical role, the department

---

[9]See Grunig and Grunig (1987) for a comprehensive review of their research in the public relations behavior of organizations.

has neglected the opportunity to develop more sophisticated public relations practices.

The department could be improved by first developing a program of research that addresses how the Commission can more effectively plan and implement communication programs in fulfillment of its mission, counseling the Commission on these programs, and then developing a method of formally evaluating the effectiveness of these efforts.

"*Central authority*. Power should be concentracted in the hands of a few top managers. Employees should have little autonomy" (p. 26). The distribution of power at the NRC reflects this asymmetrical presupposition. Although power is decentralized concerning the performance of everyday business functions, the OPA has little or no power in decision- and policy-making, the responsibilities of the Commission. Usurping the autonomy of practitioners, the Commission relegates the department to a mere support function and hinders its ability to adopt a proactive posture.

Symmetrical Presuppositions

Asserting that the long-term effects of the asymmetrical models make it impossible for organizations to be ethical and socially responsible, J. Grunig (1987) developed a symmetrical framework with presuppositions that allow public relations to "be practiced in a way that will make it a highly valued and effective force for resolving social conflict and improving the societies in which we live" (p. 39).

J. Grunig drew upon several theorists' concepts that were identical or similar to symmetrical communication in his formulation of the two-way symmetrical model. Carter's (1965) theory of communication and affective relations, into which Carter incorporated Newcomb's (1953) concept of coorientation[10], as well as Chaffee and McLeod's (1968) research on coorientation, provided a basis for J. Grunig's views. Watzlawick, Beavin, and Jackson (1967) made a distinction between asymmetrical and symmetrical communication in their theory of interpersonal communication that J. Grunig has recognized and employed. Further, he adopted Thayer's (1968) distinction between synchronic and diachronic communication elaborated in Thayer's systems theory of communication. These symmetrical theories of communication led J. Grunig (1987) to develop this presupposition: "*Communication leads to understanding*. The major purpose of communication is to facilitate understanding among people and other such systems as organizations, publics, or societies. Persuasion of one person or system by another is less desirable" (p. 34).

From a systems theory approach to organizations, J. Grunig developed four additional presuppositions that are important in establishing a public relations program based on symmetrical communication:

---

[10]According to Grunig (1987), coorientation occurs when two or more people simultaneously orient to a situation or object rather than a single person orienting to a situation or object (p. 33).

Holism. Systems consist of subsystems and are parts of suprasystems. The whole is greater than the sum of its parts, and each part of a system affects every other part. *Interdependence.* Although systems have boundaries that separate them from their environment, systems in the environment cross that boundary and "interpenetrate" the system (Preston and Post, 1975, pp. 24–27).
Open system. The organization is open to interpenetrating systems and freely exchanges information with those systems.
Moving equilibrium. Systems strive toward an equilibrium with other systems, although they seldom actually achieve it. The desired equilibrium state constantly moves as the environment changes. Systems may attempt to establish equilibrium by controlling other systems; by adapting themselves to other systems; or by making mutual, cooperative adjustments. In the symmetrical approach to public relations, cooperative and mutual adjustment are preferred to control and adaptation. (p. 34)

In addition to these systems presuppositions, J. Grunig included several presuppositions in the two-way symmetrical approach that are relevant to the discussion of an improved communication system at the NRC:

Autonomy. People are more innovative, constructive, and self-fulfilled when they have the autonomy to influence their own behavior, rather than having it controlled by others. Autonomy maximizes employee satisfaction inside the organization and cooperation outside the organization.
Innovation. New ideas and flexible thinking should be stressed rather than tradition and efficiency.
Decentralization of management. Management should be collective; managers should coordinate rather than dictate. Decentralization increases autonomy, employee satisfaction, and innovation.
Responsibility. People and organizations must be concerned with the consequences of their behaviors on others and attempt to eliminate adverse consequences.
Conflict resolution. Conflict should be resolved through negotiation, communication, and compromise and not through force, manipulation, coercion, or violence.
Interest group liberalism. Classic liberalism, which typically champions big government, can be as closed-minded as classic conservatism, which typically champions big business. Interest-group liberalism, however, views the political system as a mechanism for open competition among interest or issue groups. Interest-group liberalism looks to citizen groups to "champion interest of ordinary people against unresponsive government and corporate structures" (Boyte, 1980, p. 7). (pp. 34–35)

A program of two-way symmetrical communication for the NRC and other organizations would embrace the ideas inherent in these presuppositions and their implications for public relations. It would include participation of informed practitioners in management decision-making. Practitioners could serve not only as spokespeople for the organization but also for the public upon whom the organization has consequences.

THE PRACTICE OF TWO-WAY
SYMMETRICAL COMMUNICATION

Allowing for Organizational Inputs.   The most obvious area in which the OPA
can improve its communication efforts involves allowing members of the public
more meaningful input into decisions that affect them. Sandman (1986) has outlined some communications considerations designed to promote symmetrical communication among the community, developers, and the state concerning the siting
of hazardous waste facilities. His consideration of the community's perspective in
the decision-making process provides an illustrative example of a two-way communication perspective. And, most importantly, allowing community participation in
the siting process may result in "environmentally sound facilities, a stronger, more
empowered community, a government with credibility in the host community, and
a developer who can build a facility with minimal delays and few additional
expenses" (1986, p. 438). Perhaps Sandman's considerations are pertinent to the
regulation of the nuclear industry as well as other organizations needing to improve
their programs of public participation.

   Sandman argued that a fatal flaw in most governmental public participation is
that it is grafted onto a planning procedure that is essentially complete without
public input:

> Citizens quickly sense that public hearings lack real provisionalism or tentativeness.
> They often feel that the important decisions have already been made, and that while
> minor modifications may be possible to placate opponents, the real functions of the
> hearing are to fulfill a legal mandate and to legitimize the *fait accompli.* (p. 455)

This scenario, he explained, is likely even when the agency sees itself as genuinely
open to citizen input:

> For legal and professional reasons, experts feel a powerful need to do their homework
> before scheduling much public participation. In effect, the resulting presentation says
> to the citizen: "After monumental effort, summarized in this 300-page document, we
> have reached the following conclusions . . . Now what do you folks think?" At this
> point it is hard enough for the agency to take the input seriously, and harder still for
> the public to believe it will be taken seriously. (p. 455)

The solution is obvious, although difficult to implement, according to Sandman. He recommended that consultations with the community begin early in the
process and continue throughout:

> *Public participation should not be confined to formal contexts like public hearings,*
> *which encourage posturing. Rather, participation should include informal briefings*
> *and exchanges of opinion of various sorts, mediated where appropriate. The Com-*

mission must be visibly free to adjust in response to these consultations, and must appear visibly interested in doing so. Above all, the proposals presented for consulta-tion must be provisional rather than final—and this too must be visible. (pp. 455–456, italics added)

Sandman's recommendations seem to get at the heart of many of the NRC's cricitisms. He then provided a list of communication methods that might be helpful for "developing means to facilitate interaction, communication, trust and agreement" (p. 461). Some of these include Delphi methodology,[11] role playing,[12] focus groups,[13] and participatory planning[14].

The assistant to the director at the OPA considered undertaking communica-tion methods such as these riding the fence between promotion and regulation. Although some of these methods might be inappropriate for the NRC, the shun-ning of research undertaken to facilitate better communication with the NRC's publics provides another example of where the OPA misses the opportunity to improve its program. Research undertaken by NRC to assess how it might fulfill its mission more effectively does not necessitate promoting the nuclear industry. Instead, it provides the information needed to allow the NRC's communication system to develop into one based on a two-way symmetrical model.

Participation in Management Decision-Making. If the NRC's public relations practices stretched beyond mere technical support, the second major area where the functioning of the OPA could be improved would be easier to bring to fruition. That is, the responsibilities of the practitioners in the OPA should include the collecting of information valuable to the dominant coalition so that practitioners

---

[11]Sandman described this as a formal technique for encouraging concensus through successive rounds of position-taking.

[12]The playing out of stereotyped roles of participants in a controversy can help all sides achieve better understanding of the issues, Sandman explained.

[13]A focus group, Sandman stated, is a handful of individuals selected as typical of a particular constituency. This focus group is then asked to participate in a guided discussion of a predetermined set of topics. Often the focus group is asked to respond to particular ideas or proposals, but always in interaction with each other. The purpose of focus group methodology, he explained, is to learn more about the values of the constituency and how it is likely to respond to certain messages.

Although the assistant to the director at the OPA was quick to point out the NRC has no constituency, focus groups might still provide a useful tool for gathering information. Sandman argued that in the hands of a skilled interviewer and interpreter, focus groups can yield more meaningful information than survey questionnaires.

[14]Sandman noted that this label is sometimes given to a collection of techniques for making public participation more useful to the decision-maker and more satisfying to the public. He argued that to a large extent the value of public participation in is the agency's hands. This value depends on technique: how people are invited, on how the policy questions are phrased, on what speakers are allowed to talk about, what issues for how long, and so on.

Sandman's argument seems to provide support for the assertion that the Commission does have techniques available to it for making public participation more worthwhile.

can then participate in decision- and policy-making. Practitioners should be allowed to counsel management as the experts in the communication apsects of organizational functioning.

White (1987) argued that public relations makes its fullest contribution to management decision-making to the extent that the practice is based on complete information, gathered about the organization using a complete range of scanning techniques. Dozier (1987b) explained that scanning research involves the detection and quantification of emerging problems and opportunities facing an organization, and is thus a method of organizing inputs from the environment. In essence, scanning answers the question, "What's going on out there?" He suggested that probabilistic sampling surveys are useful scanning tools, especially if coupled with qualitative research (such as focus groups) conducted prior to the design of the questionnaire.

If, as White (1987) suggested, public relations will contribute to management decision-making to the extent that problems, threats, and opportunities faced by the organization are interpreted by practitioners for management's consideration, the OPA's limited managerial responsibilities are understandable. Without methods for gathering information valuable to the dominant coalition, the department cannot act as credible advisers. By assessing organizational inputs, the department could more effectively meet its responsibility of keeping "NRC management informed of public affairs activities" (U.S. Nuclear Regulatory Commission 1985 Annual Report, p. 203).

CONCLUSION

Technocracy is a form of power exercised in the interest of the political and economic apparatus of production and decision making. These forces of control look on society only as a totality of social means to be used in their quest for growth and reinforced power.

—Alain Touraine

As is clear from the this sentiment, expressed as the introduction to a book about nuclear power in America, the NRC must regulate an industry in the midst of suspicious hostility. The Commission has been the object of much criticism itself and its credibility has suffered markedly. As the Kemeny Commission argued in 1979, the NRC's communication system may be a primary cause of its problems. Given this, it is astounding that the public relations department of the NRC has never embraced the opportunity to improve the communications aspect of the NRC's functioning. Relying on a public information model to simply "get the word out," The OPA cuts off input from its publics—input that would help the Commission meet its commitments. The OPA's unfortunate perception of communication research as promotion renders the department unwilling to gather information about the organization and its environment. Without this information, it is unlikely that practitioners can act as counselors to the Commission and participate in decision- and policy-making as part of the dominant coalition.

The adopting of a two-way symmetrical communication model by the OPA provides an opportunity for the department to expand its activities so that it might enjoy more credibility as well as management responsibilities. And importantly, this communication model seems to offer a socially responsible framework that allows public relations to be practiced in such a way that both organizations and the public benefit. Finally, a two-way symmetrical model of communication may be the most effective. L. Grunig (1986) examined how organizations deal with activist groups and found that none of the organizations had tried a two-way symmetrical approach. The asymmetrical models failed to resolve conflict and often resulted in litigation or continued conflict. Turk (1986) found that of the state agencies she studied in Louisiana, only one used the two-way symmetrical model. The other models were ineffective. She concluded that:

> state agencies that rely upon public information officers to "get the word out" to win support for agency policies and programs may be overrating the ability of PIOs to influence the agency picture portrayed by the news media for consumption by those who get their information about state government from the media. (pp. 24–25)

The important implication of L. Grunig's and Turk's work is that the two-way symmetrical model may provide a solution for practitioners who deal with pressure from an organization's external constituents. In the model's quest for accommodation between organizations and the public, as opposed to domination of one by the other, all parties, in a sense, can win.

It may be inappropriate to say that the NRC, in its prescribed role as the nuclear industry's watchdog, should learn to "deal" with external pressures or "win" support for its policies. As former Chairman Nunzio J. Palladino said in a 1985 speech to the American Nuclear Society and the Western Society of Engineers, "Nobody loves the NRC!." However, the NRC's adopting of a two-way symmetrical approach in its interaction with members of the public should increase its sensitivity to their concerns. This sensitivity could then be carried over into the fulfillment of the NRC's regulatory duties.

REFERENCES

Bacharach, S. B., & Lawler, E. J. (1980). *Power and politics in organizations.* San Francisco: Jossey-Bass.

Boyte, H. C. (1980). *The backyard revolution: Understanding the new citizen movement.* Philadelphia: Temple University Press.

Broom, G. M., & Dozier, D. M. (1985, August). *Determinants and consequences of public* relations roles. Paper presented at the meeting of the Public Relations Division, Association for Education in Journalism and Mass Communication, Memphis, TN.

Carter, R. F. (1965). Communication and affective relations. *Journalism Quarterly, 42,* 203–212.

Chaffee, S. H., & McLeod, J. M. (1968). Sensitization in panel design: A coorientation experiment. *Journalism Quarterly, 45,* 661–669.

Child, J. (1972). Organization structure, environment and performance: The role of strategic choice. *Sociology, January,* 1–22.

Childers, L. L. (1984). *A study in the loss of trust in public officials after the Three Mile Island accident, presented in the conflict model.* Unpublished manuscript, Stetson University, DeLand, FL.

Congressional Quarterly Weekly Report 32 (October 19, 1974). President signs energy reorganization bill. 2925–2926.

Dayrit, M. (1986). *Boundary-spanning roles: Public relations and media practitioners.* Unpublished master's thesis, University of Florida, Gainesville.

Del Sesto, S. L. (1979). *Science, politics, and controversy: Civilian nuclear power in the United States, 1946–1974.* Boulder, CO: Westview Press.

Dohrenwend, B. P., Dohrenwend, B. S., Warheirt, G. J., Bartlett, G. S., Goldsteen, R. L., Goldsteen, K., & Martin, J. L. (1981). Stress in the community: A report to the president's commission on the accident at Three Mile Island. In T. H. Moss & D. L. Sills (Eds.), *The Three Mile Island accident: Lessons and implications.* New York: The New York Academy of Science.

Dozier, D. M. (1987a). *The roles of public relations practitioners.* Unpublished manuscript.

Dozier, D. M. (1987b). *Research firms and public relations practices.* Unpublished manuscript.

Ferguson, M. A. (1979, August). *Some empirically-generated public relations roles and associations with various descriptive variables.* Paper presented at the meeting of the Public Relations Division, Association for Education in Journalism, Houston, TX.

Ford, J. D., & Slocum, J. W., Jr. (1977). Size, technology, environment and the structure of organizations. *Academy of Management Review, October,* 561–575.

Geertz, C. (1973). *The interpretation of culture.* New York: Basic Books.

Gorison, S. M. (1979). *The Nuclear Regulatory Commission: A staff report to the president's commission on the accident at Three Mile Island.* Washington, DC: U.S. Government Printing Office.

Grunig, J. E. (1976). Organizations and public relations: Testing a communication theory. *Journalism Monographs, 46.*

Grunig, J. E. (1987, May). *Symmetrical presuppositions as a framework for public relations theory.* Paper presented at the Conference on Communication Theory and Public Relations, Illinois State University, Normal, IL.

Grunig, J. E., & Grunig, L. S. (1986, May). *Application of open systems theory to public relations: Review of a program of research.* Paper presented at the meeting of the International Communication Association, Chicago, IL.

Grunig, J. E., & Grunig, L. S. (1987). *Toward a theory of the public relations behavior of organizations: Review of a program of research.* Unpublished manuscript, University of Maryland, College Park, MD.

Grunig, J. E., & Hunt, T. (1984). *Managing public relations.* New York: Holt, Rinehart & Winston.

Grunig, L. S. (1986, August). *Activism and organizational response: Contemporary cases of collective behavior.* Paper presented to the Association for Education in Journalism and Mass Communication, Norman, OK.

Grunig, L. S. (1987, February). *Power in the public relations department as a function of values, professionalism and organizational structure.* Paper presented at the 16th Annual Communications Conference, Howard University, Washington, DC.

Mintzberg, H. (1983). *Power in and around organizations.* Englewood Cliffs, NJ: Prentice-Hall.

Mullenbach, P. (1963). *Civilian nuclear power: Economic issues and policy formation.* Philadelphia, PA: Wm. F. Fell.

Newcomb, T. M. (1953). An approach to the study of communicative acts. *Psychological Review, 60,* 393–404.

Otis, T. H. (1981). *A review of nuclear energy in the United States: Hidden power.* New York: Praeger.

Pfeffer, J. (1978). *Organizational design.* Arlington Heights, IL: AHM Publishing.

Pollack, R. (1986). *Testing the Grunig organizational theory in scientific organizations: Public relations and the values of the dominant coalition.* Unpublished master's thesis, University of Maryland, College Park, MD.

President's Commission on the Accident at Three Mile Island. (1979). *Report of the president's commission on the accident at Three Mile Island.* Washington, DC: U.S. Government Printing Office.

Preston, L. E., & Post, J. E. (1975). *Private management and public policy: The principle of public responsibility.* Englewood Cliffs, NJ: Prentice-Hall.

Pugh, D. S. (1973). The management of organization structures: Does context determine form? *Organizational Dynamics, Spring,* 19–34.

Retiring U.S. official assails nuclear plant safety. (1987, June 7). *The New York Times,* Section 1, p. 32.

Robbins, S. P. (1983). *Organization theory: The structure and design of organizations.* Englewood Cliffs, NJ: Prentice-Hall.

Rolph, E. S. (1979). *Nuclear power and the public safety: A study in regulation.* Lexington, MA: Lexington Books.

Sandman, P. M. (1986). Getting to maybe: Some communications aspects of siting hazardous waste facilities. *Seton Hall Legislative Journal, 9,* 437–465.

Schneider, L. A. (1985). *Organizational structure, environmental niches, and public relations: The Hage-Hull typology of organizations as predictor of communication behavior.* Unpublished doctoral dissertation, University of Maryland, College Park, MD.

Sullivan, B. S. (1985). The relationship between organizational role hierarchy and public relations job satisfaction. *International Public Relations Association Review, 9,* 14–18.

Temples, J. R. (1982). The NRC and the politics of regulatory reform: Since Three Mile Island. *Public Administration Review, 42,* 355–362.

Thayer, L. (1968). *Communication and communication systems.* Homewood, IL: Irwin.

Turk, J. V. (1986). Information subsidies and media content: A study of public relations influence on the news. *Journalism Monographs, 100.*

U.S. Congress, House, Committee on Interior and Insular Affairs. (1977). *States' rights, moratoria and NRC licensing reform, part 1.* 326.

U.S. Nuclear Regulatory Commission. (1985). *U.S. Nuclear Regulatory Commission 1985 annual report.* Washington, DC: U.S. Government Printing Office.

Walker, W., & Lonnroth, M. (1983). *Nuclear power struggles: Industrial competition and proliferation control.* London: George Allen & Unwin.

Watzlawick, P., Beavin, J. H., & Jackson, D. D. (1967). *Pragmatics of human communication.* New York: Norton.

White, J. (1987). *Public relations and management decision making.* Unpublished manuscript.

Chapter 6

Using Public Relations Theory to Evaluate Specialized Magazines as Communication "Channels"

Dennis W. Jeffers
Central Michigan University

Often, one of the most vexing problems facing public relations practitioners involves the selection of a specific media channel with which to communicate to a target audience. Practitioners who have a vital message of interest to the audience are often frustrated in their attempt to deliver it.

When distributing a news release, or otherwise seeking to communicate with a specific group, the practitioner is often advised to consider such channel-related factors as cost, credibility, and timeliness (Newsom & Scott, 1981). However, analysts have recognized that specialized media—such as specialized magazines— are often the most efficient way to reach a specific audience. Consequently, public relations practitioners are often encouraged to turn to specialized magazines (Cutlip, Center, & Broom, 1985).

The value of specialized magazines to public relations is illustrated by research conducted by Adams and Parkhurst (1984) when they sought to find out which channels farmers and ranchers turned to for agricultural information. Drawing on previous research that indicated that farmers have different sources of information for different issues or topics, Adams and Parkhurst asked Nebraska farmers and ranchers what kinds of information they considered to be important and *where* they got it. The results showed that farmers and ranchers made clear-cut distinctions between 17 channels of communication and that farm magazines were rated significantly more important than all other channels in conveying information. Other channels included the traditional interpersonal contacts (neighbors and other farmers).

The interesting aspect of the Adams and Parkhurst study is that respondents were asked which *specific* channels they used to meet *specific* information needs. For instance, ranchers had the opportunity to indicate which channel was most instrumental in providing information about livestock breeding, livestock nutrition, and livestock management. The fact that farm magazines were perceived as being most important, regardless of type of information, led Adams and Parkhurst to conclude that land grant universities should expand their use of farm magazines in their public relations effort.

Even so, given that specialized magazines are good vehicles, there is very little research that can help a practitioner make the most *effective* use of specialized magazine channels. This chapter is an attempt to remedy this situation by reporting on an *exploratory and descriptive* study of specialized magazine editors' perceptions of audience characteristics as well as the perceived role of their publication. The general framework within which the study was conducted is, like that of Adams and Parkhurst, agricultural communication—one of the most "specialized" fields of the magazine industry. Agricultural publications are often segmented both by geographic region and by unit of agricultural production. This results in hundreds of publications serving very specific audience publics (Ford, 1969; Taft, 1982).

Also, as most practitioners know, even when it is certain that the readers of a specialized publication would be interested in the practitioner's message, the practitioner must convince the editor or other gatekeeper that this is so. Gaining an understanding of audience perceptions of preferred channels is only half the battle. In order to make the best use of these channels, it is important to learn of the *perceptions of the channel gatekeepers.* By testing and extending established public relations theory, this study should shed some light on the perceptions of specialized magazine gatekeepers.

THEORETICAL AND RESEARCH BACKGROUND

In many ways, it is fruitful to think of the readers of specialized magazines as "publics." In fact, when comparing an analysis of Blumer's and Dewey's seminal definitions of publics with a contemporary analysis of the specialized magazine audience, it is clear there are many similarities (see Becker, 1983; Grunig & Hunt, 1984). Members of specialized magazine audiences do seem to be publics that are bound together by common interests and activities. They have a need to communicate about specific topics and the communication often results in specific behavior. (Perhaps the primary reason that the number of specialized magazines has increased is that advertisers realize that this "specific behavior" often involves use of their products and services.) Consequently, Grunig's situational theory for explaining the communication behavior of publics seems particularly helpful for guiding research involving the development of specialized magazine content.

James Grunig, who has been developing his theory over a number of years, says that there are four independent variables that explain when and how people com-municate about specific issues or topics and when they will have cognitions about these issues (see Grunig, 1977, 1978, 1979, 1982, 1983a; Grunig & Hunt, 1984). These variables are *problem recognition* (whether a person has a "need for information" and stops to think about an issue), *level of involvement* (whether the person connects himself with the issue), *constraint recognition* (whether the person thinks he can exert any personal control that might help resolve the issue) and the presence of a *referent criterion* (whether the person thinks he has a solution for the issue or problem).

Past research using these variables indicates that they help explain when indi-viduals (and other behavioral systems) will engage in active information-seeking or passive information-processing. And, in looking at the role of specialized publica-tions within the total media environment, it would seem that Grunig's theory has a great deal of utility for explaining the communication behavior of specialized magazine publics.

For instance, given that, overall, there is a degree of involvement on the part of the reader with the general subject matter of the specialized publication, it seems reasonable to assume that readers will be concerned about specific issues or topics within the framework of the general subject matter. Further, it seems reasonable to assume that the reader's level of involvement and perceived constraint will vary from topic to topic, just as will the readers' perceptions of problem solutions.

As for determining how this might relate to the editorial process in specialized magazines (and ultimately the practitioner's message), Culbertson's (1983) re-search on the role that editors' perceptions of audience preferences plays in editing behavior is relevant. Using a large sample of newspaper reporters and editors, he tested a news-orientation model that has three elements: the journalist's own in-terests, the journalist's perception of audience interests, and the journalist's news judgment decisions. Culbertson's model allowed for three measures: *congruency*, (similarity between the journalist's interests and those attributed to the audience), *followership*, (the extent to which the journalist makes decisions based on per-ceived audience interests), and *autonomy*, (journalistic decisions based on the journalist's own interests).

Culbertson noted that in the "traditional" method of making news decisions, there is a high degree of followership on the part of editors and, indeed, in his news orientation study he found that, overall, followership did exceed autonomy as a preferred mode of operation.

Also, Grunig (1983b), in a study in which he discussed an application of his situational theory to the reporting behavior of the Washington press corps, found much the same thing. Using a coorientational measure, he found that three out of five "gatekeeper" publics did indeed use perceptions of audience interests as a determining factor in their journalistic behavior.

In short, it is clear from the preceding discussion that the *editor's* perceptions of the audience's/public's preferences is a key element in the editing process. In fact, at another point, Culbertson (1984) suggested that there are pressures currently operating throughout the mass media industry to increase the tendency of editors to rely on their perceptions of audience interests when making editorial judgments. But, Culbertson (1983) also speculated that increased specialization by journalists may lead to greater autonomy. However, some may argue that "followership" is particularly important for specialized publications because this type of publica-tion's "reason for being" is that it does a better job of serving as the "agent" for the reader than the more general mass media.

RESEARCH HYPOTHESES

Combining the "issue"-oriented thinking of Grunig and the "followership" notions of Culbertson, the following research hypotheses were formulated:

1. Editors of specialized magazines will, indeed, perceive *varying degrees* of problem recognition, constraint recognition, involvement, and the presence of referent criteria on the part of readers *by specific issues/topics*.

2. Further, editors will have *differing perceptions* of problem recognition, con-straint recognition, involvement and the presence of referent criteria on the part of readers *for different issues/topics*.

3. Finally, the more editors perceive their readers as being involved, recogniz-ing issue/topic problems, having solutions, and being able to do something about them, *the greater the perceived role of their magazine* in the development of solu-tions to the issue/topic problems.

Implicit in these hypotheses is the assumption that specialized magazine editors are in tune with their readers: They are sensitive to which issues or topics are of concern to readers, aware of which issues readers feel they have some control of, aware of which issues readers are likely to have a high degree of involvement in, and aware of which topics/problems for which their readers have solutions.

If editors of specialized publications are really serving their readers, they are always in the process of helping readers develop solutions to their problems. Furthermore, it seems reasonable to assume that editors will claim some of the credit for helping readers find these solutions. In other words, it seems likely that editors of specialized magazines may very well believe that their publication plays an important role in this process for the reader. (There is a certain "functional" logic in this interpretation. To the extent that the magazine is meeting needs and serving a function for the reader, the more likely the magazine is to succeed as a business venture.)

In essence, if the hypotheses hold, in addition to statistically significant varia-tions of "within" and "between" issue/topic perceptual dimensions, the dependent variable of the magazine's perceived role in "providing solutions," should correlate positively with the independent variables of perceived audience "involvement," "problem recognition," and "presence of referent criteria", and correlate negatively with perceived audience "constraint."

METHODOLOGY

Sample

The type of agricultural publication selected for study is that of single-breed livestock magazines serving the beef, swine, and sheep producing industries. Consequently, a list of 34 editors was developed from the membership of the Livestock Publications Council. Headquartered in Encinitas, California, the Council was formed in 1974 and has members throughout the United States and Canada. Twenty-nine, or 85 percent, of these editors participated in the study via a mail questionnaire.

Measurement and Data Collection

As J. Grunig noted, past research involving gatekeeping has primarily relied on attitudinal variables. But his work (1983b) and the situational theory suggest that "perceptions" related to specific issues are better predictors of communicator behavior. Over the years, Grunig has developed very successful procedures for measuring the variables in his theory. As noted previously, he recently added a coorientational measure when he measured communicators' perceptions of reader conceptions of the theoretical dimensions. Essentially the same procedure was followed in this study, using items developed by Grunig to measure the theoretical variables.

Specifically, the focus of the questions centered around a list of 10 topics/issues identified by livestock industry, association, and government officials as being important to livestock breeders. These are: federal and state regulation of the livestock producing industry, the marketing of surplus dairy cattle for beef, a growing emphasis on non-red meat sources of protein, trade association service to breeders, meat imports, herd improvement techniques, breed promotional activities, animal health, interest rates and credit, and meat grading.

Using these issues as a base, Grunig's questions were adapted to measure the theoretical variables of problem recognition, constraint recognition, level of involvement, and presence of a referent criterion.

For problem recognition, editors were asked how often they thought their readers stopped to think about the issue. For constraint recognition, editors were asked if they thought their readers could do anything personally that would make a difference in the ways the issues were handled. For level of involvement, editors were asked to what extent they saw a connection between the issue and the personal situation of their readers. To detect the perceived presence of referent criteria, editors were asked how definite an idea readers had about what should be done in these areas. Finally, in order to measure the perceived role of the magazine, editors were asked what role they thought their publication has played or is playing in helping readers develop solutions to problems related to those issues.

In each case, editors were given forced choice interval level responses that corresponded with those used by Grunig. For example, for problem recognition, editors were asked how often their readers stopped to think about the specific issue—often (1), sometimes (2), rarely (3), or never (4).

Sample Size, Statistical Tests, and Theory Building

It is clear that when using inferential statistics, small samples, such as the one used in this study, are unstable (Weaver, 1981) and less powerful than large samples in their ability to demonstrate significance (Norusis, 1986).

However, there are several reasons why this study has merit in spite of the small sample size. From a statistical standpoint, the sample comes from a homogenious population which, as Culbertson (1981) noted, helps increase "precision by reducing error variance due to diverse subjects" (p. 239). Whereas, as Culbertson also pointed out, using samples from homogenious populations limits generalizibility, *it does allow researchers to identify processes taking place within the framework specified.*

This last point is particularly important for studies such as this that, as Pavlik (1987) said, help build theory by "focusing on the processes underlying the PR field" (p. 24).

RESULTS AND CONCLUSIONS

Data analysis shows that Hypothesis 1 (which deals with "within" issue/topic perceptions) is supported in that an examination of the editors' pattern of responses for each issue/topic on each of the four theoretical dimensions using goodness-of-fit chi square tests shows that the responses are not evenly distributed in 35 out of 40 categories. In other words, by and large, editors *do* perceive varying degrees of the theoretical constructs of problem recognition, constraint recognition, involvement, and presence of referent criteria by their readers in terms of each issue or topic.

Hypothesis 2 states that editors will have differing perceptions of problem recognition, constraint recognition, level of involvement, and presence of referent criteria *between* issue/topics. To test the degree of salience attributed to each issue on each of the theoretical dimensions, issue-to-issue correlation coefficients were calculated and then correlated t-tests were run on the means of those items that had significant correlations in order to determine if equal salience was attributed to each.

With the exception of the "involvement" dimension, there are few significant correlations between issue/topics. (Significant inter-issue correlation coefficients: Problem Recognition, 3; Constraint Recognition, 6; Level of Involvement, 19; and Presence of Referent Criterion, 2.) Hypothesis 2 is generally supported then, in that editors do have perceptions of readers' relationships to these issues/topics that do not have a high degree of concomitant variation. This suggests, again in general, that there is a degree of "discreetness" in editors' perceptions of these issues/topics.

But, the data are not clear-cut, and further analysis reveals an interesting finding. There are two groups of issues/topics that have high or low means on all theoretical dimensions, co-vary, and have no significant difference between means. This suggests that editors do perceive of *these* issues/topics as being of equal importance (or non-importance) to readers. Specifically, editors group Animal Health, Herd Improvement Techniques, and Breed Promotional Activities as being salient on all dimensions (Mean below 2.00) whereas the issues/topics of Interest Rates and Credit, Meat Grading and Meat Imports are grouped at the "bottom" of all dimensions (Mean above 2.00). The other four issues/topics "go back and forth" in salience, depending on the dimension.

Data needed to test Hypothesis 3 are found in Table 6.1. In general, this hypothesis is also supported. As the table shows, in 7 out of the 10 issues/topics

TABLE 6.1
Correlations of Perceived Role of Magazine with Problem Recognition, Constraint Recognition, Level of Involvement and Presence of Referent Criterion and Mean Perception of Magazine's Role in "Helping Find Solutions"

	Percent Recognition	Constraint[a] Recognition	Level of Involvement	Referent Criterion	Mean/"Helping Find Solutions"
Breed promotional activities	.28	.35*	.33*	.32*	1.276
Herd improvement techniques	.25	.38*	.22	.25	1.310
Animal health	.47**	.41**	.30*	.33*	1.679
Trade association service	.34*	.44**	.43**	.23	1.862
Meat grading	.35*	.36**	.15	.57**	2.517
Federal & state regulation	.35*	.14	.65**	−.27	2.759
Meat imports	.07	.05	.40**	−.01	2.862
Non-red meat sources of protein	.10	.35*	.42**	.45**	3.103
Interest rates & credit	.11	.42**	.38**	.33*	3.138
Surplus dairy cattle	.67**	.57**	.62**	.50**	3.517

Note: Response Categories: 1 = Very Important Role, 2 = Important Role, 3 = Little Role, 4 = No Role.

[a]Correlations for constraint recognition are "positive" because of direction of responses on questionnaire.

*p < .05

**p < .01

there are significant correlations on three out of the four theoretical dimensions with the perceived role of the magazine. Furthermore, one-way chi-squares for a matrix of the response categories are all significant. In other words, the more editors perceive of their readers as being involved, recognizing issue/topic problems, having solutions to these problems, and being able to do something about them, the greater the perceived role of the publication in the development of solutions to these problems.

An examination of the means in the same table shows that editors see their publications as playing an important role (Mean below 2.00) in helping readers find solutions to problems in the same areas that cluster at the top in the four theoretical dimensions—Breed Promotional Activities, Herd Improvement Techniques, and Animal Health.

What does all this mean for the public relations practitioner who is struggling to select the "right" channel to communicate with a target audience as part of an information campaign? Several conclusions that can be drawn from this study of the perceptions of specialized magazine editors may provide some guidance.

First, the results of this study suggest that specialized magazine editors have definite—and differing—perceptions of the relationship of readers to specific issues/topics. Furthermore, and perhaps most importantly, editors perceive their readers as being most concerned with issues and topics that are both "close by" and "personally manageable." Consequently, they see their magazine as making the greatest contribution to individual readers in these areas.

This conclusion is supported by the "rankings and clustering" of the issues/topics. Consistently, Herd Improvement Techniques and Breed Promotional Activities are issues/topics that rank high on the dimensions. These issues are ones that breeders deal with personally on their ranch or farm. (For instance, a breeder works to improve the herd through artificial insemination.) The issues that rank low on the theoretical dimensions (and hence are seen as ones that the magazine plays a less important role in providing solutions for) are ones that are "distant" and "difficult to control" by the individual breeder. Although, theoretically, the individual rancher has some impact on Interest Rates and Credit, for instance, from a practical standpoint it may be minimal.

This conclusion has both theoretical and practical implications. The results suggest that using Grunig's situational theory is useful for discriminating among issues for their own sake. For the most part, previous research using the theory has utilized issues to discriminate among publics. Practically speaking, if a public relations practitioner has information that deals with "close" and "managable" issues for the magazine's readers, he or she should find the gatekeeper to be receptive. To a certain extent, this is a "common sense" finding. But, like many common sense notions, it is not apparent to many practitioners. (Witness the number of press releases with no local angle that are distributed to community newspapers.)

The second conclusion that can be drawn is consistent with previous applications of Grunig's theory. That is, there is some validity to the notion that a specialized magazine editor perceives of these theoretical dimensions as being interrelated. As shown, the issues/topics that rank high on one dimension rank high on the others as well. (And vice-versa.)

This conclusion also has important theoretical, as well as practical, implications. From a theoretical standpoint, what this finding suggests is that even with a relatively homogenous population (in this case breeders) it is possible to identify issues on which editors, at least, perceive of their readers as falling into differing categories of "publics." Those issues in which readers are perceived as high on all dimensions are issues that Grunig would suggest lead to formation of "active" publics, whereas "low" issues would result in "latent" or "non-existent" publics.

From a practical standpoint, it is easy to speculate that editors are more concerned about providing magazine content that speaks to the "active" issues rather than the "latent" or "non-existent" issues. An important question can be raised by asking when (and how) does a "latent" issue move through Grunig's stages of "non-existent," to "latent," to "aware," to "active." Does the magazine editor initiate this process, or does he or she merely respond to other factors that change the nature of his or her readers' concerns? It may be that editors pick and choose as to *which issues* lend themselves to "followership" editing behavior and which issues are most appropriate for "autonomous" editing behavior. Furthermore, it may be that the public relations practitioner has an opportunity to influence editing behavior by influencing the "issue agenda" of the editor.

In many ways, what this study has demonstrated is that the public relations practitioner should guard against classifying communication channels on the basis of broad subject matter alone. Instead, it may be necessary to classify channels on the basis of *specific issue/topics* and their relation to the practitioner's communication objective. Certainly, this may be easier to do with specialized magazines than with other channels.

As with other exploratory studies, there are more questions raised by the results than answers provided. For instance, using the results of this study, it is not possible to say anything about the actual editing behavior of the magazine editors. A focus for an additional study would be to examine magazine content as a way of determining if editors translate their perceptions of reader attributes into specific copy dealing with these topics.

Nor is this study capable of allowing conclusions to be drawn about the congruency between editors and readers. An investigation into the editors' own perceptions on the same issues would be needed to make this comparison. Also, this study does not allow for any statements about the accuracy of the editors' perceptions. For this, a measure of the readers' thinking on these dimensions is needed.

In spite of these limitations, the results of this study suggest that the marriage of situational theory and coorientation results in a useful approach for investigating specialized magazine editing behavior and may be a useful approach for the public relations practitioner seeking to make the best "channel" choice.

ACKNOWLEDGMENT

The author wishes to thank Prof. Hugh Culbertson, Ohio University, for his assistance in preparing this article.

REFERENCES

Adams, J. L., & Parkhurst, A. M. (1984). *Farmer/rancher perceptions of channels and sources of change information* (Tech. Rep. No. 9). Lincoln, NE: University of Nebraska, Department of Agricultural Communications.

Becker, S. L. (1983). *Discovering mass communication*. Glenview, IL: Scott, Foresman.

Culbertson, H. M. (1981). Statistical designs for experimental research. In G. H. Stempel, III & B. H. Westley (Eds.), *Research methods in mass communication* (pp. 217–239). Englewood Cliffs, NJ: Prentice-Hall.

Culbertson, H. M. (1983). Three perspectives on American journalism. *Journalism Monographs, 83*.

Culbertson, H. M. (1984, August). *Breadth of perspective—An important concept for public relations*. Paper presented to Public Relations Division, Association for Education in Journalism and Mass Communication, Gainesville, FL.

Cutlip, S., Center, A., & Broom, G. (1985). *Effective public relations* (6th ed.). Englewood Cliffs, NJ: Prentice-Hall.

Ford, J. L. C. (1969). *Magazines for millions: The story of specialized publications*. Carbondale, IL: Southern Illinois University Press.

Grunig, J. E. (1977). Evaluating employee communication in a research operation. *Public Relations Review, 3*, 61–82.

Grunig, J. E. (1978). Defining publics in public relations: The case of a suburban hospital. *Journalism Quarterly, 55*, 109–118.

Grunig, J. E. (1979). Time budgets, level of involvement and use of the mass media. *Journalism Quarterly, 56*, 248–261.

Grunig, J. E. (1982). The message-attitude-behavior relationship: Communication behaviors of organization. *Communication Research, 9*, 163–200.

Grunig, J. E. (1983a). Communication behaviors and attitudes of environmental publics: Two studies. *Journalism Monographs, 81*.

Grunig, J. E. (1983b). *Washington reporter publics of corporate public affairs program*. *Journalism Quarterly, 60*, 603–614.

Grunig, J. E., & Hunt, T. (1984). *Managing public relations*. New York: Holt, Rinehart and Winston.

Newsom, D., & Scott, A. (1981). *This is PR: The realities of public relations* (2nd ed.). Belmont, CA: Wadsworth Publishing Co.

Norusis, M. J. (1986). *The SPSS guide to data analysis*. Chicago: SPSS Inc.

Pavlik, J. V. (1987). *Public relations: What research tells us*. Newbury Park, CA: Sage Publications, Inc.

Taft, W. H. (1982). *American magazines for the 1980s*. New York: Hastings House.

Weaver, D. H. (1981). Basic statistical tools. In G. H. Stempel, III & B. H. Westley (Eds.), *Research methods in mass communication* (pp. 48–86). Englewood Cliffs, NJ: Prentice-Hall.

Chapter 7

Using Role Theory to Study Cross Perceptions of Journalists and Public Relations Practitioners

Andrew Belz
Albert D. Talbott
Kenneth Starck
University of Iowa

Public relations practitioners and journalists may be said to share some of the same values while at the same time differing on others. More problematic is the particular relationship between the two groups of professional communicators. To some extent, public relations practitioners and journalists are dependent on each other. Although a good deal of interaction occurs between them, the precise nature of the relationship between those who practice public relations and those who practice journalism is vaguely defined. Specific aspects of the relationship appear to have been defined largely by the professions themselves. This relationship has raised a number of issues, including those of ethics and skills examined by Jeffers (1971). Our goal is to explore this relationship on the basis of public relations and journalism practitioners' perceptions of their field as well as of the other field.

Research on journalistic and public relations roles has often been limited to analysis of one role or the other. Kent's study (1976), for example, used role theory and Q-methodology to examine TV reporters' perceptions of role expectations. Ferguson (1979) and Dozier (1981), among others, have described the public relations role in terms of its most appropriate activities. Broom and Smith (1979) identified five major aspects of the public relations role. In a separate study, Broom (1980) compared men's and women's roles in public relations, and Dozier and Gottesman (1982) used Q-methodology to uncover various aspects of the PR role. They found four dimensions of the role, and associated these dimensions with right/left brain theory.

Occasionally, the relationship between journalists and public relations practitioners has been studied. Jeffers (1971) remarked that most of this research has focused on two aspects of the relationship—ethics and skills. Studies emphasizing ethical considerations discuss, for example, PR prizes to newspeople, news decisions by newspeople based on advertising sales, and other questions of news value. Studies emphasizing skills focus on the PR process: testing whether PR people are capable of performing journalistic procedures, testing whether PR people are aware of journalistic practices, and comparing skills between the professions.

Aronoff (1975), in a survey study, found that journalists have "negative attitudes" toward public relations practitioners. He concluded that journalists have news value orientations and perceptions of occupational status that are *opposite* to what public relations people think of themselves.

Jeffers (1971) found a skewed perception among journalists. Journalists, he said, considered practitioners whom they knew and worked with to be status-equals. However, practitioners with whom the journalists had little acquaintance were thought to be unequal in status. Jeffers linked cooperativeness to perceptions of status equality and competitiveness to perceptions of status inequality.

The notion of role interdependency has been discussed by Cutlip (1985), who described the relationship as sometimes adversarial, sometimes cooperative, and always suspicious of the other's intentions. Yet he and other authors hold out hope for a relationship governed by mutual respect.

Although Aronoff and Jeffers both found widely varying perceptions of public relations, neither study explicitly used role theory. No study has compared the *perceived* roles of journalism and public relations. In view of the considerable body of role theory available and considering the apparent relatedness of the two professions, it seemed appropriate to apply existing role theory to cross perceptions of the two roles.

Role Theory

The theoretical construct of role has been applied to a broad range of human behavior. Using the drama metaphor, role theory suggests that people play parts determined, to some extent, by others' expectations. In drama, an actor acts out a part from a written script. He or she reacts to other actors, to the director, and even to the audience's reaction. The player's action is "programmed" by these factors. As a result, the act is very similar, no matter who is filling the part.

Role theory presents a rich theoretical background for the study of two interacting roles. In particular, role research has demonstrated different types of role conflict. Interrole conflict arises when two contradictory roles are held simultaneously by the same person. Intrarole conflict, meanwhile, arises when a person is faced with contradictory expectations of the same role. Both types of role conflict are discussed by Gross, McEachern, and Mason (1966), who also present models for its resolution.

RESEARCH QUESTION

Using role theory as a central theoretical foundation, we sought to clarify basic cross perceptions between professionals in the public relations and journalistic roles. We designed the research to describe and compare predominant patterns of perception of the roles. Q-methodology was employed to carry out the research. We applied this methodology to the specific roles of journalist and public relations practitioner as they relate to each other. People from both professional roles were considered the primary creators and definers of these roles. Accordingly, they were asked to describe both roles in terms of a variety of attributes or characteristics through the use of a Q-sort. These descriptions were compared by using factor analysis to isolate the predominant patterns of perception of each role. The descriptions of these patterns or factors and the ensuing comparison of them was the primary goal of the research.

METHODOLOGY

Development of Instrument

We chose Q-methodology because it serves well as a method for tapping the subjective perceptions of people and because it allows types to form around latent perceptions. Q-methodology helps to confirm the existence of patterns of perceptions. Other methodologies could be applied to ours or a similar research question. Coorientation measurement, for example, developed by McLeod and Chaffee (1973), is a methodological tool that could be utilized to replicate this study.

The scope of the concourse—that is, the spectrum of perceptions encompassed in the statements—was designed to include the roles of journalism and public relations. By giving the title "professional communicator" to both roles, a concourse common to persons from both professions was used to describe their own and the other profession's roles.

Role theory suggests two basic aspects of role: rights and duties. These dual aspects formed part of the basis for categorizing statements in the Q-sample. Jeffers (1971) asserted that most research on the practitioner–journalist relationship focuses on skills and ethics. Kent's research (1976) on the roles of TV reporters used the categories of rights, skills, and personal characteristics.

For this study, four categories of role were formed: rights, duties, skills, and personal characteristics. These categories were used as an organizing device, rooted in theory, and not as theoretically based analytic categories to be tested. Because of the evolutionary nature of the development of the statements, it was necessary to organize them in some way to assure comprehensiveness.

We went to a variety of sources for data to specify and define these categories, including journalism and public relations textbooks that provided preliminary aspects of the journalist's and public relations practitioner's roles. Discussions of professionalism were examined to find other aspects of the two roles. Among the other documents we examined were the *Canons of Journalism*, adopted by the American Society of Newspaper Editors at its annual convention in 1975, and the Public Relations Society of America's *Code of Professional Standards*, adopted in 1959 and amended in 1963. Approximately 50 statements were developed as a result of this literature search. Achieving diversity and breadth of perspective was the primary objective in the selection of statements.

The statements were examined by practitioners in journalism and public relations to gain their suggestions. Final editing of the statements came through a pretest on five respondents. Their reactions were recorded, and the statements were modified to reduce misunderstandings. The final Q-sample numbered 54 statements.

Selection of Subjects

As in the development of the concourse of statements, diversity also was a key objective in the selection of subjects. Subjects were selected from an area approximately 125 miles in diameter in eastern and central Iowa. Journalists were chosen who had specific editorial decision-making power over public relations material. Accordingly, upon first contact with the news organization, we posed the question: "May we speak to the person who handles news releases and public relations materials?" Fourteen such journalists participated from the following kinds of news organizations:

4 Daily Newspapers (Circ. 50,000+)

1 Weekly Newspaper (Circ. 5,000−)

3 TV Stations

3 Radio Stations (Major Metropolitan Area: 50,000+)

2 Radio Stations (Small Metropolitan Area: 10,000−)

Public relations practitioners were sought who carry out the specific task of media relations. Fifteen such PR practitioners participated from the following kinds of organizations:

3 Major Corporations

2 Moderate-Size Businesses

2 Hospitals

1 University

1 Four-Year College

1 Community College
2 Local Service Organizations
1 Utility
1 Government Press Secretary

Collection of Data

Respondents were instructed to sort the Q-statements twice: Once as they perceived their own role, and once as they perceived the other professional role. Twenty-nine respondents thus produced 58 sorts. Each respondent was instructed which role to complete first (this was randomized), and was also instructed to reshuffle the statements between sortings. The items were sorted into a forced, modified normal distribution having 11 piles.

The deck of statements and the response form was either left with the respondent or mailed. None of the interviews was conducted in person by the researcher, and respondents were encouraged to carry out the task at home when ample time was available. We collected the data over a 4-month period.

Analysis of Data

This study used the QUANAL computer program, available from the University of Iowa Weeg Computer Center. It is a generalized program for Q-factor analysis utilizing Pearson product moment correlation. The principal axis factor solutions were obtained, followed by Varimax rotation. Factor scores were computed for each Varimax factor.

Results of the 58 sorts were transcribed, entered on the computer, and analyzed, using the QUANAL program. The 29 journalism role sorts were analyzed, yielding one factor. Similarly, the 29 public relations role sorts yielded two factors. Although more than one factor solution was examined for each analysis, including hand rotation, the one-factor journalism solution and the two-factor public relations solution were selected as the best summations of all attempted analyses. Stephenson's (1975) criterion for defining prototypical representatives for each of the factors was used. This criterion states that to be a prototype, the largest loading must exceed a .40 correlation. In addition, all secondary loadings, if any, must be less than a .40 correlation. To estimate the item array or factor scores for each type, the Q-sorts of the prototypes representing each factor were averaged, weighting each sort by a function of the square of the factor loading. For a brief description of Q-factor analysis as used in this study, including the weighting procedures, see MacLean, Danbury, and Talbott (1975), Nesterenko and Talbott (1976), or Talbott (1971). This is also discussed and described in works by Stephenson (1953, 1967). The arrays for each pair of types were compared by subtraction.

Tables 7.1–7.3 contain only the most agreed-with items (z scores > 1.50) and the least agreed-with items (z scores < -1.50) from each of the three factor arrays. The top and bottom items in each array thus defined constituted the items most descriptive or characteristic of each type. Tables 7.4–7.6 contain only those items for which the absolute difference between the z scores exceeded 2.00 for the pair of types being compared by subtraction. These would be the items that most differentiate one type from another.

RESULTS

We present the results of the Q analyses in four sections here. The first section examines the correlations between the two sorts. The second section concerns perceptions of the journalistic role. A single pattern, or type, emerged. The third section is a description and comparison of the two types that emerged from the analysis of perceptions of the public relations role. The fourth is a comparison of each of the PR types with the journalistic type.[1]

Individual Correlation of Sorts

Each person sorted the set of statements twice. The degree to which these two sorts were alike was given by the correlation, with 1.00 signifying identical sorts, and −1.00 signifying opposite sorts. The median correlation for all respondents was .28. The correlation is basically an index of the consistency between each person's views of the two professions. The correlations were examined to see if differences existed between PR people's responses and journalists' responses. Of the 15 persons' correlations at the median or above, 12 were public relations practitioners. Of the 14 correlations below the median, 11 were journalists. The correlations between the Q sorts of the two roles were higher for PR practitioners than for journalists. The median for the PR practitioners in the sample was .31, whereas the median for the journalists was very close to zero.

These results were an initial indication that the journalists have more widely disparate perceptions of the two roles than do PR practitioners. Within the sample, most journalists viewed the two roles as different, whereas most PR practitioners viewed the two roles as having some similarity. This confirms earlier research by Aronoff, who observed a disparity between journalists' and PR practitioners' perceptions of status and news value orientations.

---

[1]Anyone interested in a copy of a comprehensive appendix containing a set of tables detailing in full the descriptions of each of the types and the comparisons among them should contact Albert D. Talbott, School of Journalism and Mass Communication, University of Iowa, Iowa City, IA 52242.

Perceptions of the Journalistic Role

The analysis involved 29 separate sorts for the journalistic role. A single factor solution was used, which provided a strong traditional journalistic stereotype. Using .40 as a criterion, 26 of 29 persons were defined as prototypical for this type. Three persons (all PR) failed to meet the .40 criterion, but two of them had correlations close to it.

Type J-I: Consensual Perspective on the Journalistic Role.   Findings indicated that professional communicators in this sample held perceptions of the journalistic role that tend to be associated with traditional notions of journalism. A perusal of the statements most characteristic of this type (see Table 7.1) showed strong agreement that the journalistic role involves accuracy, fairness, objectivity, balance, and informativeness. It also showed disagreement that the role involves withholding information, keeping a hidden agenda, making ethical compromises, advocating a particular position, or emphasizing a specialized education.

This traditional journalistic role is not likely to go without debate. Questions have been raised about fairness, objectivity, and balance in reporting. Some argue that these traits do not exist in journalism. Criticisms of the media, such as Gans (1979), Schlesinger (1978), and Tuchman (1978), also have dealt with other,

TABLE 7.1
Description of Type J-I: Most and Least Agreed-with Items

Item	z score
5. The professional communicator gives accurate information. (D)	2.20
44. The professional communicator seeks to provide fairness in reporting. (D)	1.82
7. A professional communicator takes an objective approach to most issues; he or she tries to avoid personal opinion entering in. (PC)	1.67
10. The professional communicator provides as much balance as possible on issues about which he or she reports. (D)	1.54
42. It is the right of the professional communicator to advocate a particular position. (R)	−1.72
54. A professional communicator occasionally has to be prepared to make some ethical compromises in the interests of getting the required job done. (D)	−1.94
27. A professional communicator has a "hidden agenda" behind his or her apparent purpose. (D)	−2.07
53. The professional communicator keeps information from the audience in some cases—to help protect the organization on which he or she is reporting. (D)	−2.48

Note: Role in this study was assumed to consist of four dimensions: R = right, D = duty, S = skill, and PC = personal characteristic.

equally provocative issues, including withholding information, keeping a hidden agenda, and making ethical compromises—suggesting that traits like these may reflect some of today's journalism.

These results, however, suggest that such critical approaches are not prevalent among members of this sample. Respondents in this study held a consensus view of the journalistic role. The consensus upheld traditional journalistic standards. This may reflect the common educational background and socialization that both journalists and many PR practitioners have undergone in journalism schools. Whatever its roots, there was strong agreement about the journalistic role in this sample that cannot be ignored.

Perceptions of the Public Relations Role

This analysis involved 29 separate sorts for the public relations role. According to the criterion of .40, prototypical individuals were identified for each factor. These were individuals who were highly and clearly associated with each factor. Each of the two factors was defined by 11 prototypical respondents.

The professional role of the respondent was related strongly to the factor on which he or she had the highest factor loading. For Type PR-I, 11 of the 13 persons were journalists. For PR-II, 13 of the 16 were PR practitioners. Among prototypical individuals, all 11 for Type PR-I were journalists. For Type PR-II, 10 of the 11 were PR practitioners. There was a strong relationship between each respondent's professional role and his or her view of public relations.

Type PR-I: Journalistic Perspective on the PR Role. The 11 prototypical respondents who formed the first PR type were all journalists. These respondents perceived that public relations involved advocacy, persuasion, withholding of information, and aggressiveness (for the most characteristic items, see Table 7.2). When contrasted with the consensual view of the journalistic role, their views indicated a negative perception of public relations. Journalists did give credit to public relations people for having strong abilities to construct interesting and "digestible" messages.

Journalists also indicated that public relations is not concerned with objectivity, balance, or fairness. They stated that public relations does little to protect the public interest or to be "independent and resistant to favor seekers."

Type PR-I perceptions, like Type J-I views, are likely to be debated. Public relations manuals and textbooks, such as Cutlip, Center, and Broom (1985), and Newsom and Siegfried (1981), largely expound ideals opposite to the perceptions of this group. Nonetheless, this research indicated a very negative perception of PR by journalists.

Type PR-II: Public Relations Perspective on the PR Role. A second type was

TABLE 7.2
Description of Type PR-I: Most and Least Agreed-with Items

Item	z score
42. It is the right of the professional communicator to advocate a particular position. (R)	2.22
53. The professional communicator keeps information from the audience in some cases—to help protect the organization on which he or she is reporting. (D)	1.73
4. A professional communicator is able to persuade. (S)	1.63
22. A professional communicator may persuade his or her audience. (R)	1.51
50. The professional communicator protects the public interest. (D)	−1.59
10. The professional communicator provides as much balance as possible on issues about which he or she reports. (D)	−1.73
7. A professional communicator takes an objective approach to most issues; he or she tries to avoid personal opinion entering in. (PC)	−2.12

Note: Role in this study was assumed to consist of four dimensions: R = right, D = duty, S = skill, and PC = personal characteristic.

formed by 11 other prototypical members of the sample. But this time, 10 of the 11 were public relations practitioners. (Statements most characteristic of this type are shown in Table 7.3.)

Concurrent with PR literature, Type PR-II perceptions reflected that current PR practitioners are accurate, are able to construct clear messages, and are forthright, honest, and informative. They disagreed, as did the journalists about journalism, that public relations involves ethical compromises or hidden agendas. They also expressed disagreement that PR practitioners challenge the status quo, have the ability to suspend moral and ethical judgments for other considerations, or need a specialized education.

Type PR-II perceptions were not surprising in that they were perceptions of PR people about their own profession. Texts like Cutlip, Center, and Broom (1985) and Newsom and Siegfried (1981) confirm these perceptions of PR.

Comparison of Type PR-I and Type PR-II

The greatest difference between the two basic views of public relations (for the most differentiating items, see Table 7.4) came in the areas of ethical compromises, hidden agendas, aggressiveness, advocacy, and withholding information. The two viewpoints also differed on issues of accuracy, honesty, objectivity, fairness, and the inviolability of one's own conscience.

TABLE 7.3
Description of Type PR-II: Most and Least Agreed-with Items

Item	z score
5. The professional communicator gives accurate information. (D)	2.28
11. A professional communicator has the ability to construct clear mass communications messages. (S)	1.82
1. Forthrightness and honesty are personal characteristics of the professional communicator. (PC)	1.61
26. The professional communicator informs the audience. (D)	1.57
37. A specialized education is an important preparation for a professional communicator. (PC)	−1.72
28. The professional communicator challenges society's status quo. (D)	−1.75
19. A professional communicator is the type of person who is able to suspend temporarily moral and ethical judgments for other considerations, such as objectivity and fairness. (PC)	−1.85
27. A professional communicator has a "hidden agenda" behind his or her apparent purpose. (D)	−2.01
54. A professional communicator occasionally has to be prepared to make some ethical compromises in the interests of getting the required job done. (D)	−2.04

Note: Role in this study was assumed to consist of four dimensions: R = right, D = duty, S = skill, and PC = personal characteristic.

TABLE 7.4
Description of Types PR-I and PR-II: Most Differentiating Items

Item	PR-I	PR-II	Diff.
		z scores	
54. A professional communicator occasionally has to be prepared to make some ethical compromises in the interests of getting the required job done. (D)	1.190	−2.035	3.225
27. A professional communicator has a "hidden agenda" behind his or her apparent purpose. (D)	0.873	−2.005	2.878
9. Aggressiveness is a key trait of the professional communicator. (PC)	1.310	−1.234	2.545
42. It is the right of the professional communicator to advocate a particular position. (R)	2.218	−0.165	2.383
1. Forthrightness and honesty are personal characteristics of the professional communicator. (PC)	−1.088	1.606	−2.694
5. The professional communicator gives accurate information. (D)	−0.455	2.276	−2.731

Note: Role in this study was assumed to consist of four dimensions: R = right, D = duty, S = skill, and PC = personal characteristic.

These views were relatively distinct. The correlation between the two is only .20, reinforcing this conclusion. Most issues dividing types PR-I and PR-II have to do with ethical responsibilities of professional communicators.

Comparison of Journalistic and PR Roles

Comparison of Type J-I and Type PR-II.   The comparison of types J-I and PR-II (for the most differentiating items, see Table 7.5) reveals distinctions over issues of constitutional freedom of the press, balance, objectivity, aggressiveness, and protection of the public interest. Also, distinctions came in the areas of with-holding information, advocacy, diplomacy, previous experience, and ability to construct interesting messages.

The issues dividing these types appeared to be relatively indistinct. The empha-sis shifted from responsibilities to personal traits. For the first time in the com-parison, aggressiveness, diplomacy, and previous experience of the professional communicator appeared as key factors. Correlation of the factor arrays of types J-I and PR-II yielded a value of .49. This further supported the observation that some degree of similarity existed between these views of the two roles, with differences quite mild. In other words, the PR practitioners' view of their own role had a moderate degree of similarity with the consensual view all respondents had of the journalistic role.

Comparison of Type J-I and Type PR-I.   The sharpest contrast came between types J-I and PR-I (for the most differentiating items, see Table 7.6) over issues of objectivity, fairness, balance, accuracy, and protection of the public interest. On the negative side, differences appeared on issues of withholding information, ad-vocacy, hidden agendas, and ethical compromises.

Correlation of factor arrays for types J-I and PR-I yielded a value of −.40. This tended to support the observation that there was a very discernible contrast be-tween these views of the two roles. In other words, the journalists' view of the PR practitioner differed sharply from the consensual view of the journalistic role. This consensual view was also the way the journalists view their own role. Conse-quently, the journalists' view of the PR role was mildly negatively correlated with the way they view their own role.

DISCUSSION

The primary finding of this research was that journalists and public relations practitioners differ sharply over their perceptions of the public relations role, yet both groups have similar perceptions of the journalistic role. Several aspects of the

TABLE 7.5
Comparison of Types J-I and PR-II: Most Differentiating Items

Item	J-I	PR-II	Diff.
		z scores	
33. A right of a professional communicator is protection under constitutional freedom of the press. (R)	1.198	−1.476	2.674
10. The professional communicator provides as much balance as possible on issues about which he or she reports. (D)	1.545	−0.996	2.540
53. The professional communicator keeps information from the audience in some cases—to help protect the organization on which he or she is reporting. (D)	−2.477	−0.034	−2.443

Note: Role in this study was assumed to consist of four dimensions: R = right, D = duty, S = skill, and PC = personal characteristic.

results confirm this conclusion, most notably the clear formation of two particular views of public relations, represented by types PR-I and PR-II.

The implications of the research by role theorists Gross, McEachern, and Mason (1966) would suggest that journalists who choose to enter public relations will suffer from interrole conflict. The perceived disparity between their old journalistic role and their new public relations role—verified by this research—could produce conflict. Although the precise definition of interrole conflict states that it is conflict arising when two contradictory roles are held simultaneously, nonetheless, interrole conflict would appear to apply in job-changing situations as well.

Equally significant is the assertion that PR practitioners suffer from intrarole conflict. Gross, McEachern, and Mason (1966) stated that intrarole conflict results when a person faces varying expectations from different audiences. This research indicates that journalists hold one set of expectations from PR (Type PR-I), whereas PR people hold a different self-concept (Type PR-II). Public relations professionals appear to face conflicting expectations about their role.

Demographic information on these respondents could be relevant. Educational and professional background, age, sex, and income might provide interesting relationships with the "types." Although we have some of these data, we did not conduct such an analysis because our sample was small, being exploratory in nature. In addition, we must be cautious in making inferences about our sample subjects that were drawn purposively in accordance with Q-method procedures.

Additional research into the types would be useful. Role theory suggests that persons who have contradictory expectations placed on their role suffer from intrarole conflict. Intrarole conflict appears to be a potential problem for public relations practitioners. Journalistic standards appear to contradict both PR people's self-perception and PR people's employers' expectations. If these practitioners indeed seek to idealize the journalistic role in their own practice, and management expects them to seek primarily the organization's interest, intrarole conflict exists. The implications of this could be studied among PR practitioners. Both interrole conflict and intrarole conflict present provocative aspects of the journalist–PR practitioner relationship that deserve further study.

Research should build on this study's findings by determining the distribution of our three perceived types of professional communicators at several levels, including among practitioners, media editors, and the general population. Research on how the types are distributed in relevant populations could enhance understanding of the relationships between the professions. Such inquiry could be accomplished

TABLE 7.6
Comparison of Types J-I and PR-I: Most Differentiating Items

Item	J-I	PR-I	Diff.
	z scores		
7. A professional communicator takes an objective approach to most issues; he or she tries to avoid personal opinion entering in. (PC)	1.666	−2.117	3.783
44. The professional communicator seeks to provide fairness in reporting. (D)	1.823	−1.456	3.278
10. The professional communicator provides as much balance as possible on issues about which he or she reports. (D)	1.545	−1.733	3.277
5. The professional communicator gives accurate information. (D)	2.205	−0.455	2.660
50. The professional communicator protects the public interest. (D)	0.813	−1.586	2.399
25. The professional communicator remains independent of and resistant to favor-seekers. (D)	0.840	−1.187	2.027
3. A professional communicator has a diplomatic personality. (PC)	−0.993	1.144	−2.137
4. A professional communicator is able to persuade. (S)	−0.568	1.626	−2.194
22. A professional communicator may persuade his or her audience. (R)	−0.774	1.513	−2.286
27. A professional communicator has a "hidden agenda" behind his or her apparent purpose. (D)	−2.068	0.873	−2.941
54. A professional communicator occasionally has to be prepared to make some ethical compromises in the interest of getting the required job done. (D)	−1.942	1.190	−3.131
42. It is the right of the professional communicator to advocate a particular position. (R)	−1.724	2.218	−3.942
53. The professional communicator keeps information from the audience in some cases—to help protect the organization on which he or she is reporting. (D)	−2.477	1.728	−4.205

Note: Role in this study was assumed to consist of four dimensions: R = right, D = duty, S = skill, and PC = personal characteristic.

by utilizing a survey instrument defining the three types, with appropriate response categories allowing respondents to associate themselves with a particular type (Talbott, 1963).

REFERENCES

Aronoff, C. (1975). Credibility of public relations for journalists. *Public Relations Review, 1*, 45–56.

Broom, G. M. (1980, August). *A comparison of roles played by men and women in public relations*. Paper presented to the Public Relations Division, Association for Education in Journalism Annual Convention, Boston, MA.

Broom, G. M. & Smith, G. D. (1979). Testing the practitioner's impact on clients. *Public Relations Review, 5*, 47–59.

Cutlip, S. (1985, April). The role of corporate public relations in the nation's public information system. *Proceedings of the Fifth Annual Donald S. MacNaughton Symposium* (pp. 71–95). Syracuse University, Syracuse, NY.

Cutlip, S., Center, A. H., & Broom, G. M. (1985). *Effective public relations* (6th ed.) Englewood Cliffs: Prentice-Hall.

Dozier, D. M. (1981, August). *The diffusion of evaluation methods among public relations practitioners*. Paper presented to the Public Relations Division, Association for Education in Journalism Annual Convention, East Lansing, MI.

Dozier, D. M., & Gottesman, M. (1982, July). *Subjective dimensions of organizational roles among public relations practitioners*. Paper presented to the Public Relations Division, Association for Education in Journalism Annual Convention, Athens, OH.

Ferguson, M. A. (1979, August). *Some empirically-generated public relations roles and associations with various descriptive variables*. Paper presented to the Public Relations Division, Association for Education in Journalism Annual Convention, Houston, TX.

Gans, H. J. (1979). *Deciding what's news: A study of CBS Evening News, NBC Nightly News, Newsweek, and Time* New York: Vintage Books.

Gross, N., McEachern, A. W., & Mason, W. S. (1966). Role conflict and its resolution. In B. J. Biddle & E. J. Thomas (Eds.), *Role theory: Concepts and research* (pp. 287-296). New York: Wiley.

Jeffers, D. W. (1971). Performance expectations as a measure of relative status of news and PR people. *Journalism Quarterly, Summer*, 300.

Kent, P. L. (1976). Television reporters' perceptions of role expectations. Unpublished doctoral dissertation, University of Iowa, Iowa City.

MacLean, M. S., Jr., Danbury, T., & Talbott, A. D. (1975). *Analysis of Q-sort data*. Worked Example Series: No. 1, Iowa City: Iowa Center for Communication Study, School of Journalism and Mass Communication.

McLeod, J. M., & Chaffee, S. H. (1973). Interpersonal approaches to communication research. *American Behavioral Scientist, 16*, 469–499.

Nesterenko, A., & Talbott, A. D. (1976). *Centroid Factor Analysis*, Worked Example Series: No. 3, Iowa City: Iowa Center for Communication Study, School of Journalism and Mass Communication.

Newsom, D., & Siegfried, T. (1981). *Writing in public relations practice: form & style.* Belmont, CA: Wadsworth Publishing Co.

Schlesinger, P. (1978). *Putting "reality" together: BBC news.* London: Constable.

Stephenson, W. (1953). *The study of behavior.* Chicago: The University of Chicago Press.

Stephenson, W. (1967). *The play theory of mass communication.* Chicago: The University of Chicago Press.

Stephenson, W. (1975). *Newton's fifth rule.* Unpublished manuscript.

Talbott, A. D. (1963, August). *The Q block method for indexing Q typologies.* Paper presented to the Theory and Methodology Division, Association for Education in Journalism Annual Convention, Lincoln, NE.

Talbott, A. D. (1971, February). Q technique and its methodology: A brief introduction and consideration. Paper for Symposium entitled *The use of Q-methodology for research in educational administration.* 1971 Annual Meeting of the American Educational Research Association, New York (ERIC Document Reproduction Service No. ED 060 040).

Tuchman, G. (1978). *Making news: A study in the construction of reality* New York: The Free Press.

Chapter 8

The Gap Between Professional and Research Agendas in Public Relations Journals

Glen M. Broom
Mark S. Cox
Elizabeth A. Krueger
Carol M. Liebler
San Diego State University

Introduction of a new journal devoted to research in public relations signals the continuing professionalization of the field and expanding body of knowledge underlying the practice. It also is an appropriate context for again considering the knowledge base of public relations and for reporting an empirical study of what some perceive as a gap between professional and research agendas. This chapter is intended as something of a "situation analysis" with respect to the professional and scholarly literature on public relations available to researchers, practitioners, teachers, and students. Concern about the relationship between public relations research and public relations practice motivates the analysis. The empirical portion of our analysis is an inventory of the content of *Public Relations Journal* and *Public Relations Review*. The analysis begins, however, with a review of recent assessments of public relations research and its relationship to the practice.

The Problem and Literature

Several scholars have contributed to our understanding of the foundation of knowledge underlying public relations. Ehling (1975) led the way in recent times by presenting a framework for defining the boundaries of public relations knowledge. His theoretical analysis included concepts of purposive behavior, conflict, social groups, and community as they relate to public relations.

When Ehling's work appeared in the second issue of *Public Relations Review* in 1975, James Grunig and his graduate students at the University of Maryland were surveying the literature in several disciplines to identify theoretical concepts useful in research on organizational communication and public relations (Grunig & Hickson, 1976). They found that most of the research related to public relations was being done by researchers in other fields, and that "little such research, or even theorizing, is being done by researchers whose primary interest is in public rela- tions" (p. 36). Their findings, however, dealt more with the type and quality of research rather than the specific content topics.

By the time Grunig presented an update on the status of public relations research at the 1978 Association for Education in Journalism Annual Convention in Seattle, *Public Relations Review* was in its fourth year of publication. Even though this publication had increased the number of research-based articles, he found little evidence to change his earlier feelings of discouragement with what was available to his students. He concluded that the status of public relations research was, "Not good" (Grunig, 1978, p. 22).

In another session at the same convention, Grunig (1979) pointed out the gap between the views of practitioners and academics on both the role of research and the nature of problems addressed in research. He suggested that the differences result from the academic researcher's need to pursue ideas and theories that are relevant to a number of situations and organizations. This is in contrast to the practitioner's understandable concern with specific situations and the day-to-day problems of one organization.

Tirone (1979), speaking at the same convention, suggested that public relations researchers turn their attention to "field research directed toward resolution of 'practical problems'" and to use "less rigid" tests of significance (p. 23). He argued that public relations researchers should concentrate on "common-sense, practical research," saying he was inclined to leave the "crooked paths to unexpected conclusions" to "social psychologists of a mind to retravel them" (p. 23). He concluded that "we have . . . a great deal to be modest about in discussing re- search done by public relations" (p. 24). Yet in his scenario for the professionaliza- tion of public relations, he called for graduate degree curricula based on a "body of knowledge to carry forward" (p. 22).

Next on the program, Lindenmann (1979) cited the evidence of increasing research activity in public relations and publication of *Public Relations Review* as encouraging signs of the development and enhancement of public relations as a profession. Unlike Tirone, however, he called for a move away from the "wheel- spinning stage to a truly effective system and theory-building stage" (p. 35) in the research effort. Whether the research is directed toward applied problems or in- spired by scientific curiosity, Lindenmann saw the need to show how the research relates to the central body of theory and "to what is happening elsewhere" (p. 29).

Whereas Lindenmann proposed dialogues between academic researchers and researchers in the profession, McElreath (1980) used a delphi study to bring together the views of both professionals and academics into a list of "Priority Research Questions in Public Relations for the 1980s." Thirty scholars and profes- sionals responded to McElreath's initial open-ended survey. In the second wave, the same panel rank ordered the edited and categorized research suggestions submitted in the first survey. The final report presented the ordered listings of topical questions (from a purposive sample of unknown representativeness) intended to "point out what needs to be investigated" (p. 6).

In summary, researchers in both academic and professional settings have been critical of public relations research and called for changes in its content and quality. They also agree on the need to develop a conceptual framework for organizing and relating the research efforts. Although not agreeing on the severity of the problem, all perceive "two worlds" of concerns and a gap between the practitioners' information needs and theory-based research findings rewarded by academic institutions and research journals.

Their conclusions are based on analyses of the literature of other disciplines, theses and dissertations reporting public relations research, and personal experiences, as well as surveys of practitioners and scholars. None, however, turned to the major public relations media that reflect and influence the concerns of practitioners and researchers.

To the extent that the surveillance and agenda-setting functions of the mass media generalize to the professional literature, the major public relations publications should indicate both the specific concerns of the field and their relative saliences. It was this imagery of the role of public relations literature that led us to undertake a content inventory of *Public Relations Journal* and *Public Relations Review*.

The Publications

Unlike those preceding us, we were able to study the content of eight volumes of *Public Relations Review*. The *Review* represents a significant development in the professionalization of public relations. It also indicates that the profession is in its embryonic stage in that only since 1975 has it had a journal devoted to research and comment of a scholarly nature.

The *Review* is a refereed scholarly journal published by the Foundation for Public Relations Research and Education, with its editorial office in the College of Journalism, University of Maryland. Circulation in 1983 averaged approximately 1,750 for the four issues, with a large secondary readership as a library reference.

Public Relations Journal, on the other hand, began its 40th year of publication in 1984 with a paid circulation of 15,400. The *Journal* is the professional magazine of the major professional society, Public Relations Society of America, with its editorial office in New York City. As Editor Leo J. Northart said in the December 1981 issue:

> The content of the *Journal* is determined by your information needs, which are further determined by personal and written or phone contacts, requests to PRSA's Information Center, and by keeping abreast of the subject areas and content of

seminars and literature in the field. The comments I receive indicate that we are on target for the great majority of our readers. (p. 32)

Content generally follows the "themes" established for the monthly issues: public relations and change, education and placement, new technology, investor relations, research and evaluation, international public relations, internal communication, corporate annual reports, audiovisuals, management of the function, corporate advertising, and expectations of the future that will affect the practice.

Although there are other important publications in public relations, these two are probably the major references—other than textbooks—used by students of public relations. They also represent both the professional and academic concerns selected by a knowledgeable editorial staff at the *Journal* and a nationally recognized editorial review committee associated with the *Review*.

The Content Analyses

After several pretests, seminar discussions, and revisions, we developed a conceptual framework of three major divisions of content subdivided into 10 categories. An additional five categories described the range of analysis techniques used by the authors.

Content Coding Categories

The 10 *content* categories represent components of the conceptual framework and spell out the operational definitions—content cues and indicators—used to specify the content of articles.

Context Content

Context content deals with macro- and micro-level analyses of public relations in the larger society and in organizations.

Social Context. Articles discuss the impact of social, cultural, political, and economic conditions on public relations; the role of public relations in society; and macro-level analyses of the functions and dysfunctions of public relations in the larger social system.

Organizational Context. Articles discuss attributes of organizations, institutionalized roles, and intra- and inter-departmental relationships as they relate to the public relations function in organizations. Articles report how public relations functions differ across organizations; how organizational factors affect public relations functions, titles, and structures; and how the function is integrated into the larger organization (including agency–client relationships).

Profession Content

Profession content includes the professionalization of public relations practice, education for the profession, and the practitioners themselves.

Professionalization.   Articles relate to the professional standing of the practice, the professionalization of the practitioners, licensing, ethical standards, and the development of professional societies. Articles compare the professionalization of different fields and discuss issues related to the body of knowledge underlying the profession, the role of education in professional development, and the "state-of-the-profession."

Education.   Articles analyze the education of practitioners, focusing on the educational process, institutions offering public relations education, the programs offered, students, and educators. Articles discuss the content of curricula and courses, as well as the nature of the educational experiences needed by students and professionals.

Practitioners.   Content deals with attributes of the practitioners themselves. The set includes reports of individual differences among practitioners, such as educational and professional backgrounds, incomes, titles, places in the organizational hierarchy, opinions, attitudes, and behaviors. The often-reported profile surveys also go here. Research in this category includes studies of the determinants of job performance and the relationships among other individual attributes.

Process Content

The *process* of public relations describes the involvement of practitioners and others in management problem-solving, beginning with gathering information and ending with evaluating results of programs. Process content is organized according to the steps in that process.

Formative Research, Information Input, and Intelligence.   Articles discuss attributes of the information-gathering processes related to organizational intelligence. Sometimes called "formative research," this content deals with research and fact-finding for the purpose of guiding program planning. Articles discuss survey methods for monitoring public opinion, methods for using results of social science research, other techniques for environmental surveillance, and futures research as a part of the public relations function.

Management, Planning, and Programming.   Articles deal with attributes of the process of making public relations decisions. They discuss how information is factored into organizational decisions, how programs are formulated, and how the public relations function is managed. This set could include a discussion of how management techniques apply to programs or specific tasks, a case study illustrating the value of crisis planning, or a systematic study of program planning. The emphasis is on how to make decisions and plans, not on the specific content of those decisions and plans.

Action/Message Strategies and Techniques. Articles on program content are in this category—action strategies employed, as well as message content and techniques used. The category includes characteristics of things done and things said, alternative message strategies tested and/or used, specific strategies aimed at different publics, actual programs implemented, and management actions taken. This category deals with "what was done" and "how it was said."

Media Usage and Techniques. This category deals with attributes of the delivery systems used to get messages to target publics. Articles report media strategies, compare alternative media, match media to publics, introduce new media and media techniques, discuss media planning and costs, and explore the workings of media systems and institutions used in public relations programs. This content includes such things as using slides to tell a story, improving meetings, and dealing more effectively with editors and reporters.

Program Impact, Effects, and Evaluation Research. This category includes discussions of the need for and the techniques used in program evaluation, as well as articles on effects of specific programs. It focuses on the outcomes of public relations, their measurements, and the determination of program effectiveness. The range of content could include a normative piece on the necessity of "summative research" in managing a public relations program, a methodological discussion of a particular technique for measuring program effects, or a data-based report of the impact of a program on specific variables of interest in a target public.

Treatment Coding Categories

The treatment approaches in the analyses and research presented by authors range from straightforward presentations of undocumented opinions and personal philosophy, to rigorous application of scientific methods to test theory-based hypotheses. We categorized the alternative treatments in five modes:

Philosophical or Theoretical Commentary. Articles present the personal knowledge, opinions, and theoretical propositions of the authors. Personal observations, philosophical discussions, and polemic presentations are typical styles used in articles put into this category.

Historical Analysis or Research. Analyses based on biographical recollections, chronologies of long-past events, and causal explanations inferred from data in archival records are characteristic of this treatment category. The simplest treatment might be the straightforward presentation of the log of events related to an important event or person. The most rigorous treatment conforms to generally-accepted scientific methodology, but observations come from historical records rather than the researcher's firsthand or mediated surveillance of the current situation.

Legal Analysis or Research.   Legal treatments of the substantive content involve two major approaches. The first style is the traditional legal advocacy based on normative assumptions and selected documentation. The second is the scientific marshalling of evidence to test propositions related to questions of legal precedent and process, legal reform, and impact of law in society and on public relations. Evidence in such studies may include court opinions, legislative documents, constitutions, regulations, and scholarly commentaries.

Case Study or Descriptive Research.   This treatment category includes reports based on relatively objective and systematic observations of phenomena. The articles describe events, behaviors, people, and systems and look for associations among their attributes. The typical research design in this category does not allow for causal explanations, but represents the first step toward such understanding. Articles in this category range from narrative reports of situations to the presentation of data gathered using scientific techniques.

Basic or Applied Analytical Research.   This treatment category includes research presentations in which the scientific method is used to test hypotheses deduced from theory. Using controlled, objective observation and measurement procedures, empirical evidence is gathered in an attempt to explain the relationships among phenomena. The result is a contribution to the systematic body of theory related to public relations. The purpose of the research effort may be either to improve the practice or to expand the knowledge base on which the profession is based.

The Pretests and Pilot Test

Pretesting indicated a reliability problem in coding the two journals' content. We found that often the manifest content of *Review* articles was not limited to only one of our content categories. Inter-coder agreement in the first pretest ranged from .40 to .70, with a mean of .55. Study of the articles on which we did not agree revealed the problem of multiple content. In our discussions and reviews of articles, however, we found that the detailed dissections of articles usually led to a consensus on the major thrust of the content. Subsequent pretests and the pilot test indicated that as we practiced assigning articles to categories, the impact of our varied backgrounds and levels of familiarity with public relations concepts and issues diminished with each trial.

In order to produce a final coding of the content we decided to use a two-step process. First, we did individual coding and then together analyzed articles on which our individual codings differed. The result of this process is a consensus inventory of the content of the *Review*.

While the same two-step process was used to resolve other differences in coding, the pilot test indicated relatively high levels of agreement on the treatment approaches used by the authors of *Review* articles. The six inter-coder reliability scores on the treatment categories ranged from .80 to .90, with a mean of .87. Our reliability scores for *Journal* content averaged .74. Because we found little variance in the treatment approaches used by authors in this publication, we decided to code only the content in the *Journal*.

The Census and Sample

The complete population of articles published in the *Review*, Volumes 1–8 (1975–1982), was analyzed, producing a census of this publication. Three "articles" were later dropped from the data because they were simply introductions to or overviews of articles to follow. The census included 134 *Review* articles.

Approximately 700 substantive articles—not counting regular columns, descriptions of upcoming PRSA conventions, and listings of newly accredited members—were published in the *Journal* during the concurrent period, 1975–1982 (Volumes 31–38). To select a systematic sample of approximately the same number of articles included in the *Review* census, we selected every fifth article after beginning the count in each volume on a randomly selected number within the interval. The resulting sample included 140 articles.

The Content

The results of the content analysis showed that *Journal* content reflects practitioners' day-to-day concerns with how to do their jobs: Two thirds of the articles dealt with the process of public relations. Two of the process categories included 42% of the sample–Action/Message Strategy and Techniques, and Media Usage and Techniques. Another process category—Management, Planning, and Programming—tied with Social Context as the next most frequent content in the *Journal*. (See Table 8.1.)

In spite of the concerns about measurement and evaluation often expressed in public relations circles, the *Journal* included relatively little substantive content dealing with research in either the formulation or evaluation of public relations programs. Only education received less coverage.

There was no apparent shift in emphasis over the 8 years studied. Overall, 23% of the articles related to the context of public relations, 12% to the profession itself, and 65% to the process. Two years, 1977 and 1980, deviated from the overall distribution, with 1977 articles devoted disproportionately to process and 1980 equally divided between context and process.

TABLE 8.1
Public Relations *Journal* Content

	1975	1976	1977	1978	1979	1980	1981	1982	Total	Percent of Total
1. Social context	2	2	2	4	1	5	1	4	21	15%
2. Organizational context		3	1		1	2	3	1	11	8
3. Professionalization	2	1		1	2		1		7	5
4. Education				2				1	3	2
5. Practitioners	1			1		2		2	7	5
6. Formative research, information input, and intelligence		1	1	1	1	1		2	7	5
7. Management, planning, and programming	4	2	4	1	4		2	4	21	15
8. Action/message strategy and techniques	3	5	6	4	4	2	2	3	29	21
9. Media usage and techniques	4	2	1	6	4	4	7	2	30	21
10. Program impact, effects, and evaluation research	1		1		2				4	3
Totals	17	16	16	20	19	16	17	19	140	100%

By contrast, *Review* content was almost equally distributed over the three major conceptual categories, with 30% of the articles related to the context of public relations, 36% to the profession, and 34% to the process. (See Table 8.2.) Four years stand out as departures from this pattern and more or less cancel each other out in the overall distribution. In 1976 and 1979, the emphasis was on the profession. More than half of 1977 articles dealt with the process. In 1978, more than half covered topics related to the context of public relations.

Within these major conceptual areas, the Social Context category (24% of the articles) and Professionalization (17%) stand out as the major topics in the *Review*. Articles are almost equally distributed over the remaining categories, with the smallest percentage in Program Impact, Effects, and Evaluation Research. (Table 8.3 presents the complete content x treatment matrix for the *Review* articles.)

The primary treatment approaches used by the authors of *Review* articles were Philosophical or Theoretical Commentary (35%) and Case Study or Descriptive Research (35%). Legal Analysis or Research was the least-used approach with only two percent of the articles in this treatment category. The remaining articles were equally divided between Historical Analysis or Research and Basic or Applied Analytical Research.

Year-by-year analysis revealed only 3 years in which there were major deviations from the overall pattern: Half of the 1978 articles were Historical treatments, two thirds of the 1979 articles were in the Philosophical or Theoretical Commentary category, and 12 of 23 1982 articles used the Case Study or Descriptive Research treatment.

Other than the many empty cells in the matrix, several patterns deserve attention. Social Context content took the form of Philosophical or Theoretical Commentary and Historical Analysis or Research. Media Usage and Techniques, as well as Program Impact, Effects, and Evaluation Research articles were done primarily as Case Study or Descriptive Research and Basic or Applied Analytical Research.

Comparisons of Content

Journal and *Review* content compared across the three major conceptual divisions indicates a statistically significant difference. (See Table 8.4.) The agenda portrayed by the *Journal* is much more heavily weighted on the process than is the agenda reflected by the *Review*. And whereas the *Journal* devotes relatively little of its content to analyses of the profession, the *Review* features this conceptual area as the dominant content.

Likewise, comparison of distributions across the 10 content categories yielded a statistically significant difference. The most striking differences occur in the comparisons of the Social Context and Professionalization categories, to which the *Review* devotes major attention. A similar disparity in the opposite direction is found in the differences in content emphases for Action/Message Strategy and

TABLE 8.2
Public Relations Review Content

	1975	1976	1977	1978	1979	1980	1981	1982	Total	Percent of Total
1. Social context	3	3	5	7		2	3	9	32	24%
2. Organizational context		2	1	1	1	1	2		8	6
3. Professionalization	1	5	2	2	6	1	5	1	23	17
4. Education	2	1	2			3		6	14	10
5. Practitioners	1	2		2	3	1	1	1	11	8
6. Formative research, information input, and intelligence	2		4	1		2		1	10	8
7. Management, planning, and programming	2	1	2		3	1	1	1	11	8
8. Action/message strategy and techniques		1	1	2		1		3	8	6
9. Media usage and techniques		3		1	2		3	1	10	8
10. Program impact, effects, and evaluation research	1		4			2			7	5
Totals	12	18	21	16	15	14	15	23	134	100%

Table 8.3
Public Relations Review Content by Treatment

	Philosophical or Theoretical Commentary	Historical Analysis or Research	Legal Analysis or Research	Case Study or Descriptive Research	Basic or Applied Analytical Research
1. Social context	16	8	1	6	1
2. Organization context	3			3	2
3. Professionalization	11	3		7	2
4. Education	4			10	
5. Practitioners		4		5	2
6. Formative research, information input, and intelligence	6			4	
7. Management, planning, and programming	6		1		4
8. Action/message strategy and techniques		2		4	2
9. Media usage and techniques	1	1	1	4	3
10. Program impact, effects, and evaluation research				4	3
Totals (N = 134)	47	18	3	47	19
Percent of Total	35%	14	2	35	14

Techniques, and Media Usage and Techniques. These two categories dominate *Journal* content but receive relatively little attention in the *Review.*

In summary, different agenda of concerns are reflected by the articles in the *Journal* and *Review* during the 8 years of concurrent publication. Whereas *Journal* articles are primarily concerned with the public relations process (65% of the articles), the *Review* devotes almost equal attention to public relations, context, profession, and process. Specifically, *Journal* content deals primarily with Action/Message Strategy and Techniques, and Media Usage and Techniques. The *Review*, by contrast, assigns an equally disproportionate amount of its content agenda to Social Context and Professionalization. And even though the *Review* was, at the time, the only scholarly journal in the field, the dominant treatments of content take the form of Philosophical or Theoretical Commentary and Descriptive Research or Case Study approaches.

Conclusions

We began with the concerns expressed regarding the content and quality of public relations research. Our objectives in the content analyses were to empirically determine and compare the manifest agenda of *Public Relations Journal* and *Public Relations Review*. We found major differences.

It was not the province of this study, however, to explain why these differences occur or to judge the relative merits of the two publications. We surmise that the *Journal* accurately reflects practitioners' primary concerns with day-to-day problems in implementing public relations programs. The *Journal* agenda also exposes the paucity of information about and authors who can discuss the uses of research in the formulation and evaluation of programs.

The latter observation probably explains equally well why the *Review* contains so little content on research. This scholarly publication's attention to the Social Context and Professionalization of public relations may indicate the authors' responsiveness to practitioners' concerns about their roles and status in society. We think that these content emphases mirror the historical concerns of an emerging profession searching for a collective identity and justification for the practice. The *Review* agenda portrays such a preoccupation with professional introspection.

We offer three qualified conclusions: First, the commentaries and research published in the *Review* are not responsive to the interests of practicing professionals in implementing programs. Second, both publications provide little to help

TABLE 8.4
Comparisons of *Journal* and *Review* Content

	Percent of Content			
	Journal		*Review*	
	(n = 140)		*(n = 134)*	
Social context	15*		24	
Organizational context	8		6	
Total Context		23**		30
Professionalization	5		17	
Education	2		10	
Practitioners	5		8	
Total Profession		12		36
Formative research, information input, and	5		8	
intelligence	15		8	
Management, planning, and programming	21		6	
Action/message strategy and techniques	21		8	
Media usage and techniques	3		5	
Program impact, effects, and evaluation research				
Total Process		65		34
		100%		100%

*$\chi^2 = 43.7$, $df = 9$, $p < .001$, two-tailed test, comparing distributions across 10 content categories.
**$\chi^2 = 28.9$, $df = 2$, $p < .001$, two-tailed test, comparing distributions across three conceptual categories.

students, teachers, practitioners, and managers understand and use research in public relations. And third, as Grunig (1978) observed about public relations research in general, the *Review* offers relatively little cross-situational, theory-building research that adds to the systematic body of knowledge on which the practice is based.

The qualification we must put on these conclusions is that they are conditioned to some unknown degree by how representative *Journal* and *Review* content is of professional and scholarly concerns. We picked these two publications, however, because we judged them to be the most accurate barometers of the field.

To the extent that the eight volumes of the *Review* and *Journal* reflect what is available from public relations scholars, however, this new journal will have to recruit the several young, research-oriented academics entering public relations education, and actively solicit manuscripts from other communication scholars whose research has relevance to public relations. Of course, there is at least one other alternative: Those of us in public relations research and education could turn our attention to theory-building research related to the process of public relations.

Before you conclude that we see ourselves above these concerns, we end by pleading a collective "mea culpa." We would code this article as "Descriptive Research" about "Professionalization."

REFERENCES

Ehling, W. P. (1975). PR administration, management science and purposive systems. *Public Relations Review, 1,* 15–42.

Grunig, J. E. (1978, August). *The status of public relations research.* Paper presented to the Public Relations Division, Association for Education in Journalism Annual Convention, Seattle.

Grunig, J. E. (1979). Special section: The two worlds of PR research. *Public Relations Review, 5,* 11–14.

Grunig, J. E., & Hickson, R. H. (1976). An evaluation of academic research in public relations. *Public Relations Review, 2,* 31–43.

Lindenmann, W. K. (1979). The missing link in public relations research. *Public Relations Review, 5,* 26–36.

McElreath, M. P. (1980). *Priority research questions in public relations for the 1980s.* New York: Foundation for Public Relations Research and Education.

Northart, L. J. (1981). "Editor's Notebook: Some thoughts for Year-End," *Public Relations Journal, 37*(12), 6–7, 32.

Tirone, J. F. (1979). Education, theory, and research in public relations. *Public Relations Review, 5,* 15–25.

Chapter 9

Police in America: A Study of Changing Institutional Roles as Viewed by Constituents

Hugh M. Culbertson
Hochang Shin
Ohio University

In part, today's incredible world is incredible because society's needs are changing rapidly. Institutions must change to meet these needs without losing credibility.

Practitioners need to play leadership roles in helping clients contribute and adjust to such changes. In line with recent research, as well as theorizing, by Grunig and Hunt (1984), Broom and Dozier (1986), and others, this involves gauging and interpreting:

1. Societal changes.
2. Possible and actual reactions of client organizations to these shifts.
3. Public opinion on the appropriateness and importance of the changes.
4. The extent to which public opinion should govern client policies and priorities.

The study reviewed in this chapter looked at public priorities and views relating to a small-town police department in Athens, Ohio. Specifically, the focus was on police as educator and service provider—in contrast to the more traditional roles of detective and "crook catcher."

LITERATURE REVIEW AND HYPOTHESES

Associationist attitude theory is used to predict and understand public priorities. Before reviewing this theory and stating research hypotheses, we look briefly at police functions in America today in order to understand the subordinate status of the service role within the police officer's world view. That status, in turn, serves as a basis for predictions about belief salience, suggesting in part that service-and-education-related beliefs about police gain special salience when linked to problems of crime, the long-accepted focus of police work.

Historically, and even at present, people who define police roles have emphasized crime detection and apprehension as core, high-status activities. Training usually focuses on law enforcement as opposed to peace-keeping and service efforts. Also, awards and recognition in the field go largely for brave, clever apprehending of criminal suspects.

Movies and television have no doubt led the public to accept such a view. Westerns and detective stories have often glorified fearless sheriffs, marshals, and cops.

In a 1982 nationwide survey, 57% of those answering said that the police should respond only to calls that, according to the caller, involve an actual or suspected crime (Flanagan, 1985). In a related vein, over three fourths of those covered in 1974 and 1981 surveys felt that the courts and police were too lenient in dealing with criminals (Erskine, 1974, 1982). Such a view seems to downgrade the role of a cop as a community servant—taking heart-attack victims to the hospital, rescuing cats from window ledges, and so on.

Despite all of this, research indicates that American police men and women spend about 80 to 90 percent of their time maintaining order, not enforcing the law (Bard, 1973). In short, they engage mostly in what they and the public regard as secondary service activities. Such efforts apparently have assumed added importance in police work for at least two reasons.

First, there's been growing realization that, to do its job, a law-enforcement agency must be respected and seen as legitimate by diverse racial, ethnic, and socioeconomic groups. Such acceptance, in turn, requires ongoing two-way communication between policemen and their constituencies. Citizens must feel that cops are present to serve them—not simply to write parking tickets and catch an occasional heavy (Cain, 1973).

Second, indications are that public service builds public support and cooperation partly because it permits cops to relate to citizens in non-punitive, helpful ways (Pugh, 1986). In a recent national survey, those who supported police most strongly tended to favor a broad, service-oriented definition of police activity (Flanagan, 1985).

However, police personnel playing such a role must overcome a number of barriers:

1. Widespread operation in police cars, rather than on foot as in days gone by. This switch, carried out largely for efficiency, has reduced personal contact with ordinary citizens. These folks, in turn, tend at times to see police as remote and non-responsive (Cain, 1973).

2. Professionalization, which supposedly leads police to behave in line with

bureaucratic rules and abstract calculations. That, in turn, can contribute to beliefs that cops are not attentive to unique local needs (Fink & Sealy, 1974).

3. Lack of social-science and humanities training helpful in human relations. As recently as 1968, only 10 percent of the nation's police personnel had college degrees (Reichley, 1968). There has been some improvement here. Forty-six percent of all cops reportedly had completed at least some college training by 1974, compared with just 20 percent 14 years earlier (U.S. News and World Report, 1978). However, numerous observers urge more training (Pugh, 1986).

4. Perspectives that differ from those of other "human service providers" to whom police must often refer troubled people. For instance, Walthier, McCune, and Trojanowicz (1973) asserted that police are trained to value bureaucratic activities and formal standards along with competitiveness and assertiveness. Social workers, on the other hand, tend to disdain these things. Such divergence may make cooperation between the two groups difficult and sometimes ineffective.

5. Low status and few resources for work in police–community relations (PCR). Too often, PCR personnel within police departments have little training for or clear definition of their jobs. Further, they tend to view such assignments as demotions. As a result, police public relations is sometimes said to emphasize hype and surface appearance rather than real two-way communication (Trojanowicz, 1973).

6. Lack of status and respect for police in general. Cops tend to come from lower socioeconomic strata. Yet they are seen by citizens with whom they deal most often—presumably also from lower strata—as representing powerful elites. In a real sense, then, they are caught in the middle with little or no support base (Whittington, 1971).

Despite these and other constraints, police departments have made substantial strides in community relations.

Neighborhood Watch programs have provided a vehicle for police and citizens to work together in crime prevention. Such efforts appear to have succeeded in cities and towns from Detroit (Viviano, 1981) to New York (Newsweek, 1985). Also, the New York Police Department has involved nearly 200,000 civilians in projects ranging from senior escort services to precinct youth councils (Ebony, 1985).

In line with such developments, substantial numbers of Americans have realized that society as a whole bears some responsibility for crime. Broken homes, unemployment, and other social problems are thought to pave the way for lawbreaking (Erskine, 1974). Such a view should create a favorable climate for police to play a peacekeeping role.

Prior research has indicated rather broad, if not intense, acceptance of police as human-service providers. However, few studies appear to have dealt explicitly with cops' educational activities and public reactions to them. This investigation attempts to begin filling that gap.

The inquiry utilized associationist attitude theory, developed in the 1960s by Rosenberg (1960) and Rokeach and Rothman (1965), and more recently by Anderson (1978), Fishbein and Ajzen (1981), and Woelfel, Cody, Gillham, and Holmes (1980). The basic notion here is that an attitude's stability, salience, and perhaps behavioral implications depend in part on beliefs that link the attitude to other entities in one's environment. Study of such linkage requires analysis of:

1. *Linked objects* with which a person associates the attitude object, giving special attention to the salience and evaluation of those objects. (For example, a favorable evaluation of police may not be very change-resistant—or lead to much supportive behavior—if one links police to apprehending murderers and nothing else. However, additional linkages to, say, theft prevention and drug avoidance may add to both loyalty and active support.)

2. *Linkage beliefs* associating attitude object with linked objects. In a recent study, Culbertson and Stempel (1985) proposed that linkage beliefs could be of at least three types: (a) *frequency of association* between attitude and linked objects. If frequency has been high, the two objects may seem likely to go together in the future; (b) *similarity* of the two objects, a notion stressed by pioneer cognitive psychologist Fritz Heider (1958); and (c) *part–whole relations* in which either attitude or linked object is seen as part of the other. Also, both objects may share a given component or part.

Culbertson and Stempel (1985) found evidence that, in assessment of osteopathic medicine, certain experiences involving contact with that branch of health care varied as predicted with *similarity* and *frequency-of-association* linkage beliefs. Our study focuses largely on *part–whole* concepts and their implications.

Linkage theory incorporates the notion, made explicit by Grunig (1976) and Dervin (1983), that attitudes and their behavioral implications hinge on beliefs that change from one situation to another. Linkages, it's suggested, are among the elements that change.

Our study examines *part–whole* linkage beliefs as anchors for attitudes about police education and service activities. Specifically, it hypothesizes that public acceptance of a given activity will be high where that activity overlaps with a specific area of concern about crime that has recently been publicized widely in the area—and/or a broad topic (crime in general) that has long been defined as central to police operation.

The study dealt with three sets of *linked objects:*

Set 1. Three crime problems that have gained extensive publicity recently. First were acts of kidnapping and violence directed against children. A television movie about the death of a boy named Adam, first shown in the mid-1980s, presumably helped move this topic onto the public agenda. Missing-children signs had since shown up on gas-station walls and cereal boxes, and in many other places. Second was drug and substance abuse, object of constant news coverage in the mid-1980s, much of it about athletes and other prominent people. The third problem was sexual abuse, including rape and sexual harassment in the work place. This topic had gotten much attention nationally and even more locally over a period of several years. Athens had witnessed several highly publicized rape trials— along with widespread discussion of "date rape" on campus—during several months prior to the survey.

Set 2. The general concept of crime detection and apprehension of criminals. As noted earlier, American police and citizens have long regarded this area as the core responsibility of police. A 1982 national survey showed that about 57 percent of Americans would look with favor—at least, in the abstract—on restricting police response almost entirely to this realm (Flanagan, 1985).

Set 3. General service to the public. Despite the finding just noted, the American people do appear to view this realm with some favor. For example, in the same survey, 41 percent of those who said they'd limit police response to crime calls still felt that cops should help heart attack victims. And 69 percent felt that cops should break up a noisy family argument late at night (Flanagan, 1985).

Furthermore, a majority in other national surveys have agreed that arrest and punishment alone would not eliminate crime (Erskine, 1974). Thus, although it is apparently less salient and widely approved than law enforcement, service is generally seen as a needed, accepted police activity.

In this study, citizens assessed police education and service activities of four types. Hypothesis 1 held that importance ratings fall in a rank ordering from type 1 (highest) through type 4 (lowest), depending on perceived association in the public mind with the three linked objects noted previously. The types are as follows:

Type 1. *Activities relating to specific, widely publicized crimes* (drug, child, and sexual abuse). Work on educating citizens and helping them protect themselves in these areas deals with elements of (i.e., overlaps psychologically with) crime detection/apprehension, as well as with specific crimes. As a result, importance ratings should be high.

Type 2. *Crime prevention* activities such as night-time patrols in town, Neighborhood Watch, checking vacant lots, and consultation with property owners on crimeproofing. Such efforts link clearly with crime in general (linked object 2), but not with specific, widely publicized crimes. Thus importance ratings should be fairly high, but below those for type 1.

Type 3. *Service to the community not tied clearly to crime.* Activities here included bicycle safety lectures for kids, escorts for funeral and other processions, traffic control for major events, and unlocking car doors. Such efforts overlap clearly with the community service role shown by past research to be quite widely approved, but with only modest priority, throughout the country. Thus, impor-tance ratings here should be only moderate.

Type 4. *General communication activity.* Included here were speaking to service clubs and other groups, and setting up a booth at an annual fall craft festival. These efforts were expected to receive low priority because they did not link up clearly with any aspect of the police role described in the literature as receiving high priority.

In another area, we hypothesized that linkage to self would help predict and explain priorities. Such linkage has played an important role in recent public relations theorizing, especially in James Grunig's concept of involvement (Grunig & Hunt, 1984). The underlying notion is that a citizen will attach high priority to police activities that relate closely to his or her role in life—and to his or her feelings of need and personal vulnerability.

Hypothesis 2 suggests that women attach more importance than men to child-related police activities. This stems from the assumption that women tend more than men to define child-rearing as central to their roles. The hypothesis relates to 6 police activities studied—drug education in elementary, middle, and high schools, as well as for parents; bicycle safety lectures in elementary schools; and fingerprint-ing children annually during crime prevention week.

Hypothesis 3 holds that women also exceed men in importance attached to sexual assault programs, as well as regarding rape and assault as the most serious crime problems in Athens. Women, normally the victims in such cases, should have a deep concern with these areas.

Hypothesis 4 asserts that retirees should attach higher importance than other

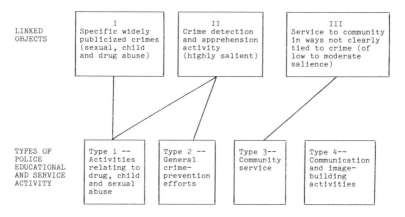

FIG. 9.1.   Types of police activity rank ordered by association with linked objects of varied salience. (Lines denote presumed overlap, at a psychological level, between particular types of police activity and linked objects.)

groups to programs relating to home theft and vandalism. Activities here include consultation on theft reduction and routine checks of vacant property. Retirees should be especially apt to see theft and vandalism as serious crime problems. This prediction stems from the assumption that these folks feel vulnerable because they travel a lot, leaving their property unattended, or are physically infirm.

Exploratory data analyses will also be examined for other results consistent with the expectation that people attach highest priorities to those areas which they are apt to link clearly to themselves and their own life settings.

METHODS

Questionnaire Construction

The Athens police chief and colleagues developed a list of programs carried out by the city's police department. In several meetings with the chief, the researchers and interviewers became familiar with the needs addressed by and philosophy behind these programs.

Questionnaire items were developed to gauge public reaction in two areas:

1. *Overall Importance.*   In all, 24 Athens Police Department activities and programs were described with enough detail that even uninformed citizens would have an idea of objectives and types of effort involved. Respondents then indicated whether they felt that a given program or activity was very important, fairly important, or not important.

2. *Level of Department Activity.*   Here, seven types of activities and programs were described. Interviewers asked for assessments of whether the department was doing about the right amount in each area, should do more, or should do less.

In addition, questions dealt with age and occupation (defined in the respondent's own words and placed in several categories as noted in the list that appears in the sampling section). Also, respondents were asked what they felt was the most serious crime problem in Athens. Responses were quite varied, but most fell into nine categories defined by the researchers after data were collected.

An initial questionnaire required about 15 minutes to complete—long enough to discourage many prospective respondents. After preliminary pre-testing, items were pruned and combined so that administration required only about 5 minutes.

Interviewing

Phone interviews were completed by 13 members of the Ohio University chapter of the Public Relations Student Society of America (PRSSA). Most were juniors and seniors who had completed at least one course in social science research methods. All crew members practiced interviewing on each other, as well as on friends and roommates. And all underwent a training session of more than 1 hour just prior to interviewing.

Most calling was done between 6:30 and 10:00 p.m., Monday through Thursday, when people of all ages and both sexes tended to be at home. About 80% of the data were collected during four evenings from phones in the School of Journalism Building at Ohio University. The senior investigator, who was also PRSSA faculty advisor, supervised interviewers closely and continuously. Interviewing was done in late February 1987.

Interviewers took careful notes on cues that might call the validity of some responses into question. Based on this information, the advisor and callers decided what data should be retained for analysis. A few doubtful answers and one entire questionnaire with incongruous responses were discarded.

Sampling

Random digit dialing was used to cover households with unlisted numbers. Three established exchanges in the city were covered. In all, 214 interviews were completed.

The Athens telephone directory was scoured to identify fourth and fifth digits actually used for residential phones within each exchange. It was found, for example, that all residential numbers with the 592 exchange had fourth and fifth digits spread quite evenly within the range of 11 to 66. All numbers within that range (i.e., 11, 12, 13, etc. up to 66) were listed in order. Then a table of random numbers was used to select the sixth and seventh digits of each number called.

About one third of the initial calls activated non-working-number recordings and were removed from the sample. Where no answer or recording was obtained, interviewers tried again at least 24 hours later. If that attempt came up dry, a third try was made a day later. Numbers not reached within that time were regarded as "non-responses."

About 62% of all attempted interviews were completed. This response rate is seen as adequate. It was computed by dividing the number of interviews completed by attempts. (Attempts equaled those completed plus refusals and non-responses that did not elicit non-working-number recordings[1].)

Twenty-two percent of all calls that reached working residential numbers did produce refusals. This figure is fairly high as surveys go. It suggests the data may not reflect fully the thinking of a small "anti-police" minority in the area. However,

---

[1]Obviously some non-answered calls which did not activate recordings may have gone to business phones. Previous experience showed that, in Athens, about 30% of all numbers are assigned to businesses (which, of course, were not within the population studied). Thus in computing a response rate, the number of non-refusal, non-answers was multiplied by .70.

interviewers estimated that about half of all refusals stemmed primarily from lack of time for an interview—not from anti-police feelings. Thus, it appeared that overall non-response bias was fairly minor.

About 10 percent of all persons called did indicate that they lived outside the city. In such a case, the interviewer asked if the respondent shopped and recreated regularly—and had children who attended school—in Athens. Where a *yes* answer was given, the interview was completed, because the respondent appeared to be a "customer" of the Athens Police Department in a meaningful sense. In about half of such instances, a *no* response led to termination of the interview and elimination of that person from the intended sample.

The sample was compared with the overall population of Athens, as described in the 1980 U.S. Census, to give a rough indication of representativeness. Although differences did exist, they were substantial in only a few cases. Fortunately, the data suggested that sample subgroups seldom differed markedly with regard to priorities and perceptions studied. Some discrepancies and comparisons do warrant comment:

1. The median age of 29 years in the sample, compared with 21.7 years for the population, really doesn't represent an unintended bias. We arbitrarily eliminated those who had not graduated from high school or reached the age of 18, because people below that age cannot vote and may have little to go on in responding.

2. A fairly modest under-representation of university students also squared with the survey plan. A new telephone exchange just coming on line for Ohio University dormitories was excluded. Dorm residents were thought to have little interest or involvement in city government and its priorities. The exchanges that were covered presumably insured that off-campus students were well represented. In fact, students made up 36% of the sample, compared with 43% of the city's population.

3. Women made up 56% of the sample but only 48% of the 1980 population. Past experience suggests that, in this area, women are more apt than men to answer phones. Early interviewing leaned heavily toward females. After that, interviewers were instructed to alternate between men and women where possible.

4. University personnel and overall managerial-professional people were both over-represented, making up 32% of the sample but only 18% of the population. These groups may have high interest in surveys so they seldom refuse to answer. However, they differed little from the rest of the sample in overall response patterns.

5. White-collar workers made up 11% of both the population and the sample. Also, unemployed persons constituted 5% of the sample, compared with 6% of the population. Both of these subgroups gained appropriate representation.

Analysis

Initially, factor analyses were run separately on importance and level-of-activity items. Principal axis solutions were followed by varimax rotation. Six factors based on the importance items, along with three on activity, were produced and had eigenvalues greater than 1. Variance accounted for amounted to 61% of that among importance items and 64% with activity.

In testing hypothesis 1, an item was used to measure a given variable only if it met two conditions. First, the item had to have a primary loading, after rotation, on the factor tapped by that variable of a least .58, and no other loadings above .40. Second, the item had to cluster conceptually with other items tapping the factor. In light of these constraints, two one-item indexes were used.

Repeated-measures multiple analysis of variance (MANOVA) was performed to test hypothesis 1. Also, Guttman's scalogram analysis tested whether importance ratings reflected a single underlying dimension of police acceptance.

Chi-square and discriminant-function analyses were also run to explore hypothesis 2 through 4 and to look for patterns that were consistent with the idea that people prioritize police activities with regard to their own personal lives.

RESULTS

Hypothesis 1 specified that police-department activities on drug, sexual, and child abuse (type 1) would receive the highest importance ratings, followed in order by general crime prevention (type 2), community service (type 3), and communication and image-building (type 4). The hypothesis is confirmed in Table 9.1. In fact, only one index (traffic control) had a mean that was equal to or greater than any mean with a lower-numbered type.

The repeated-measures multiple analysis of variance (MANOVA) procedure within the Statistical Package for the Social Sciences was used to compare overall means for adjacent types within the rank-ordering. Differences were statistically significant and in the predicted direction in each case. Specifically, type 1 exceeded type 2 ($F = 22.38$; $df = 1$, 191; $p < .001$). Type 2 exceeded type 3 ($F = 30.75$; $df = 1$, 191; $p < .001$). And type 3 outdid type 4 ($F = 13.52$; $df = 1$, 191; $p < .001$).

In a further step, Guttman's scalogram analysis was run on means averaged across specific indexes within each given type. Ten sets of cutting points were tried, and the most appropriate set from a conceptual standpoint yielded a coefficient of reproducibility of .90, as well as a coefficient of scalability of .68. Nie, Hull, Jenkins, Steinbrenner, and Bent (1975) indicate that a defensible Guttman scale is achieved when these statistics reach .90 and .60, respectively.

This suggests that a single underlying dimension orders assessment of all four

TABLE 9.1
Mean Importance Ratings for Four Types of Police Activity

Activity	Mean	Standard Deviation
Type 1—Education relating to drug, child, and sexual abuse		
Sexual assault (1 item dealing with department's sexual assault program run with two social-service agencies)	2.73	0.443
Drug education (4 items focusing on high, middle, and elementary school children as well as parents)	2.62	0.422
Child safety (2 items, one on teaching children to react when approached by strangers and one on an annual project to obtain children's fingerprints)	2.61	0.486
Type 2—General crime prevention		
Theft prevention (3 items on a neighborhood watch program, consultation to crime-proof homes and businesses, and routine checks of vacant homes and businesses)	2.35	0.453
Business-section patrols (2 items dealing with regular patrols in general, and in the evening, for the city's business district)	2.33	0.525
Type 3—Community service		
Traffic control (2 items on traffic control at Ohio University events and at several local athletic contests)	2.35	0.555
Unlocking (1 item on unlocking car doors for motorists)	2.16	0.797
Transportation (2 items on escorting funeral processions and giving bicycle-safety lectures in elementary schools)	1.96	0.562
Type 4—Communication and image building		
Public relations (2 items on operating a booth at a local craft festival and speaking at local events)	1.85	0.522

Note: All items involved 3 choices, with a value of 3 assigned to "very important," 2 to "fairly important," and 1 to "not important." Means given are averaged means for all items within a given index.

types of educational and service activity quite well. Most people who emphasized type 4 activities (communication and image building) appeared to be "diehard fans" who gave high priority to varied police efforts in service and education. A second group downgraded type 4 but placed above-average emphasis on the other types. A third group gave high importance only to types 1 and 2 (activities relating to specific crimes and to crime in general, respectively). A fourth batch of respondents emphasized only type 1. And a fifth subset, called "diehard foes," turned thumbs down on most or all educational and service activities by local cops.

Table 9.2 describes all five types of respondents and reports on cross-tabulations of type against sex and age. Cases not fitting the scale were excluded here from analyses. Specific findings were as follows:

1. Women tended more often than men to qualify as across-the-board fans of

TABLE 9.2

Percentages of Men and Women, as Well as Persons of Different Ages,
Who Fall within Five Scalogram Types Based on Acceptance of Police Activities

Type	Sex*		Age**			
	Men	Women	18–22	23–29	30–42	43–88
A—Give low ratings on all four types of activity	19.7	7.9	8.5	13.9	17.9	9.7
B—Give high ratings on specific, widely publicized crime programs, low ratings on all other activities	32.8	27.0	36.2	44.4	20.5	12.9
C—Give high ratings on specific crimes, general crime prevention, low ratings on other activities	21.3	23.6	21.3	16.7	33.3	19.4
D—Give high ratings on specific and general crime activities, community service, low on other activities	16.4	25.8	19.1	19.4	25.6	25.8
E—Give high ratings on all four types of police activity, including communication and image building	9.8	15.7	14.9	5.6	2.6	32.3
	100%	100%	100%	100%	99.9%	100.1%
	(n = 61)	(n = 89)	(n = 47)	(n = 36)	(n = 39)	(n = 31)

Note: Ratings that provided basis for scalogram analysis were on a 3-point scale with 3 = very important, 2 = fairly important, and 1 = not important. Cutting points in scaling were per-item scores of 2.50 on communication and image building, 2.40 on community service, 2.40 on general crime prevention, and 2.42 with regard to education on specific, widely publicized crimes.

*Chi-square = 5.17, 2 df, p = .075. Types A and B were combined, as were types D and E, to provide adequate cell expected values.

**Chi-square = 14.19, 6 df, p = .03. Types A and B were combined, as were types D and E, to provide adequate cell expected values.

police educational and service activity by a nearly significant amount. In all, 42% of the women, but only 26% of the men, fit into types D and E, which favored all crime prevention and community service activities. On the other hand, 53% of all men, but only about one third (35%) of the women, fell in the rather skeptical types A and B.

2. In general, older respondents favored police activities more than did younger ones by a significant margin. Specifically, young adults (age 29 and under) tended more often than their elders to fit into type B, which gave above-average support only to programs against specific, widely publicized crimes. Also, one third of those between 30 and 42 years old fit within type C, which supported crime prevention but nothing else. And a surprising 58% of older adults between 43 and 88 years of age responded in accordance with types D and E, reflecting support for most types of police activity.

Further research is needed to determine why women and older people tend to be strong supporters of police activity in the educational and service realms. Perhaps these segments of the population feel vulnerable to crime. It could be that political conservatism plays a role. Also, women are sometimes said to favor nurturance and negotiation, rather than force and arrests, in solving human problems.

Hypothesis 2 specified that women attach greater importance than men to police activities that relate to children and their safety. Table 9.3 provides clear overall support here. On each of the six items relating to drug education, bicycle safety, and child fingerprinting, women tended more often than men to give "very important" ratings. Differences proved significant at 3% or lower levels of confidence in all cases but bicycle safety, where $p = .07$. Also, partial correlations in the right-hand column of Table 9.3 indicate that these relationships changed very little when age was controlled.

Table 9.4 reports the results of a discriminant function analysis supporting hypothesis 2. This procedure defined a single underlying variable or discriminant function that correlated significantly and positively with importance attached to five of the six child-rearing activities (with bicycle safety lectures narrowly missing significance). In the table, each standardized coefficient is analogous to a standardized beta in multiple regression, reflecting level of association between the function and a given activity variable with the other activities controlled.

As expected, females scored higher than males on this variable. It appears, then, that a single children-oriented factor does have special relevance to women as noted in hypothesis 2.

Hypothesis 3 asserted that women exceed men in importance attached to sexual assault programs, as well as in regarding rape and assault as the most serious crimes in Athens. The data provided no support here. Specifically:

1. Just under three fourths of those in both sexes (74% of men and a like proportion of women) saw the department's sexual assault program as very important.

TABLE 9.3
Percentages of Men and Women Who Rated Selected Department Activities
Relating to Children as Very Important

Activity	Men's Ratings	Women's Ratings	Probability**	Point Biserial Correlation with Sex***
Drug-education programs held annually in elementary schools	61%	80%	.01	.22(.21)
Drug-education programs held annually in middle school at teacher's request	59%	77%	.02	.22(.22)
High school drug-education programs stressing the impact of drug-related arrests, especially on careers*	64%	81%	.02	.21(.21)
Lectures and literature alerting parents and adults to signs of drug use among kids, teens*	46%	67%	.01	.27(.25)
Bicycle safety lectures given annually in elementary schools	26%	36%	.07	.12(.10)
Child fingerprinting done annually in schools and during crime prevention week in Athens Mall	47%	66%	.03	.19(.22)

Note: Men responding to each item ranged from 91 to 92, women from 117 to 119. These figures were used as bases in computing the above percentages.

*For these items, "not important" and "fairly important" categories were combined to give adequate cell expected values in chi-square computation. In such cases, chi-squares with 1 df were computed. With the other four items, these categories were kept separate, yielding computations with 2 df.

**Probabilities based on chi-square computations.

***In each cell of this column, the first number is the point-biserial correlation between sex and importance attached to a given police activity. The number in parentheses is a partial r_{pb} with age controlled.

2. Almost identical percentages of men (12%) and women (16%) regarded rape and sexual assault as the most serious crime problem in Athens. This difference did not approach significance.

Apparently, then, both men and women had great concern about rape and steps to prevent it. Obviously many, if not most, men are close to women who stand as potential rape victims.

Hypothesis 4 asserted that retirees would tend more than others to regard theft and vandalism as Athens' most serious crimes—and that they should attach relatively high importance to crime prevention efforts. Table 9.5 gives partial support here, although the small number of retirees in the sample made significance difficult to achieve. Specifically:

TABLE 9.4

Standardized Coefficients and Function-Variable Correlations in Discriminant
Analysis of Police Priorities Expressed by Men and Women*

Activity**	Standardized Coefficient	Correlation Between Function and Activity Variable
Lectures and literature alerting parents and adults to signs of drug use among kids, teens	.50	.72
Child fingerprinting done annually in schools and during crime prevention week in Athens Mall	.43	.51
Drug-education programs held annually in middle schools at teacher's request	.24	.57
Drug-education programs held annually in elementary schools	.21	.55
High-school drug-education programs stressing the impact of drug-related arrests, especially on careers	.20	.57
Bicycle safety lectures given annually in elementary schools***	.16	.34

*Mean scores on the standardized discriminant function were $-.423$ for males, .326 for females. This difference was significant with chi-square $= 23.76$, $df = 6$, $p < .001$.

**Activities ordered by the stepwise selection method.

***Males and females differed on this item at $p = .08$, two-tailed test. All other items had differences significant at $p < .01$.

TABLE 9.5

Percentages of Retirees and Others Who Rate Theft or Vandalism as Most Serious
Crime, and Who Rate Theft-Prevention Activities as Very Important

Rating	Retiree Ratings	Others' Ratings	Probability of Difference Occurring by Chance
Theft or vandalism as city's most serious crime problem	65%(n = 17)	42%(n = 180)	.12
Routine checks of vacant homes and businesses when residents are away rated as very important	67%(n = 21)	38%(n = 190)	.02
Visits and consultations by police to help reduce theft from homes and businesses through such techniques as better lighting and moving displays as very important	55%(n = 20)	31%(n = 189)	.07

Note: Numbers in parentheses are bases on which percentages were computed. In importance ratings reported in second and third rows, "fairly important" and "not important" categories were combined to achieve adequate expected values for chi-square computation.

1. Almost two thirds of all retirees, but only 42% of other respondents, regarded theft or vandalism as the city's most serious crime problem. This difference, althouh substantial in magnitude, did not reach statistical significance.

2. Just two thirds of all retirees, but only 38% of others, gave "very important" ratings to routine checks of vacant homes and businesses. This relationship was significant at $p = .02$.

3. Fifty-five percent of the retirees, but only 31% of their younger compatriots, attached high importance to visits and consultations with police to "crimeproof" homes and business. The difference narrowly missed significance ($p = .07$).

Analysis of scalogram data also supported hypothesis 4. In a cross-tabulation, retirees, unemployed people, and housewives were combined into a single occupational category. A very large 57% of all such respondents who conformed to scalogram types fell in types D and E, qualifying them as strong "fans" of police education and service activity. That compared with only 30% among those in other job categories. At the other extreme, only 17% of the "non-employed" persons, compared with 48% of others, fit in the "skeptical" types A and B (chi-square = 10.71, 2 df, $p < .01$). Obviously, non-employed persons felt special need for police educational and service activities.

In a search of further evidence relating to "self-centeredness" in assigning police priorities, additional discriminant analyses were carried out. Police importance and activity factor scores were entered computationally as discriminating variables to ascertain how they might predict placement of respondents into job, sex, and age categories. A number of exploratory findings supported the self-centeredness thesis:

1. Women tended more often than men to see a need for residential patrols in daytime, when housewives are especially likely to be at home, as well as at night. Furthermore, women's previously noted emphasis on drug education and child safety appeared to translate into a more frequent call than men gave for additional drug-related activity by the police department.

2. Young adults, age 30–42, tended more than others to place high priority on child-safety activities (training on how to deal with strangers as well as fingerprinting of children). Obviously, these people tend to be parents or look ahead to parenting. On the other hand, older people, ages 43 through 88, tended more than any other group to downgrade the importance of child-safety efforts.

3. Older folks, on the other hand, emphasized traffic control at events such as parades (which they undoubtedly often attend). Further, these people gave high priority to residential patrols. (As noted earlier, retirees tended to stress theft and vandalism protection, probably because they felt vulnerable to these crimes.)

4. Those who regarded vandalism as the town's most serious crime problem tended more often than most others to call for additional activity in theft prevention and downtown patrols.

5. However, those who felt that violent crimes (theft, burglary, rape, and murder) were especially threatening downgraded theft prevention while calling for additional residential patrols. Apparently, these folks felt a need for police as protective big brother or sister near their homes—even in daytime.

Taken as a whole, these data suggest that folks take a rather personal view of police activity. That is, they emphasize the meeting of their own needs and the prevention of problems to which they, as individuals, feel quite vulnerable.

SUMMARY AND CONCLUSIONS

American police departments continue to solve crimes and bring criminals to justice. However, cops have gradually reached the point where they spend about 80% of their time on crime prevention, education, helping the ill, and other community services.

This study looked at public reaction to changing police roles from the viewpoint of associationist attitude theory. A general-population sample in Athens, Ohio rated the importance of education and service activities offered by that town's police department.

Factor analysis of ratings on 24 police activities helped identify four general activity types. Citizens attached high priority to efforts linked directly to crime— shown in previous research to be the primary police concern as viewed by Americans. Priorities were especially high where education and service addressed widely publicized crime problems. At the other extreme, little importance was attached to police–community relations and image-building. Moderate, but slightly higher, emphasis went to general community service (traffic control, unlocking car doors, bicycle safety lectures, etc.).

Guttman's scalogram analysis revealed that a single underlying dimension ordered priorities quite effectively. Thus, the few people who stressed police "image building" also emphasized all other types of activity studied. Others bought into crime prevention but not community service or image-building. Still others gave high rating to prevention of widely publicized crimes but no other education or service activities. And so on.

Women and older folks were often genuine "fans," stressing most or all activities studied.

In another area, it was hypothesized—and generally found—that sample subgroups placed highest emphasis on police activities that seemed especially relevant to them and their roles. For example, women stressed child-related activities. Also, retirees tended more than others to endorse activities addressing threats of theft and vandalism—areas in which the elderly no doubt feel quite vulnerable. Surprisingly, however, men and women were equally concerned with the police department's sexual-assault program.

Overall, respondents attached high importance to police education and service activity. Almost half of all ratings were very important, 37% fairly important, and just 15% not important. However, some soft spots did show up in the data. Results tentatively suggest that police administrators might:

1. Work to let the public know that police–community relations takes effort— and that this pays off in crime prevention and detection. Low ratings assigned to community activity may stem in part from a failure by most people to link this area to the cop's main mission of dealing with crime. Such a linkage surely can be shown, but this apparently hasn't happened in Athens.

2. Consider the possibility—implied by these data—that police public relations needs to be a step-by-step process. Diehard foes of the police department might first be convinced that crime-prevention efforts are important. Only those sold on that area, in turn, seem open to calls for general community service. And only the service-oriented appear to be receptive to appeals for communication activity. Such a sequence is only suggested here—data collected at several points in time would be needed for confirmation. However, if established, this pattern could say a lot about program planning. In short, police departments may need to talk about different things with different audiences and at different points in time.

3. Take a fresh look at demographics in defining the audience. Women and the elderly, in particular, appeared to be strong fans of police service activity. These groups apparently had an inclination to accept—and perhaps take part in—such efforts.

4. Consider carefully the fears and crime-related concerns of businessmen, students, and others within the community. The data at least hint that a given police activity will gain added support if people relate it clearly to their own personal security and well-being as individuals.

5. Make a special effort to inform people as to just what are the most frequent and destructive crimes in a community. Residents of Athens varied greatly as to perceptions in this area. And the data suggest that, once a given type of crime is shown to be a serious problem, people will endorse police activity linked to prevention of that type.

In conclusion, this study has obvious limitations. It deals with citizen priorities in just one small town—and at one time. It assumes certain levels of salience accorded to linked objects, and certain strengths of linkage beliefs, based mainly on prior research at the national level. Ideally, such cognitions should be measured directly within a given data set used to test predictions. Also, it would be wise to assess perceived *quality* of police performance along with *importance* of broad types of activity. There is no doubt that quality and importance interact to affect public acceptance of programs in ways not tested here.

However, the project plowed important ground by studying public reaction to a client institution's changing roles. Such change has often been ignored in "snap shot" studies of an organization's popularity or acceptance at one point in time.

Data here support a thesis that is popular with historians. Society is changing rapidly, and institutions must play new roles to meet changing needs. Apparently, citizens of at least one small town accept such change—but only insofar as they link it to an institution's heritage and traditional roles. The politician or bureaucrat who innovates without regard for the past is apt to be seen as incredible, all right— but *low* in importance. And public officials seen as doing rather trivial things are not apt to come across as highly credible.

ACKNOWLEDGMENTS

The authors express appreciation for valuable insights provided by Ted Jones, chief of police in Athens, Ohio. Also, data-collection help came from Heidi Tracy, Teresa Kuchinsky, and other members of the Public Relations Student Society of America chapter at Ohio University.

REFERENCES

Anderson, N. H. (1978). Cognitive algebra: Integration theory applied to social attribution. In L. Berkowitz (Ed.), *Cognitive theories in social psychology* (pp. 1–101). New York: Academic Press.

Bard, M. (1973). The role of law enforcement in the helping system. In J. R. Snibbe & H. M. Snibbe (Eds.), *The urban policeman in transition: A psychological and sociological review* (pp. 407–420). Springfield, IL: Charles G. Thomas.

Billie Holliday of the NYPD. (1985, September). *Ebony*, pp. 46–50.

Broom, G. M., & Dozier, D. M. (1986). Advancement for public relations role models. *Public Relations Review,12*, 37–56.

Cain, M. E. (1973). *Society and the policeman's role*. London: Routledge & Kegan Paul.

Culbertson, H. M., & Stempel, G. H., III (1985). Linking beliefs and public relations effects. *Public Relations Research and Education*, 2, 23–35.

Dervin, B. (1983). *A theoretical perspective and research approach for generating research helpful to communication practice*. Paper presented to Public Relations Division, Association for Education in Journalism and Mass Communication, Corvallis, OR.

Erskine, H. (1974). The polls: Fear of violence and crime. *Public Opinion Quarterly, 38*, 131–145.

Erskine, H. (1982, September). Opinion Roundup. *Public Opinion*, 5, 26.

Fink, J., & Sealy, G. (1974). *The community and the police: Conflict or cooperation?* New York: John Wiley & Sons.

Fishbein, M., & Ajzen, I. (1981). Acceptance, yielding and impact: Cognitive processes in persuasion. In R. E. Petty, T. M. Ostrom, & T. C. Brock (Eds.), *Cognitive responses in persuasion* (pp. 339–359). Hillsdale, NJ: Lawrence Erlbaum Associates.

Flanagan, T. J. (1985). Consumer perspectives on police operational strategy. *Journal of Police Science and Administration, 13*, 10–21.

Grunig, J. E. (1976). Organizations and public relations: Testing a communication theory. *Journalism Monographs, 46*.

Grunig, J. E., & Hunt, T. (1984). Managing public relations. New York: Holt, Rinehart & Winston.

Heider, F. (1958). The psychology of interpersonal relations. New York: Wiley.

Nie, N. H., Hull, C. H., Jenkins, J. G., Steinbrenner, K., & Bent, D. H. (1975). Statistical package for the social sciences. New York: McGraw-Hill.

Police under fire: Fighting back. (1978, April 3). U.S. News and World Report, pp. 37–40.

Pugh, G. M. (1986). The good police officer: Qualities, roles and concepts. Journal of Police Science and Administration, 14, 1–5.

Reichley, A. J. (1968, December). The way to cool the police rebellion. Fortune, pp. 108–113, 150.

Rokeach, M., & Rothman, G. (1965). The principle of belief congruence and the congruity principle as models of cognitive interaction. Psychological Review, 72, 128–172.

Rosenberg, M. J. (1960). A structural theory of attitude dynamics. Public Opinion Quarterly, 24, 319–340.

The "blues" on beat street. (1985, January 28). Newsweek, p. 49.

Trojanowicz, R. C. (1973). Police community relations: Problems and process. In J. R. Snibbe & H. M. Snibbe (Eds.), The urban policeman in transition: A psychological and sociological review (pp. 119–138). Springfield, IL: Charles G. Thomas.

Viviano, F. (1981, September). What's happening in murder city? The Progressive, pp. 38–42.

Walthier, R. H., McCune, S. D., & Trojanowicz, R. C. (1973). The contrasting occupational cultures of policemen and social workers. In J. R. Snibbe & H. M. Snibbe (Eds.), The urban policeman in transition: A psychological and sociological review (pp. 260–280). Springfield, IL: Charles G. Thomas.

Whittington, H. G. (1971). The police: Ally or enemy of the comprehensive community mental health center? Mental Hygiene, 55, 55–59.

Woelfel, J., Cody, M. J., Gillham, J., & Holmes, R. A. (1980). Basic premises of miltidimensional attitude change theory: An experimental analysis. Human Communication Research, 6, 153–167.

Chapter 10

Horizontal Structure in Public Relations: An Exploratory Study of Departmental Differentiation

Larissa A. Grunig
University of Maryland

In 1984, J. Grunig and Hunt devoted fewer than two pages in their book on public relations management to what they called "the division of labor on a single level of authority" (p. 101). Why such scant attention to the horizontal set-up of the typical public relations department? Did they consider structure relatively unimportant to the effectiveness of public relations? No. Although J. Grunig and Hunt considered this horizontal differentiation vital to the operation of a public relations subsystem within the larger organizational system, they could find no systematic studies or even anecdotal descriptions in this area.

To help fill that gap in the understanding of public relations practice, this chapter reports the findings of an exploratory study of the horizontal structure of public relations departments in the Washington, DC area. Research was conducted to answer two basic questions: How are the tasks in a public relations department carved up and why is the structure as it is? Methodology was global—involving survey data, personal interviews, and an analysis of organizational publications.

Interpreting the findings of the study depends at least in part on an understanding of the following related areas: systems theory, the determinants of structure, and both vertical and horizontal structure. Each is dealt with in turn in the following conceptualization. After a description of the method employed and the findings that resulted, the chapter concludes with implications for managers who need to design or to restructure their public relations departments. By determining an appropriate horizontal structure, managers can help meet the needs of their organization in adapting to and dealing with the external environment.

CONCEPTUALIZATION

The Systems Perspective

Systems theory, although frequently criticized as too abstract to be applicable to the actual situations facing managers in organizations, provides a perspective that is critical to this study. Useful components of that perspective include its interdisciplinary nature; its assumptions about the interconnectedness of the system, its subsystems, and its suprasystem; and its implications for contingency theory.

The interdisciplinary nature of systems theory is consistent with the approach that this chapter takes. In particular, the research presented here builds on the literature of organizational sociology and of business. The key concept of structure illustrates this theoretical melding.

"Structure" is a macro-level concept borrowed from sociology; it is equivalent to the micro-level concept of "design" described in the literature of business management. One prominent scholar of organizations, Robbins (1987), incorporated the two terms in the title of his recent text: *Organization Theory: Structure, Design, and Applications*. He explained that both terms encompass division of labor and a hierarchy of authority. However, "design" emphasizes the managerial process associated with achieving organizational goals (see pp. 5–6). The sociological perspective on structure, on the other hand, implies that no one person (even a top-level manager) is as important in configuring the organization as is the organization's dominant coalition.

Embracing the systems concept also leads to an appreciation of the interconnectedness or *gestalt* of organizations, their external environments, and their internal departments. This holistic notion is especially important in any study of public relations, because one main function of this managerial subsystem is coordination. Understanding that the environment influences the organization, and vice versa, has implications for an interactive, balanced form of communication that J. Grunig (1984) called "two-way symmetrical." The goal of this model of public relations is cooperation between the organization and its relevant external publics.

Not all organizations, though, require such a sophisticated form of public relations. J. Grunig (1984) contended that some may be successful by adopting an imbalanced model, which he called "two-way asymmetrical." Still others may succeed when using the more anachronistic one-way forms of public relations: either "press agentry/publicity" or "public information." But how can a manager determine the most appropriate model of public relations for his or her organization?

Contingency theory provides the answer. Organization theory, in the systems perspective, concludes that different parts of the organization may be structured in different ways, contingent on the environment. Thus, it stands to reason that different models of public relations may be adopted when dealing with different aspects of the organization's suprasystem, or its external environment. Some recent research validates this assumption[1]. Might it not also be the case that different horizontal structures for public relations departments are appropriate in organizations with significantly different environments? The answer, from a contingency approach, is yes—that there is no single best way to organize.

Determinants of Structure

Organizational scholars such as Burns and Stalker (1961), Hage and Aiken (1969), and Perrow (1967) built on the foundation laid by Weber (1947) in his early work in the structural paradigm[2]. They first looked at technology (Woodward, 1965) and size (Pugh, Hickson, Hinings, & Turner, 1968) as causes of social structure. Then, with the ensuing investigations of Lawrence and Lorsch (1967) and Thompson (1967), they added environmental factors into the equation[3].

Thus, this structural-functional school brings together the fragments of a field derived from different antecedent perspectives. It represents a logical and testable theory that integrates the limited conclusions of other scholars into generalizations that can benefit researchers and practitioners of public relations alike. It stresses the commonalities—rather than the differences—in organizations. Because of its emphasis on the relatively stable nature of concentration of power, it offers potent predictions.

The basic question that structural-functionalism addresses is the same question that Weber asked 40 years ago: What is the best form of organization and why? To answer, most structural theorists have tried to isolate structural variables that (unlike Weber's) are independent of any culture or historical period. Possible determinants of that structure are described next.

---

[1]J. Grunig and L. Grunig (1986) recently presented a program of research that includes correlations between model of public relations practiced and dominant environment: political/regulatory, which emphasizes public affairs, and product/service, where public relations supports the marketing function. Studies that they reviewed suggested that chosen domain did, at least to some extent, predict model of public relations—particularly when the emphasis in public relations is on marketing.

[2]Weber's ideal construction, the bureaucracy, has been called the first structural-functional theory of organizations (Hage, 1980, p. 15). However, his bureaucracy must be considered one type of organization, rather than a way to describe other organizational types by degree (Pugh, Hickson, Hinings, MacDonald, Turner, & Lupton, 1963). As a result, other theorists searched for variables that might form a continuum of organizational types ranging between extremes that might include all organizations. See, for example, Burns and Stalker (1961), with their attempt at an inclusive continuum between the polar extremes they called "organic" and "mechanistic" managerial systems.

[3]In fact, as early as the 1950s, Parsons (1956a, 1956b) had emphasized organizational interchanges with the environment as a means by which the organization obtains the resources necessary to legitimize its existence. As an advocate of the General Systems School, he agreed with Pareto (cited in Henderson, 1967) on the importance of an organization's equilibrium with its environment.

Environment.   The environment, frequently mentioned already in this chapter as a key factor, may be only one determinant of organizational structure. In fact, Robbins (1987, chapter 7) contended that the environment represents a significant contingency only when that environment is fraught with uncertainty. One important aspect of environmental uncertainty is dynamism. Thus, according to Robbins, structuring an organization dependent on its environment is more important with a dynamic than a static suprasystem. Given the rate of change in the environment for most organizations today, of course, dynamism is the assumption rather than the exception.

Strategy.   Robbins (1987, chapter 4) considered strategy, a second possible determinant of structure, of little importance. He explained that strategy, or an organization's plan to achieve its ends, impacts only certain structural dimensions rather than all aspects of organizational design. He further explained that empirical research on long-range planning and on patterns of decision making fail to support strategy as a major structural influence.

Organization Size.   Size is a third determinant of organizational structure. Robbins (1987, chapter 5) argued that the impact of the number of employees on structure is not clear—largely because most research in this area has been done on large- and medium-sized companies. However, he concluded that size alone is not a significant predictor of organizational structure. Instead, size seems to interact with factors that include organizational type, environment, technology, complexity, and whether the size is growing or shrinking. Size alone affects only certain dimensions of structure: vertical differentiation, formalization, and decentralization.

Technology.   Technology has been found to be more of an influence than an imperative on organizational structure. Contrasting these two possibilities helps make sense of a heterogenous body of research in both the technological and structural schools.

More than 20 years ago, Woodward (1965) contended that technology was the most critical variable in determining structure. Robbins (1987, chapter 6) subsequently pointed out that because technology and structure are both multidimensional concepts, technology can have an important effect on structure without being imperative. Perhaps more insightful, Pfeffer (1978) explained the relationship among technology, environment, and structure when he talked about organizational management: "Choice of a domain, and a set of activities and tasks, tends to constrain the organization's technology, but the domain is still chosen" (p. 99). In other words, technology constrains managers because they have little choice over their organization's technological processes. They do have a choice of environment, however, and that environment influences their organizational activities.

Hage and Hull (1981) developed a structural typology of organizations wherein each organizational type develops within an environmental niche. They contended that two factors—scale and complexity—subsume other structural considerations. Scale represents the repetitiveness of events that characterize an organization's operation rather than to a raw number such as employees, number of sales dollars, or number of clients. Complexity refers to the technical sophistication or knowledge base inherent in that operation.

Juxtaposing these two variables results in four normative models[4]—each cell representing an environmental niche. That is, large scale of the environment is positively related to large size of the organization, low certainty, non-variability of environmental tasks, codified (analyzable) knowledge, and a stable, static environment. Small environmental scale is positively correlated with small organizational size, high environmental uncertainty, task variability, uncodified knowledge, and a shifting, dynamic environment. In addition to incorporating key structural components, then, this typology emphasizes the consequences of the environment on organizational structure—making it especially relevant to any study of horizontal differentiation.

"Traditional" or "craft" organizations have small scale and a low knowledge base. "Mechanical" organizations are large-scale, low complexity structures. "Organic" organizations are small in scale but high in complexity. "Mixed mechanical/organic" organizations are large-scale, high-complexity operations[5]. Aiken and Hage (1971) suggested that as the speed of technological change increases, so will cooperative relationships between an organization and its environment—via the communication link. This cooperative situation could encompass both organic and mixed mechanical/organic organizations, because both are characterized by high rates of knowledge change and growing complexity.

Implications for public relations personnel, as boundary spanners, are obvious. However, any public relations theory emerging from this structural-functional approach (which focuses on how organizations design their internal departments contingent on the environment) must be considered more normative than descriptive: Previous studies have failed to support many hypotheses, and the size of many correlation coefficients is small[6].

Power-Control. Robbins (1987, chapter 8) contended that factors just described explain only about half of the variance in organizational structure[7]. Al-

---

[4]Hage and Hull based their work largely on the mechanistic-organic continuum first proposed by Burns and Stalker (1961).

[5]Consistent with contingency theory is the qualification that different parts of an organization may be structured differently, dependent on the parts of the environment that they interact with. For example, the R & D component of an organization frequently operates as an organic unit, whereas production in that same organization typically is mechanistic.

[6]For the results of a program of research based on this approach, see J. Grunig and L. Grunig (1986).

[7]One recent study on the relationship between power and model of public relations practiced seems to support this conclusion for the domain being studied here. See L. Grunig, 1987.

though those factors (strategy, environment, size, and technology) all may con-strain the amount of discretion that managers enjoy, their power allows them the necessary room to maneuver. Further, organizational politics—reflected in power— explains the lack of rationality inherent in much contemporary organiza-tional structure. Robbins (1987) argued that decisions about structure result from struggles between internal coalitions each arguing for a structural arrangement that best meets their own needs. He further explained that members of the power elite select both technologies and environments that they figure will help them maintain control—typically routine technology and a relatively stable environment.

Structure

Vertical Structure. Recall that organizational structure encompasses two di-mensions: vertical and horizontal. The former refers to a hierarchy of authority (Robbins, 1987).

Vertical structure is determined by four major variables: complexity, centraliza-tion, formalization, and stratification (Hage, 1980). Complexity is measured by education of employees, their professionalism, and the specialization of roles with-in the department. (It is most directly related to horizontal structure.) Centraliza-tion represents the degree to which decision making is concentrated at the top of the hierarchy. Formalization involves the existence of and adherence to written rules and regulations[8]. Stratification represents the extent to which differences between ranks are emphasized.

J. Grunig and Hunt (1984) believed that these four variables would help predict the model of public relations that an organization is likely to adopt. Their assumption led to at least one earlier study that characterized public relations departments in terms of their vertical structure. Schneider (1985; a.k.a. L. Grunig), for example, found that structural components within the public relations depart-ment vary significantly by Hage–Hull organizational type. However, their com-monalities outweigh their differences. For instance, *centralized* decision making characterizes most departments included in her sample. Most departments are highly *formalized* as well. The majority operates under an organization chart that nearly everyone in the department follows. Most also have written job descriptions to which they adhere to a lesser degree.

Findings related to *stratification* are less consistent across all organizations. Although more than half of all respondents perceived some differences in status among the employees in their department, a third consider those differences to be overly conspicuous.

---

[8]Recent theorizing has suggested "organizational culture" as a viable substitute for formalization. Robbins (1987) reasoned that because it increases behavioral consistency and implies control without written documentation, culture may in fact be more effective because "culture controls the mind and soul as well as the body" (p. 362).

Dimensions of *complexity* also are mixed. For example, Schneider found a high level of education among most practitioners surveyed; and they described a similarly high level for others in their departments. However, relatively few are trained in the field of public relations. They lack education in the skills that would separate them from employees in less complex departments. (Over half, though, expressed some degree of professionalism—slightly more than previous studies[9] predicted.) Further, the public relations departments investigated have relatively little specialization. Instead, generalists predominate—public relations practitioners who see their jobs as being almost evenly divided among responsibilities as different as media and government relations, who write for several channels (television, radio, newspapers, magazines, and newsletters), and who attend both to internal and external audiences.

Horizontal Structure.   Systematic determination of horizontal structure—a process that goes beyond casual observation or even experience—begins with a taxonomy of possibilities. J. Grunig and Hunt (1984) listed what their experience suggested were typical: structure by publics, by management process, by communication technique, by geographic region, by account executive system, by organizational subsystem, and/or by combination of these methods. All of these categories represent a division of labor within the public relations department on a single level of authority.

Schneider's (1985) last finding, related to vertical structure, in particular, does not support J. Grunig and Hunt's (1984) assertion that "structure by publics" (p. 101) is most common in business firms. This first of their seven types of horizontal structure organizes the public relations department by publics that may include the media, the employees, the community, the government, the owners, and any special-interest groups opposing the organization. Schneider, though, found that most practitioners she surveyed considered themselves generalists whose bosses expected them to interact simultaneously with the media, community, government, stockholders, and employees.

A second horizontal framework, "structure by management technique," (J. Grunig & Hunt, 1984, p. 102) organizes the work of the public relations department by such managerial processes as planning, evaluation, communication, and research. J. Grunig and Hunt suggested that this structure also would be appropriate for business firms, especially those that have been decentralized and thus involve more people in decision making.

"Structure by communication technique" involves organizing the PR department according to techniques such as audio-visual and print. J. Grunig and Hunt predicted that this structure would dominate in organizations with a stable environ-

---

[9]See, for example, Ingram (1975); McKee, Nayman, and Lattimore (1975); J. Grunig (1976); Wright (1976, 1979); and Werle (1980).

ment or in organizations whose top brass considers public relations a relatively low-level, technical function.

A fourth horizontal structure, "by geographic region" (J. Grunig & Hunt, 1984, p. 102), sets up public relations components to serve each region, state, or country where the organization does business. J. Grunig and Hunt pointed out that this structure typically operates in conjunction with one of the other structures. They also considered it especially appropriate with environments that are complex because of their geographical dispersion.

The "account executive system," J. Grunig and Hunt reasoned, would be advantageous especially to consulting firms that assign different employees to each client. Its flexibility lends itself to different needs and structures of the client organizations.

"Structure by organization subsystem" is a variation of the account executive system just described. In essence, PR practitioners within an organization serve as account executives to other organizational subsystems. Their job is largely to publicize the activities of departments in their assigned "beats." J. Grunig and Hunt hypothesized that this structural approach would predominate in governmental and educational organizations.

The final horizontal structure that J. Grunig and Hunt proposed is a "combination of methods." They deemed it the most common of all, contending that few organizations would design their PR departments using only one of the aforementioned structures.

The preceding page represents almost all that has been written to date on the horizontal structure of public relations departments. Suggestive though these ideas are, they have not been empirically verified—nor have alternative structures been proposed nor tested. Additional ways of organizing a public relations department may well exist. One final limitation is that they fail to consider other organizational subsystems that also may deal with communication between organizations and their environments.

In some organizations, the public relations department encompasses issues management (IM)[10], government relations, employee communication, media relations, marketing, and advertising. In others, of course, these functions are separated into distinct departments. Marketing and advertising, in particular, are often directly involved with public relations. Cutlip, Center, and Broom (1985) contended that marketing, in fact, often is confused with public relations. They explained:

> Confusion results from notions that advertising is the sole province of marketing and publicity is the job of public relations. Advertising designed to establish, change, or

---

[10]One recent study explored the structural relationship between IM and PR. Wartick and Rude (1986) concluded that although related, the two functions should remain separate and clearly distinguishable within the organization. In so doing, each department has a higher profile than when integrated into a single public affairs/public relations office.

maintain relationships with key publics (usually by influencing public opinion) should, by its nature and objectives, be supervised by the public relations department. It will require the advertising department's expertise to produce and place the advertisements, but the outcome sought has more to do with public relations than with promoting goods and services. Conversely, publicity about products and services designed to increase sales or use is clearly part of the marketing function. Because public relations staffers are typically more skilled at writing and placing publicity, they are enlisted to help with this aspect of the marketing effort. (pp. 88–89)

Cutlip, Center, and Broom (1985) concluded that although marketing and public relations may be combined in a single department, separate offices for the two functions are more common. They did not speculate on the typical structural relationship between advertising and public relations.

By looking at the relationship between marketing and public relations and between advertising and public relations, one can explore the interdependency between communication subsystems of the organizational system. This line of inquiry extends the knowledge of systems theory as it applies to public relations. It also should enhance the understanding of the horizontal distribution of tasks considered under the rubric of organizational public relations. As such, this study takes into account all communication functions—especially marketing and advertising—that might be considered part of public relations.

Establishing a list of typical horizontal structures that includes relationships between the public relations departments and other factions engaged in related communication activities undoubtedly is a Herculean task. But might it be impossible, if organizational systems and their subsystems are as unique as fingerprints?

Robbins (1987) explained that although organizations do exhibit unique configurations, they share *patterns* of structure for three main reasons. First, the natural selection model holds that the environment lends itself to only a few organizational forms. Second, organizations search for internal consistency—structural characteristics that work well together to be in synch with their environment. Finally, organizational structure is as much a victim of fashion as are hemlines or hairstyles. That is, the number of viable configurations is limited to what is in vogue because managers are prone to follow what is trendy—be it participatory management, bureaucracy, or matrix management.

Assumptions and Research Questions

The first logical question to pose is whether the J. Grunig–Hunt taxonomy of horizontal structures represents the universe of structures actually found in public relations departments. If not, what other structures exist? If so, which structures predominate? And, why is one structure—or combination of structures—chosen over another?

The assumption, gleaned from the admittedly thin body of suppositions about horizontal structure, is that "combination of methods" is most typical. Presumably, this is especially the case with organizations whose environments are the most complex: the organic and the mixed mechanical/organic.

It also might be the case, however, that organizations with the largest-scale environments—the mixed mechanical/organic and the mechanical—have the need for the most comprehensive public relations efforts possible. If so, one would expect to find a combination of several horizontal structures. Also, the relationship between public relations and other communication functions such as advertising and marketing might be more integral than in small-scale organizations: craft or organic. Mechanical organizations, in particular, might rely on a two- or three-pronged approach that includes PR, marketing, and/or advertising to help dispose of their products into the large market that they typically enjoy.

If significant correlations emerge between horizontal structure and/or the involvement of public relations with other communication functions in the organization and the four Hage–Hull organizational types, one could assume that environment does dictate the structure of public relations programs. If not, then future research should consider other possible determinants. Because the Hage–Hull typology encompasses two of those possibilities (organizational size and technology), the most likely explanation would be either strategy or power-control.

METHODOLOGY

The global approach of this study included both in-depth personal interviews with public relations managers and a self-administered, eight-page questionnaire. Trained interviewers talked with two high-ranking individuals in each of 48 public relations departments[11]. Interviews lasted between 1 and 2 hours. In addition, as Pavlik and Salmon (1983) recommended, current organizational publications such as company newsletters, annual reports, memoranda, organization charts, news releases, and public service announcements were examined.

Forty-eight organizations in the Washington, DC, area (12 representing each of the four Hage–Hull types) were included in the purposive sample. Internal media and mass media were analyzed for an initial assessment of Hage–Hull organizational type[12]. Traditional or craft types included a small hospital, a county police force, and a professional basketball team. Mechanical organizations included the

---

[11]In some cases, it was not possible to question two PR practitioners in a single organization. This was especially true in the mid-sized companies—those large enough to employ at least one public relations expert but too small for a comprehensive department. For this reason, the total number of respondents was 87 rather than the 96 possible if two practitioners had been available from all 48 organizations studied.

[12]All 48 organizations were deemed to be in equilibrium with their environments. That is, none was likely to go out of business at the time of the research. Because the Hage–Hull typology is a normative model, this assumption of stability is crucial.

U.S. Air Force, a teachers' union, and a power company. Organic organizations included a private school, a wholesaler and retailer of innovative running gear, and a NASA subcontractor. Mixed mechanical/organic organizations included the world's largest teleprocessing network, a chemical manufacturer, and an aerospace conglomerate.

Interviews, questionnaires, and publications all contributed to the understanding of how horizontal structure varies by organizational type. The theorizing of Hage and Hull framed the study because their work suggests an explanation for whatever structure is exposed: the environment, in their opinion, dictates the structure for organizations in equilibrium with their suprasystem.

This combination of qualitative and quantitative research should provide for more powerful analyses than would either approach by itself (Sanders, 1982; Stinchcombe, 1965). Although the historical-critical method contributed the bulk of the data here, the survey instrument helped guard against bias and subjective, perceptual data as reported by interviewees.

One major thrust of this descriptive study is determining what exists in terms of typical horizontal structures of public relations departments. Research results described next also should relate those configurations to some preceding event or cause. The comprehensive methodology described previously allows for such inferences of causality. The major disadvantage of the global method is that it limits the number of cases that can be studied. This inherent bias, in turn, limits the generalizability of conclusions.

FINDINGS

Horizontal Structure

This exploratory study began with J. Grunig and Hunt's (1984) list of horizontal structures as possible answers to the following survey question: "How is the public relations department in your organization set up?" Response categories included *by region of the country, by public (employees, community, stockholders, government, media, etc.), by technique (print, audiovisual, exhibits, etc.), by internal "client" (different departments such as R&D or production), by combination of the above (please also check all that apply),* and *other (please specify)*[13].

Frequency responses show that, as predicted, a *combination* of methods is by far the most common horizontal structure (53%). The most typical combination is by public and by technique. Second most common is by public and by internal client and—mentioned equally frequently—by communication technique and by client.

---

[13]Because this question calls for objective answers, the survey instrument was chosen over the personal interview for more efficient analysis of responses. The questionnaire incorporated a brief description of what was meant by each type of horizontal structure.

Other method was checked by 16% of the respondents. Their responses to this open-ended category include the following:

- all corporate or headquarters function
- no real public relations department
- no formal PR department
- management responsibility
- one professional does it all
- generalists who specialize as needed
- by type of media
- publications, media relations, editorial

These cryptic comments add little valuable information to the study. Only the last two (by type of media and publications, media relations, editorial) are descriptive enough to be useful. However, the fact that 16% of the survey respondents consider the structure of their public relations operation to be something *other* than the possibilities listed (as suggested by J. Grunig and Hunt, 1984) invites further study[14].

Next in frequency of response to the question of horizontal structure was by *public* (12%), followed by *technique* and *internal client* (5% each), and *region of the country* (4%). Because of the small number of respondents in each of these four categories (10, 4, 4, and 3, respectively), the statistical procedures that would allow for generalizations by organizational type were not pursued. However, this initial investigation adds to what little is known about the way in which the workload is organized within public relations departments in general.

This information, though, must be interpreted in light of the following qualification: The two respondents in a single organization disagreed about their horizontal structure in 12 cases (one quarter of the sample). This calls into question Blau and Schoenherr's (1971) contention that objective attributes of an organization could be answered adequately by any single member of that organization. As such, it represents one limitation of the study. At the same time, it may help explain why no more significant findings emerged.

Recognizing and identifying horizontal structure may be impossible because no clear-cut differentiation of tasks on the one level of authority exists. Perhaps public relations practitioners—even those working in the same department of the same organization—may not even agree on what public relations is. The following sections dissect the interaction between what is generally accepted as "public relations" and related functions that include marketing, advertising, development, and public affairs.

---

[14]Of course, some respondents work in organizations with no real public relations department and so for them, the question may be irrelevant. Other practitioners checking the *other* option did not elaborate at all in the blank provided.

TABLE 10.1
Relationship between PR and Marketing

Extent of Relationship	Number	Percentage
1. Close	19	24%
2. Some	22	27%
3. Little or none	14	17%
4. No marketing department	21	26%

Relationship to Marketing

The job titles of many respondents allude to marketing as well as to public relations. Perhaps a close involvement with marketing could distinguish one organizational type from another. Thus, the connection between public relations and marketing was classified along a continuum from *close* to *little or no* relationship. The midpoint would indicate *some* involvement between the two departments in a given organization. Interview responses were coded according to these categories[15]. A fourth category encompassed organizations with no marketing department or marketing function at all. Results are shown in Table 10.1.

The significance of the mean score, 2.51 on a 1–4 scale, is affected by the addition of a fourth category that is somewhat different from the degree of involvement indicated by the first three categories. However, the absence of any marketing activity allows for even less involvement than would be possible if the organization has a marketing department. So, in a sense, it can be considered a fourth degree of involvement. Because about a quarter of all respondents work in organizations with no marketing, this alternative seemed vital to include.

Looking at some examples of the rationale given for these responses provides a fuller picture of the relationship. An expression of a *close* relationship between public relations and marketing came from the manager of public relations at Goodyear Tire & Rubber Co.. He said: "In this company, public relations acts as aggressive support for the marketing effort. Our News Bureau is especially involved." The vice president for public relations of a PR and advertising firm described their close relationship as "cross-selling" between public relations and marketing. The director of the communications department of the Mormon Church said that whatever marketing done there is the responsibility of her department[16].

A response typical of *some* involvement between public relations and marketing came from the public affairs manager at duPont's Washington office. He explained that although marketing is a separate, autonomous function within every manufac

---

[15]Because this question calls for perceptual data, the personal interview was deemed the more appropriate vehicle than the survey instrument for finding answers.

[16]The only marketing that the church does is what this interviewee termed the "soft sell" of the church's image.

TABLE 10.2
Mean Scores of Marketing and Advertising Variables Broken Down
by Organizational Type

	Entire Population (N = 76)	Organizational Type			
		Craft (N = 16)	Mechanical (N = 20)	Organic (N = 23)	Mixed (N = 17)
Relationship to marketing F = 5.08 (3 df), p < .003	2.51	1.62	2.95	2.70	2.59
Relationship to advertising F = 2.64 (3 df), p < .056	2.53	1.94	2.90	2.70	2.41

turing department, a public affairs representative is assigned to assist each one. The same is true at Satellite Business Systems, where public affairs provides an in-house counseling service to the Marketing Division.

At the American College of Cardiology, the communications department has *little or no* involvement in marketing. As its director of communications explained, "Marketing and other promotional activities are done by the concerned departments, not by the communications department." This separation is common in almost one of every five organizations sampled.

Table 10.2 shows that significant differences exist between marketing and the four types of organizations ($p < .003$). Table 10.3 exposes the extent of the differences. Public relations departments in mechanical organizations tend to be significantly closer to the marketing function than are departments in any other organizational type ($Tau = .21, p < .01$). Public relations practitioners in tradi-

TABLE 10.3
Correlates of Marketing and Advertising Variables
with Organizational Type (*TAU*)

Organizational Type	Relationship to Marketing	Relationship to Advertising
Traditional	−.36***	−.25**
Mechanical	.21**	.18*
Organic	.10	.09
Mixed	.02	−.05

*p < .10
**p < .01
***p < .001

tional organizations, the other low-complexity type, are least involved with typical marketing functions ($Tau = -.36, p < .001$).

Organizational publications collected during the interviews do nothing to dispute this finding or to add insight. However, respondents offered few publications with any marketing orientation. (Written materials that would be considered marketing-oriented include consumer surveys, press releases about new products, and direct-mail publicity or promotion.)

These data help confirm the finding that pertains to all four types of organizations: Fewer than a fourth of the public relations practitioners who responded indicated that they perceive a close relationship to marketing.

Relationship to Advertising

Another way of exploring the interdependency of subsystems in an organization and to help determine the horizontal structure typical of public relations departments is to focus on the relationship between PR and advertising. As with marketing, the connection could be classified along a continuum from *close* to *little or no* relationship. The midpoint would indicate *some* interaction between these two functions. And as with the question related to marketing, a fourth category provided for interviewees whose organizations do *no* advertising. Results are shown in Table 10.4.

As with marketing, responses are fairly evenly split among the four options. Mean is 2.53 on a 1–4 scale, again affected at least somewhat by the addition of the fourth category—one that is not truly comparable with the other three points on the scale. This mean is almost the same as that of the average involvement between public relations and marketing (2.51). This indicates that about the same level of involvement is typical between public relations and both marketing and advertising: The distinctions between functions are clear but some interaction is not unusual. In systems terms, the boundaries between the departments are semipermeable.

A response indicative of *close* involvement of public relations in advertising came from the director of public affairs at the American Red Cross. She explained that advertising is her responsibility because of the public-service nature of adver-

TABLE 10.4
Relationship of PR to Advertising

Extent of Relationship	Number	Percent
1. Close	19	24%
2. Some	20	25%
3. Little or none	19	24%
4. No advertising department	18	22%

tising the Red Cross does (especially for blood and health programs). At Goodyear, the public relations department is integrally involved in one of its two types of advertising: corporate image (handled completely by public relations), rather than product (where public relations has almost zero responsibility). In small organiza- tions, such as a NASA subcontractor, it is not unusual for advertising, public relations, and even marketing to be handled by the same person.

Some involvement with advertising characterizes the larger public affairs office, such as that of Ford Motor Co.. Although each function has its own vice president and is formally a separate operation there, public affairs becomes involved in the planning of advertising for what its director of Washington Public Affairs called "corporate image." Another response, coded *some* involvement, came from the public affairs administrator of Satellite Business Systems. He described the set-up there as follows:

> Advertising is a separate division under the vice president for National Networks. SBS also relies on a New York-based ad agency. Public Affairs, though, provides in- house consultation to advertising. For example, our department introduced the sen- tence, "We invite comparison" to focus attention on the advantages of its services and rates for long-distance telephone. Now, advertising has picked up this language and is beginning to use it.

Public relations departments in many other organizations, though, have *little or no* involvement in advertising—either because they are independent of their com- pany's own advertising department or because the company relies on an ad agency.

Table 10.2 shows that organizational types vary significantly ($p < .056$) in terms of the involvement of their public relations departments in advertising. Correlations reported in Table 10.3 indicate that mechanical organizations, in particular, involve their public relations staffs in advertising ($Tau = .18, p < .05$). Traditional organizations are the least likely to do so ($Tau = -.25, p < .01$). Organic and mixed types of organizations are not significant predictors of public relations involvement in advertising.

Two kinds of advertising are evident in the publications collected: institutional ads and public service announcements (PSAs). At least 1 of the 13 corporate- image ads came from each type of organization. PSAs were somewhat more com- mon: 25 in all, and again, each type of organization contributed at least a few. This shows that many public relations practitioners are involved in work more typical of an advertiser, at least to some extent. In neither case, however, does the number, quality, nor content seem to vary appreciably across organizations. As a result, an analysis of these advertisements does not add to any understanding of how public relations people in different kinds of organizations interact with their colleagues in advertising.

Relationship of PR to Other Communication Functions

The survey instrument only assessed the relationship between public relations and advertising and marketing. During the in-depth interviews with practitioners, however, other relationships became apparent. This information carries important implications for the job satisfaction of respondents. This section presents representative remarks.

For example, a vice president in charge of public relations for a savings and loan company expressed his frustration at "having to wear too many hats"[17]. The director of information for a public school system called his job "unmanageable" because it included public affairs as well as public relations. Because his work is "fragmented," the director of corporate relations for a multinational conglomerate felt frustrated. He explained that "public relations work is done in several departments, not under one umbrella."

Many practitioners in non-profit organizations, in particular, reported that their position includes fund-raising. The American Heart Association's director of public relations is typical. He explained that although he likes his work, he would be even more satisfied if a separate position could be created for public relations; he finds it difficult to do everything related to both development and public relations. In fact, practitioners in non-profit settings tended to complain that they are overworked in general because they lack the financial resources to hire the staff necessary for doing what one called "quality" work[18].

CONCLUSIONS

Most public relations departments studied are organized by a combination of horizontal structures—predominantly by public, by technique, or by internal client. The predominance of this combined approach indicates an appropriate area for future research. Specifically, determining why certain types of structure tend to be used in combination with others would add to the body of knowledge about how the work in public relations is organized.

A very few interviewees reported a single horizontal structure. In these cases, 12% of the sample, that structure is by public (such as media, government, community, or employee). However, 16% of the respondents did not recognize their division of labor as any one of the possibilities suggested in response to this

---

[17]To a few interviewees, however, "wearing many hats" leads to satisfaction because it creates a feeling of being essential. It also involves practitioners in a variety of tasks and with a variety of people and keeps them busy—additional determinants of job satisfaction (L. Grunig, 1987).

[18]As a public relations practitioner at the Corcoran Art Gallery explained: "I enjoy my job, but it's frustrating to be understaffed. There's no time to really do a *good* job."

question. This finding also suggests a fruitful area for future study: identifying alternatives to the taxonomy first enunciated by J. Grunig and Hunt (1984). Only one structure suggested, by type of media, makes sense on its face. If the model of public relations valued in the organization is public information, then concentrating on different media would be appropriate.

Findings related to the interdependence of public relations and marketing and advertising show approximately the same level of involvement in both cases. About half of all respondents said that their department is significantly involved in marketing or advertising of both.

The relationship with marketing is most often characterized as supporting, assisting, or counseling. It is most pronounced in the mechanical organization. This supports the contention that structural-functionalism represents a valid way to study organizations. Apparently, disposing of products or services in a large-scale environment requires the involvement of more than a single subsystem, that of marketing or advertising. Conversely, public relations professionals in the small-scale operation characterized as "craft" or "traditional" have the least involvement in the kind of communication with customers or clients typically thought of as marketing.

Advertising undertaken by public relations practitioners, too, is most common in the large-scale, mechanical type of organization. Rather than product advertising, it tends to be of an image, institutional, or public service nature. The role of the public relations department, typically, is more in planning than in production. Public relations is least involved in advertising in the traditional type of organization.

The relationship between PR and advertising–marketing correlates significantly with both Hage/Hull organizational types with low complexity—negatively in the case of traditional organizations and positively with mechanical ones. Scale of the environment alone, then, is not the significant predictor. If it were, all four types of organizations would show significant associations: PR's involvement with advertising and marketing would correlate significantly and positively with the mixed organizational type as well as with the mechanical and it would correlate significantly and negatively with the organic as well as with the traditional.

Instead, correlations are significant only with the low-complexity type. These organizations tend to be product—rather than service—oriented[19]. Disposal of the products is paramount. The model of public relations that dominates in the traditional organization is press agentry. This persuasive model encompasses aspects of marketing and advertising, making the separation of these communication functions unnecessary.

Indeed, about one-fourth of the organizations in the sample have no marketing or advertising department. However, because of the predominance of organiza-

[19]Examples of traditional organizations included in the sample are a bagel bakery, a chain of printing establishments, and an art gallery. Mechanical organizations included a supermarket chain, automobile and truck manufacturers, and a department store chain.

tions reporting interaction among these internal subsystems when they exist, systems theory is supported as a valid way of looking at public relations behavior in
organizations.

However, the major assumption of the study was unsupported: that horizontal
structure of public relations departments would vary significantly by Hage–Hull
organizational type. This calls into question the environmental imperative. It also
questions the efficacy of the J. Grunig–Hunt taxonomy of horizontal structures, of
course. But the most important question is why no clear pattern of structure—
much less relationship between structure and environmental niche—emerged.

To answer, first recall that in more than a few instances, two interviewees from a
single organization disagreed in their determination of horizontal structure. Is
structure unrecognizable even to the people working within it? Or is the way
public relations actually is practiced—rather than the way it theoretically or normatively can be described—idiosyncratic, unique to each organizational system
and even to the individual frame of reference of practitioners within the public
relations subsystem?

The two questions are related. Perhaps the answer to the first query is "yes,"
horizontal structure is unrecognizable even to public relations practitioners working together in the same department. The reason it may unrecognizable is that
those practitioners may not share an understanding of what public relations is.
Their conception of the tasks involved in public relations may differ so radically as
to call up completely different schema when asked by an interviewer to define the
allocation of those tasks in their office.

Given the spread of responsibilities that many respondents described, this
assumption warrants further study. To one practitioner, public relations may mean
fund-raising as well as the more typical activities that include employee communication, media relations, and counseling management. To another, PR may encompass legislative interaction as well as community and stockholder relations.
Most significantly, those two practitioners may be colleagues in the same department.

Finally, the determination of horizontal structure may be an irrational one.
Robbins (1987) suggested that dominant coalitions have the power to influence
structural decisions. He further suggested that individual members of that power
elite may not have a consistent set of goal preferences. In the case of horizontal
structure in public relations, they may not consider all logical alternatives—much
less select the most efficacious one. This would be most likely to happen if public
relations practitioners are not represented in the dominant coalition.

IMPLICATIONS

The lack of clear-cut job responsibilities in the average public relations department
studied presents several problems. In some cases, it leads to job dissatisfaction:

ambiguity and overwhelming numbers of responsibilities upset the equilibrium of some practitioners interviewed. In other cases, the work that PR professionals do in a single department may overlap.

Perhaps most serious, a lack of enunciated responsibility may lead to gaps in the public relations program. If everyone in the department concentrates on fund raising, no one may be working with the community public. An emphasis on media relations may preclude important interaction with the government.

On the other hand, a lack of identifiable horizontal structure actually may strengthen the practice of public relations in some organizations. Formalized differentiation may create cumbersome, inflexible patterns of activity that interfere with the department's ability to respond quickly, inexpensively, and effectively to changing environmental stimuli. An ad hoc horizontal structure—or a lack of structure—offers the advantage of a simple, flexible, responsive approach to external dynamism. This is especially the case when the PR department is staffed with professionals—educated, experienced practitioners who can rise to the non-routine occasion and who would recoil from a more formalized configuration. These experts work well in teams, coordinating their efforts through mutual adjustment. Such unstandardized practice of public relations seems especially important when the department's environment is a dynamic, complex one.

The question, then, is whether any horizontal structure is incompatible with a public relations department in an organization whose environment is constantly in flux and whose employees have professional—rather than technical—capabilities. The answer suggested by the findings in this study is a qualified "no." Structure appropriate for the environment could be defined initially by a coalition or team of public relations experts—members of a department whose main concern is meeting organizational goals through the communication function broadly defined to include whatever other aspects are necessary—marketing, advertising, lobbying, and so on. Members of the department should share an understanding, then, of what public relations is. Their definition would not be so general as to be unmanageable nor so narrow as to shut out two-way interaction with a range of relevant publics.

As long as the public relations professionals themselves have a hand in determining that structure, odds are that the structure of choice may work well—at least for a time. Any structure or combination of structures adopted should be reexamined in light of significant changes in the environment. For example, structure by public may be the most appropriate when the company is new and growing by adding to its market share by cultivating customers. Later on, as it diversifies and moves into new markets, structure by geographical region may be important to factor into the structural equation. In other words, think of structure as a blueprint for a house that may need to be remodeled as the family's lifestyle shifts.

By considering alternative configurations—such as the J. Grunig–Hunt list or options mentioned by respondents to this study—managers of public relations programs should have a valid basis on which to structure their department that is compatible with its organizational environment, technology, goals, and ideology.

REFERENCES

Aiken, M., & Hage, J. (1971). The organic organization and innovation. *Sociology, 5,* 63–82.

Blau, P. M., & Schoenherr, R. A. (1971). *The structure of organizations.* New York: Basic Books.

Burns, T., & Stalker, G. M. (1961). *The management of innovation.* London: Tavistock.

Cutlip, S. M., Center, A. H., & Broom, G. M. (1985). *Effective public relations* (6th ed.). Englewood Cliffs, NJ: Prentice-Hall.

Grunig, J. E. (1976). Organizations and public relations: Testing a communication theory. *Journalism Monographs, 46.*

Grunig, J. E. (1984). Organizations, environments, and models of public relations. *Public Relations Research and Education, 1*(1), 6–29.

Grunig, J. E., & Grunig, L. S. (1986, May). *Application of open systems theory to public relations: Review of a program of research.* Paper presented at the meeting of the International Communication Association, Chicago.

Grunig, J. E., & Hunt, T. (1984). *Managing public relations.* New York: Holt, Rinehart, & Winston.

Grunig, L. S. (1987, July). *An exploration of the causes of job satisfaction in public relations.* Paper presented at the meeting of the International Association of Business Communicators, London.

Hage, J. (1980). *Theories of organizations: Form, process, and transformation.* New York: Wiley.

Hage, J., & Aiken, M. (1969). Routine, technology, social structure, and organizational goals. *Administrative Science Quarterly, 14,* 366–377.

Hage, J., & Hull, F. (1981). *A typology of environmental niches based on knowledge technology and scale: The implications for innovation and productivity.* Working Paper 1. University of Maryland: Center for the Study of Innovation, Entrepreneurship and Organization Strategy.

Henderson, L. J. (1967). *Pareto's general sociology: A physiologist's interpretation.* New York: Russell & Russell.

Ingram, W. R. (1975). Building a viable PR function. *Public Relations Journal, 31*(5), 13–14.

Lawrence, P. R., & Lorsch, J. W. (1967). *Organization and environment: Managing differentiation and integration.* Cambridge, MA: Harvard Graduate School of Business Administration.

McKee, B. K., Nayman, O. B., & Lattimore, D. L. (1975). How PR people see themselves. *Public Relations Journal, 31*(11), 47–52.

Parsons, T. (1956a). Suggestions for a sociological approach to the theory of organizations—I. *Administrative Science Quarterly, 1,* 63–85.

Parsons, T. (1956b). Suggestions for a sociological approach to the theory of organizations—II. *Administrative Science Quarterly, 1,* 225–239.

Pavlik, J. V., & Salmon, C. T. (1983, August). *Theoretic approaches in public relations research.* Paper presented at the meeting of the Association for Education in Journalism and Mass Communication, Corvallis, OR.

Perrow, C. (1967). A framework for the comparative analysis of organizations. *American Sociological Review, 32,* 194–209.

Pfeffer, J. (1978). *Organizational design.* Arlington Heights, IL: AHM Publishing.

Pugh, D. S., Hickson, D. J., Hinings, C. R., MacDonald, K. M., Turner, C., & Lupton, R.(1963). A conceptual scheme for organizational analysis. *Administrative Science Quarterly, 8,* 289–316.

Pugh, D. S., Hickson, D. J., Hinings, C. R., & Turner, C. (1968). Dimensions of organization structure. *Administrative Science Quarterly, 13,* 65–105.

Robbins, S. P. (1987). *Organization theory: Structure, design, and applications* (2nd ed.). Englewood Cliffs, NJ: Prentice-Hall.

Sanders, P. (1982). Phenomenology: A new way of viewing organizational research. *Academy of Management Review, 7,* 353–360.

Schneider, L. A. (1985). The role of public relations in four organizational types. *Journalism Quarterly, 62*(3), 567–576, 594.

Stinchcomb, A. L. (1965). Social structure and organizations. In J. G. March (Ed.), *Handbook of organizations* (pp. 142–193). Chicago: Rand McNally.

Thompson, J. D. (1967). *Organizations in action.* New York: McGraw-Hill.

Wartick, S. L., & Rude, R. E. (1986). Issues management: Corporate fad or corporate function? *California Management Review, 29,* 124–40.

Weber, M. (1947). *The theory of social and economic organization.* New York: Oxford University Press.

Werle, C. (1980). Public relations' silent majority. *Public Relations Journal, 36*(10), 30–31.

Woodward, J. (1965). *Industrial organizations: Theory and practice.* Oxford: Oxford University Press.

Wright, D. K. (1976). Social responsibility in public relations: A multi-step theory. *Public Relations Review, 2*(4), 24–36.

Wright, D. K. (1979, August). *Premises for professionalism: Testing the contributions of PRSA accreditation.* Paper presented at the meeting of the Association for Education in Journalism, Houston.

Chapter 11

Putting the "Public" First in Public Relations: An Exploratory Study of Municipal Employee Public Service Attitudes, Job Satisfaction, and Communication Variables

Dennis W. Jeffers
Central Michigan University

The headline on a recent *Time* magazine cover story about service in our economy summed up the frustrations of millions of Americans when it implored: "Pul-eeze! Will somebody help me?" ("Pul-eeze!," 1987) The article went on to detail the decline of the service ethic in our society and suggested that if the U.S. economy is to thrive, the service concept will have to be "serviced."

The experts agree. Management consultants James Quinn and Christopher Gagnon (1986) noted that service industries offer even more opportunity for growth—and for mismanagement—than product-based industries. They also believe that it is essential to take a hard look at services, how we manage them, and how much they contribute to the nation's economy.

Quinn and Gagnon lamented that many persons still characterize the service sector in our economy as being devoted to making hamburgers and shining shoes. They said that, in reality, the service sector is highly complex, sophisticated, and accounts for more than 68% of the gross national product (GNP) and 71% of the nation's employment.

Fortunately, at the same time that the service sector is becoming more complex, so is the thinking about how to improve performance within it. For instance, suggestions range from restructuring large organizations into "co-corps," which operate for the purpose of benefitting the public instead of making profits (Collier, 1979), to devoting more study to "emotional labor."

The latter term was coined by Hochschild (1983) to describe a "part of a distinctly patterned yet invisible emotional system—a system composed of individual acts of 'emotion work,' social 'feeling rules,' and a great variety of exchanges between people in private and public life" (pp. x–xi). Hochschild's research with flight attendants and bill collectors documents the fact that in a service industry "the emotional style of offering the service is part of the service itself" (p. 5).

With the problem of "poor service" perceived as being so pervasive, there is no doubt that public relations practitioners throughout all segments of our society will be called on to help provide remedies. It could be that programs devoted to helping organizations improve their services to the public may become the new growth area for public relations.

Public relations practitioners venturing into this arena will not find the environ-ment alien. In fact, management principles designed to improve service within an organization sound very similar to principles designed to improve public relations. When describing their "service management concept," Albrecht and Zemke (1985) said:

> First, as a result of working in and with organizations, we are biased to believe that high quality service at the front line has to start with a concept of service that exists in the minds of top management. This service concept must find its way into the structure and operation of the organization.
>
> We also believe in the value and importance of measuring service. An intimate and objective knowledge of how you are doing—in the customer's eyes—is critical. Market research, the service audit, and a process for measuring service quality and feeding back this information to the frontline people are crucial ingredients in moving an organization to a high level of service orientation. (p. vi)

Albrecht and Zemke's notion of providing employee feedback—and hence, training—is seen by most experts as a crucial component in the process of improv-ing organizational service. Organizations frequently cited as having outstanding service are the same ones cited for having outstanding employee training and development programs (Branst, 1984). As indicated previously, it can be argued that the public relations practitioner is the best person within an organization to provide this employee feedback and training. Consequently, this chapter is de-signed to support that view and offer guidance for those practitioners undertaking such a venture.

RESEARCH QUESTIONS

If the concept of improved public service is important to the private sector, it is even more important in the public sector. Government at all levels—federal, state, and local—is increasingly challenged to be more responsive to the public. And, often, "responsive" translates into providing more services with less tax dollars.

The pressure to improve service is particularly intense on the local municipal level—not only because taxpayers have a greater opportunity to be "responsive" themselves (by not passing millages) but also because of the closer social contact that exists among those who live in the same community. Citizens simply expect better service from municipal workers who are their friends and neighbors.

Nevertheless, public service by municipalities is considered to have declined along with that provided by other organizations. Often, employee unionization is cited as the reason for this decline (Davis & West, 1985; DiTomaso, 1978; Seroka, 1979). In some studies, however, more employee-centered variables (such as job satisfaction) are linked to municipal worker efficiency (Pintor, 1976).

If, as suggested previously, public relations practitioners are going to be called on to help improve organizational public service performance by municipalities, there is a good deal of formulative research that needs to be done. Specifically, public relations practitioners need to begin answering the following questions:

1. What are some of the components of "public service" that municipal employees link to an overall municipal public relations program? In other words, what actions/activities do employees themselves consider to be important to an overall public relations effort.

2. What is the underlying structure of city employee attitudes regarding these public service activities? In other words, given that public service actions are important to an overall public relations effort, what is the state of employee attitudes regarding these variables?

3. What is the relationship between that attitudinal structure and other job-related variables, such as job satisfaction? Job satisfaction is an often investigated variable in organizational communication research and, as noted earlier, other research has linked it to public employee performance.

4. Finally, are there identifiable municipal employee communication patterns that might be used by public relations practitioners to improve the public service attitudes, and perhaps, performance?

This chapter reports on the results of one exploratory study designed to contribute answers to these questions.

RESEARCH SETTING, UNDERLYING THEORY, AND METHODOLOGICAL APPROACHES

Responding to the pressure to improve service by employees, a number of municipalities, linked to a mid-western state association of municipal governments, instituted a series of workshops designed to achieve objectives consistent with Albrecht and Zemke's recommendations. First started in late 1985, the workshops are continuing in 1987 and have been designed with help from the Center for

Communication at a mid-western state university. Faculty members from several communication-related departments at the university lead the workshops, which have two objectives: First, to provide "frontline" training to municipal employees in communication techniques, principles of public relations, and the role of good public service in a municipal government's public relations program. Second, to provide a vehicle for gathering data related to the research questions highlighted previously. This latter objective helps to close the "feedback" loop by providing researchers with information to help improve training.

To date, over a dozen sessions have been held in municipalities that range in classification from "small town" to "metropolitan area." In essence, the process has been a learning experience for all concerned. Hundreds of municipal employees have received training and the researchers have gained valuable insight and knowledge about this relatively unexplored area of public relations. One goal of this chapter is to share some of this knowledge in the hope that it stimulates further research.

The methodology involved in this research process has been traditional in nature in that both qualitative and quantitative techniques were used. Specifically, for the first year of the project, *qualitative* techniques were used to identify and distill major themes, issues, and concerns of municipal employees regarding public service and public relations. Later, *quantitative* techniques were used to further investigate and validate the qualititative findings. In essence, qualitative methods were used to gather data needed to answer the first research question and quantitative methods were used to gather data for the last three research questions.

Qualitative Methods

As indicated heretofore, a qualitiative approach was used for approximately the first year that the training sessions were held to determine what actions and activities municipal employees considered relevant to an overall public relations effort.

Although the specifics vary slightly in each situation, the general framework for the training sessions is as follows: The sessions are held in a municipal facility and are designed to be 4 hours in length, allowing two sessions a day. Employees are given release time to attend one or the other session and generally are not separated by department or classification. Depending on the size of the municipal workforce, the number of session participants ranges from 25 to 100. The workshop format utilizes a combination of lecture, small group, and individual teaching techniques by two to four instructors.

At each session, participants are asked to identify issues that they consider important to their role as municipal employees and public servants. Further, they are asked to describe situations (both positive and negative) that they consider relevant to the city's overall public relations effort. In addition to utilizing this information for pedagogical purposes during the sessions, researchers categorize and record these employee observations.

Quantitative Methods

Whereas the qualitative techniques used in the study are "atheoretical," the quantitative techniques have been developed from a definite theoretical perspective. To guide this phase of the study, Grunig's situational theory (Grunig & Hunt, 1984) is considered to be particularly appropriate.

This theory is well documented, as Grunig and others continue to utilize this perspective in a variety of settings. However, it is considered especially relevant for organizational communication-related research (such as this project) because this is the area where it has received the most refinement.

Essentially, Grunig says that persons communicate, and have attitudes about, specific situations—not broad generalizations. His research has shown that at least three variables (sometimes four) are responsible for how often and how much persons will communicate about the specific issues. These include the degree to which the person considers the issue a "problem" (problem recognition), whether the person feels that he or she can do anything about the issue (constraint recognition), and how "involved" the person considers himself or herself to be with the issue (level of involvement). Grunig considers communication to include both information seeking and information processing.

Grunig's approach was considered to be especially relevant for this study in light of his recent work that related measures of job satisfaction (an important variable in this study) to his theoretical measures (Grunig, 1983).

Consequently, once researchers felt confident about their identification of the issues, concerns, and situations that municipal employees considered to be relevant to public service, measuring instrument items were developed to gather data about the underlying attitudes regarding these issues. Because this was an exploratory study, the researchers decided to concentrate on one major cluster of these concerns (explained later) in an effort to provide a sharper focus for later research. These items provided data to contribute answers to the second research question. To gather data relevant to the third and fourth research questions, specific techniques used by Grunig to measure his theoretical variables, as well as job satisfaction, were adapted for this study.

The result of this effort was an instrument that combined measures of "public service" attitudes and job satisfaction, as well as measures of information seeking, information processing, problem recognition, constraint recognition, and level of involvement with/about *specific issues* related to public service. (This approach is considered to be consistent with Grunig's theory. Instead of asking city employees how they "feel" about public service, a better approach is to gather measures about issues/topics that *relate* to public service.) In addition, a number of demographic variables were measured as well.

To gather data needed to contribute answers to the research questions, the measuring instrument was administered to employees of a municipality with a total population of nearly 40,000 in late spring, 1986. While all municipalities have unique characteristics, the one chosen for this case study is "typical" in many ways of other mid-western cities of the same size. There are slightly over 100 employees (ranging from the city manager to public works laborer) divided into four divisions.

Sixty-nine, or over 70% of eligible employees completed the questionnaire at one of two workshop sessions conducted as described earlier. Sixty-two percent of the respondents were male and nearly 40% were between the ages of 36 and 45. Fifty-six percent have worked for the city 10 years or less. The amount of time spent with the public each day ranges from "none" (6.2%), to "all day" (16.9%), with most (27.7%) having 2 to 3 hours of public contact.

The respondents were representative of those employed in all four divisions: Public Works (44.3%), Public Safety (18%), Finance & Records (13.2%), and Community Affairs (24.6%). In fact, a municipality of this size was chosen for the case study aspect of the study in order to insure a high percentage of representative employee participation. For this formulative study, the trade-off that results in a smaller N for greater accuracy was deemed important by the researchers for purposes of validity. Consequently, caution should be exercised when generalizing the results of this study beyond the municipality investigated.

The rationale for each set of items and the statistical procedures used to analyze them are explained as each set of variables is presented.

RESULTS AND DISCUSSION

Question 1: Public Service Activities/Actions

Analysis of the interactions with municipal employees as part of the training workshop process indicates that there are two major categories, or clusters, of activities/actions that employees link to public service and an overall public relations campaign.

The first, which could be labeled as an "External" cluster, deals with activities related to "contacts" with the public by municipal employees. Some examples of these kinds of activities include:

- Providing solutions to citizen problems.
- Dealing with a wide range of "types" of citizens.
- Promoting citizen understanding of city policies.
- Establishing working relationships with citizens.

An anecdotal example that illustrates these kinds of activities would be a situation where street department employees are completing road work in a neighborhood and are asked by a senior citizen to trim a tree branch in her backyard that she believes is causing a dangerous condition. Adhering to city policies, the workers would be prohibited from assisting the citizen. Yet, the citizen views municipal workers as "public servants," and indeed, the employees recognize that solving her problem (which may take only a few minutes) would generate a good deal of positive feelings about the city. Nevertheless, the employees have to make a decision about "how and what" to tell the citizen to prevent creating negative feelings. (They may just go ahead and trim the branch in spite of departmental policy, or, tell the citizen "no" for liability reasons.)

The second, which could be labeled as an "Internal" cluster, appears to relate to organizational structural factors that Grunig identifies in recent research (Grunig, 1983). Some examples of these kinds of activities listed by city employees include:

- Inefficient/inadequate training of employees.
- Implementing effective management techniques.
- Eliminating the overlapping of job responsibilities.

An anecdotal illustration of these kinds of activities is found in the example of Public Safety division employees reporting situations to the Public Works division that citizens consider to be "problems," and becoming frustrated because Public Works inefficiency prevents the citizens' concerns from receiving attention. Ultimately, Public Safety employees begin to "go around" the Public Works department and solve the problems themselves. Rightly or wrongly, Public Safety employees perceive they are demonstrating a greater degree of "public service", and they resent the lack of commitment by Public Works employees. Consequently, they believe that any public relations effort by the city is negatively affected by poor performance on the part of one division or department.

Because of the wide scope of the two major activity/action categories, the decision was made to focus this preliminary investigation on the first, or External, cluster of activities during the case study phase. By focusing on these variables first, the researchers believed that they could enhance the feedback necessary to provide "front-line" training.

Question 2: Attitudes Toward Activities/Actions

Thus, to obtain a measure of employee attitudes toward these specific actions, a series of Likert-type statements was developed from discussion items that emerged during previous training sessions. The items reflected specific "public contact" concerns expressed by employees during previous sessions and called for "Strongly Agree" to "Strongly Disagree" responses (5-point scale). To minimize a response set, the "direction" of some items was reversed. However, all items were coded so that the higher the mean, the more positive the response.

The Public Contact items are the first nine listed in Table 11.1 and an examination of the mean shows that, in general, employees in this municipality have "positive" attitudes about their contacts with local citizens. For instance, they do

TABLE 11.1
Public Contact and Job Satisfaction Item & Index Means, Factor Loadings and Communalities

Item	Mean	Interaction Factor	Intrapersonal Factor	Perception Factor	Job-Satisfaction Factor	Communality
Public Contact						
1. I'm not embarrassed to have to say "no" to requests from citizens.	3.81	.74	.06	−.03	−.17	.58
2. I prefer a business-like relationship with citizens who try to tell me their personal troubles.	2.79	−.71	.04	.21	.02	.55
3. I don't mind it when people interrupt my work with requests for information or help.	3.97	.59	−.11	−.05	.02	.52
4. I feel uncomfortable when I have to admit to a citizen I don't know the answer to a question directed at me.	3.03	.06	.84	.11	.04	.73
5. I'm frustrated with my limited authority to provide solutions to citizen inquiries.	2.88	−.07	.74	.03	.11	.57

6. Most citizens understand the reasons for our department policies.	2.92	.20	.03	-.65	.13	.49
7. I feel that most of the public I deal with is made up of cranks, oddballs, and deadbeats.	4.00	-.07	.27	.64	.20	.53
8. My boss appreciates what I have to put up with from the public.	3.61	-.30	.38	-.59	.34	.69
9. After the first few hours of the day I'll hear the same old stories from every citizen who comes along.	3.46	-.30	.24	.54	.38	.58
Job Satisfaction						
10. I look forward to coming to work almost every day.	3.56	.15	-.01	.01	.85	.75
11. On the whole, my job is challenging and interesting.	4.06	-.23	.33	.00	.73	.69
Index Mean		3.52	2.96	3.47	3.80	

Note: Scale: 1 = Negative   5 = Positive

not believe that the citizens they deal with are "cranks, oddballs, or deadbeats," nor do they mind interruptions by requests for information or help.

However, because this was an exploratory study, it was considered important to investigate the underlying attitudinal dimensions reflected in the responses. Consequently, these items were factor analyzed and those results are presented in Table 11.1 as well.

As can be seen, three distinct factors emerged for these Public Contact items. The first, labeled a "Public Interaction" factor, contains items that center around the actual interaction of city employees with citizens. It reflects concerns about the type of relationship they have with citizens on a day-to-day basis. The second dimension is labeled as an "Intrapersonal" factor[1] because it contains items that describe how the employee feels internally about his or her dealings with the public. The third dimension is labeled as a "Perception of Others" factor. Items that load on this factor describe how the employee views others in the public service relationship.

For use in further analysis, items that loaded on each of the factors were used to create scales or indices for each dimension. The means for each Index can be found in Table 11.1. This process makes it easier to see that, for employees in this municipality, attitudes about Public Contact activities are generally positive. The only exception is the Intrapersonal dimension, which is slightly negative.

Question 3: Job-Related Variables

There were two job-related variables thought to have a relationship to Public Contact and public service attitudes. The first was job satisfaction. As noted earlier, previous research has linked job satisfaction to public employee performance. Also, as Grunig relates, job satisfaction and organization communication are often linked. (Although, he believes job satisfaction is more a product of structural factors than organizational communication.)

The second job-related factor investigated was the time that each employee spends with the public each day. In any municipality, some employees have a lot of public contact, others have very little. It makes sense to suspect that the amount of daily contact may have some relationship to attitudes about that contact.

To measure job satisfaction, two items that Grunig used for the same purpose were incorporated into this study. These items were included in the factor analysis of Public Contact items and, as expected, they loaded on a separate factor. Consequently, a Job Satisfaction Index was created. The items, means, and factor loadings are presented in Table 11.1. As can be seen, the employees in this city are relatively satisfied with their job.

---

[1]Although, as a general rule, it is best to define factors that have at least three loadings, because this was an exploratory study and both loadings are in the same direction, this factor was defined with two. See R. Wimmer and J. Dominick (1983, p. 237).

As for the other job-related variable, as explained earlier, employees were asked to indicate the amount of time they spend with the public each day. The largest percentage spend 2 to 3 hours with the public each day.

Table 11.2 presents the results of correlating the Public Contact indices with Job Satisfaction and time spent with the public. The data show that there is a positive correlation between Job Satisfaction and the Intrapersonal and Perceptions of Others attitudes. Although it is impossible to assign any causality, it does appear that if a city employee has positive internal feelings about his or her relationship to the public and positive feelings about others in the process, the more likely he or she is to be satisfied with the job.

In many ways, this is not surprising. But, as noted following, it does suggest that those who are concerned about improving employee attitudes about public service may want to investigate the relationship further.

What is surprising, perhaps, is the lack of a linear relationship between the Public Contact attitudes and time spent with the public. Conventional wisdom, (and, indeed, even some management research) would suggest that "burn-out" occurs with increased public contact. Further investigation may reveal that this municipality utilizes techniques (such as rotating employees on the front desk) to minimize negative reactions.

Question 4:
Communication Variables

To date, most of the research using the situational theory has been conducted for the purpose of identifying "publics." Grunig collects data on the three or four theoretical variables (as independent variables) and relates them to the dependent communication variables. He further discriminates among respondents to identify those types (or publics) that communicate in similar ways. Because this process is so well established, what has been overlooked is the utility of the theoretical and communication variables for their own sake. In other words, given that the variables and the types of publics they identify are valid and consistent (as demon-

TABLE 11.2
Correlations of Public Contact Indices with Job Satisfaction
and Time Spent with Public

	Job Satisfaction	Time Spent
Public Interation Index	.01	.16
Intrapersonal Index	.26†	.13
Perception of Others Index	.41††	.13

†$p = .05$
††$p = .01$

strated in Grunig's 15 years of research with situational theory) there is merit in utilizing them in ways other than for the identification of publics.

In this study, the theoretical and communication variables are useful for describing the communication behavior of the employees as a whole, and *validating the identification of issues suspected of relating to the other variables of importance*— specifically, attitudes about Public Contact and Job Satisfaction.

Here, based on their interactions with municipal employees, researchers believed there were four issues or items that might be related to Public Contact attitudes and Job Satisfaction:

1. City ordinances and regulations.

2. The best way to handle citizen complaints.

3. The *quality* of city services to residents.

4. Obtaining an adequate budget to properly perform services.

The rationale for suspecting why these issues are important to municipal workers is not hard to discern. Much of a city worker's behavior is governed by ordinances and regulations. In many cases, the ordinances are the employee's "reason for being." Unfortunately, many city residents are not always happy with the ordinances or the way they are enforced. Consequently, dealing with complaints is a major component of a city worker's job. Nevertheless, discussions with municipal workers indicate that most are truly concerned about providing quality service to citizens. Yet, they seem to believe their efforts are often hampered by the lack of an adequate budget.

The procedures used to measure the theoretical and communication variables are those recommended or utilized by Grunig. For the theoretical variables, respondents are asked how often they stop to think about the issues (problem recognition), whether they can do anything personally that would make a difference in the way the issues are handled (constraint recognition), and to what extent they see a connection between themselves and the issue (level of involvement). Responses are coded on a 4-point scale.

For the communication variables, respondents were asked how they would treat the receipt of a memo about each of the issues (information processing): read it immediately, put it aside to read when time is available, skim it briefly, or not read it at all. In addition, they were asked how likely they would be to attend a voluntary meeting after work hours about each of the issues (information seeking): very likely, somewhat likely, not likely, not attend.

Table 11.3 confirms that these are important issues to municipal employees. In general, these city employees think about the specific issues frequently (high problem recognition), believe they *can* do something about the issues (low feelings of constraint), and consider themselves to be involved with the specific issues (high involvement). In addition, city employees are active information "processors" and "seekers" of information about the four issues.

TABLE 11.3
Means of Situational Theory and Communication Variables
for Public Contact Related Issues

	Issue			
	City Ordinances	Handling Complaints	Quality of Service	Obtaining Budget
Variable				
Problem recognition	3.18	3.48	3.47	2.83
Constraint recognition	2.52	2.92	2.61	2.15
Level of involvement	3.00	3.28	3.10	2.48
Information processing	3.54	3.75	3.56	3.18
Information seeking	2.97	3.12	3.02	2.82

Note: 4-point Scale.

A closer examination reveals some interesting findings, however. For instance, the most "active" issue is the one dealing with complaint handling. Employees consider this to be the issue that they think about the most and the one with which they are most involved. Fortunately, they also believe they *can* do something about how complaints are handled. And, just as the Situational Theory would predict, this is the issue about which employees are most likely to communicate.

The issue associated with the greatest degree of constraint has to do with obtaining an adequate budget. For whatever reasons, city employees feel that they have less control over this issue than any of the others. Predictably, they are less likely to process or seek information about this issue, compared to the others.

Table 11.4 presents the relationship of the theoretical and communication variables to the Public Contact indices. The two indices that contain significant correlations are Intrapersonal and Perceptions of Others—the same two that are positively correlated with Job Satisfaction.

The cluster of attitudes that co-varies the most with the theoretical variables is the Perception of Others group. Two of the significant correlations (both negative) relate to the same issue: city ordinances. What this suggests is that employees with a greater sense of involvement and a lack of constraint on this issue are the same ones with less positive attitudes about others in their public contact relationships. Nevertheless, Table 11.4 shows that those employees who score "positively" on this dimension are most likely to process or seek information about obtaining an adequate budget, complaint handling, and the quality of city services.

It is worthy of note that the single issue with the largest number of significant correlations is the one that relates to "obtaining an adequate budget to properly perform city services." Again, without assigning any degree of causality, the results suggest that those employees who are most likely to communicate about underlying budget concerns are the same ones who feel good about their dealings with the public and have positive perceptions of others involved in the process.

Table 11.4 also shows the relationship of Job Satisfaction to the theoretical and

TABLE 11.4
Correlations of Situational Theory and Communication Variables
with Public Contact and Job Satisfaction Indices

	Interaction Index	Intrapersonal Index	Perception Index	Job Satisfaction
Problem Recognition				
City ordinances	.00	.11	−.01	.09
Handling complaints	.15	.11	.12	.18
Quality of service	.13	.24‡	.18	.40‡‡
Obtaining budget	−.04	.28‡	.37‡‡	.31‡‡
Constraint Recognition				
City ordinances	.11	.11	−.27‡	−.18
Handling complaints	.07	.08	.12	.16
Quality of service	−.01	.02	.05	.10
Obtaining budget	−.04	.18	.11	.21
Level of Involvement				
City ordinances	−.06	.16	−.25‡	.06
Handling complaints	−.04	.05	−.02	−.04
Quality of service	.08	.19	.21	.12
Obtaining budget	.06	.19	.21	.09
Information Processing				
City ordinances	.18	−.04	−.04	.14
Handling complaints	.07	.03	.19	.34‡‡
Quality of service	.11	−.06	.16	.32‡‡
Obtaining budget	.03	.07	.32‡‡	.34‡‡
Information Seeking				
City ordinances	.09	.19	.11	.39‡‡
Handling complaints	−.02	.13	.26‡	.50‡‡
Quality of service	.05	.21	.32‡‡	.49‡‡
Obtaining budget	−.11	.15	.31‡‡	.38‡‡

‡p = .05
‡‡p = .01

communication variables. One of the most interesting findings of this study is the strong relationship between information processing and information seeking with job satisfaction. The strong positive correlations show that the more satisfied an employee is with his or her job, the more likely he or she is to communicate about the specific issues. Job satisfaction is also strongly correlated with problem recognition for "quality of service" and "obtaining an adequate budget" issues.

CONCLUSIONS AND OBSERVATIONS

There are a number of conclusions that can be drawn and observations that should be made from the results of this study. These should be of use to both public relations practitioners and researchers interested in improving municipal public service/public relations programs.

- The results of this study support the often-stated notion that "actions speak louder than words" in public relations. In spite of the fact that public relations techniques are most often "communication-related" techniques, this study demonstrates that non-communication actions and activities (identified here in External and Internal clusters) are linked to the overall public relations effort of a municipality by those intimately involved—municipal employees. What this means for a municipality, of course, is that a public relations program will be seen as ineffective by employees if the municipality is providing poor public service to the community.

- The clusters of relevant activities are complex and multi-faceted. The Public Contact cluster, selected for investigation in the case study, appears to have at least three dimensions. Of these, the Intrapersonal and Perceptions of Others dimensions seem to be the most important. Consequently, the fact that the mean for the Intrapersonal index is slightly negative for this group of employees should raise a red flag for city officials concerned about improving attitudes toward public service.

- It is important to investigate the relationship of the Internal cluster of activities to public service/public relations. It may be, as Grunig has suggested, that these structural variables are the more important ones for researchers concerned about organizational communication and effectiveness. Certainly, municipal employees link these kinds of activities to an overall public relations effort.

- The positive correlation of Job Satisfaction with the Intrapersonal and Perceptions of Others dimensions suggests that those concerned with improving municipal employee attitudes about public contact and public service may want to investigate the relationship further.

  For instance, it may be that by developing training programs designed to improve the employee's internal feelings and help him or her understand how the public may view city employees, job satisfaction could increase. Or, it may be more constructive to "massage" the relationship from the other direction: Undertake programs to improve job satisfaction (by altering Grunig's structural variables, for instance) and the employee's attitude toward the public may improve.

- Using Grunig's situational theory to validate the identification of important issues seems to be fruitful. For example, in this study, the methodological approach associated with the situational theory identified the budget issue as being particularly important to these employees. The correlational analysis of this issue with the other variables holds a number of implications for training programs. For instance, it may be that efforts to explain and encourage communication about budgetary matters would pay off in greater employee job satisfaction and enhanced attitudes about public service.

Further, it is not necessary to only use Grunig's methodology to identify employee publics or groups. For instance, in this municipality, there are significant correlations between job satisfaction and two of the public contact dimensions. Consequently, to identify specific employees who might benefit from additional public contact training, city officials could look at the demographics of those who score below the mean on Job Satisfaction—and hence, lower on the Intrapersonal and Perceptions of Others scales.

• This study confirms the importance of employee communication to job satisfaction. It is important to note, however, that the relationship investigated here was between communication behavior (not the more commonly investigated variable of communication satisfaction) and job satisfaction. But, clearly, city officials who lament, "if dissatisfied employees would only read the information we provide them, then they would see what we are talking about," need to realize that dissatisfied employees are less likely to process information, much less seek it. This finding does not discount the importance of communicating with city employees, it only means that additional techniques to improve job satisfaction should be considered as well.

• Finally, it almost goes without saying that it is important for researchers to pursue the relationship between public service attitudes, job satisfaction, and internal communication if they are to help municipalities work to improve public service and public relations. The results of this study have to be considered preliminary until others validate them with research in other cities.

REFERENCES

Albrecht, K., & Zemke, R. (1985). *Service America!: Doing business in the new economy.* Homewood, IL: Dow Jones-Irwin.

Branst, L. (1984). Disneyland—A kingdom of service quality. *Quality, 23,* 16–18.

Collier, A. T. (1979, November–December). The co-corp: big business can reform itself. *Harvard Business Review,* p. 121.

Davis, C. W., & West, J. P. (1985). Adopting personnel productivity innovations in American local governments. *Policy Studies Review, 4,* 541–549.

DiTomaso, N. (1978). Public unions and the urban fiscal crisis. *The Insurgent Sociologist, 8,* 191–205.

Grunig, J. E., & Hunt, T. (1984). *Managing Public Relations.* New York: Holt, Rinehart & Winston.

Grunig, J. E. (1983, May). *A structural reconceptualization of the organizational communication audit, with application to a state department of education.* Paper presented to the International Communication Association, Honolulu.

Hochschild, A. R. (1983). *The managed heart: Commercialization of human feelings.* Berkley: The University of California Press.

Pintor, R. L. (1976). Satisfaction in work and formalism as bureaucratic phenomena: An analysis of attitudes in Chile. *Revista Espanola de la Opinion Publica, 44,* 101–145.

(1987, February 2) Pul-eeze! Will somebody help me? *Time,* pp. 49–57.

Quinn, J. B., & Gagnon, C. E. (1986, November–December). Will services follow manufacturing into decline? *Harvard Business Review,* pp. 95–103.

Seroka, J. H. (1979). Local public employee unionization: Trends and implications for the future. *The Policy Studies Journal, 8,* 430–437.

Wimmer, R. D., & Dominick, J. R. (1983). *Mass media research.* Belmont, CA: Wadsworth.

Author Index

Subject Index